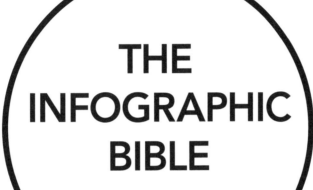

THE
INFOGRAPHIC
BIBLE

Visualising the drama
of God's word

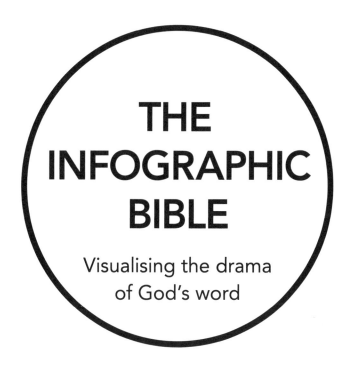

THE INFOGRAPHIC BIBLE

Visualising the drama
of God's word

Karen Sawrey

WILLIAM
COLLINS

William Collins
An imprint of HarperCollins*Publishers*
1 London Bridge Street
London SE1 9GF

WilliamCollinsBooks.com

First published in Great Britain in 2018 by William Collins

1

© Karen Sawrey 2018

Karen Sawrey asserts the moral right to be identified as the author of this work in accordance with the Copyright, Designs and Patents Act 1988

Cover design by Karen Sawrey

www.karensawrey.com

A catalogue record for this book is available from the British Library

ISBN 978-0-00-755461-4

Set in Avenir, Avenir Next Condensed, 1592 GLC Garamond and Arrus.

Printed and bound in China

MIX
Paper from
responsible sources
FSC™ C007454

FSC is a non-profit international organisation established to promote the responsible management of the world's forests. Products carrying the FSC label are independently certified to assure consumers that they come from forests that are managed to meet the social, economic and ecological needs of present and future generations, and other controlled sources.

Find out more about HarperCollins and the environment at www.harpercollins.co.uk/green

to my beloved Jesus
also
my 'beaut' of a family, especially
Reggie, Smith, Flynn and Bay

remember nothing is impossible!
[LUKE 1:37]

About the author

Conceptual designer, illustrator and lover of all things paper and ink, Karen Sawrey is passionate about engaging a visual generation with creative ways to see and digest information. Karen has over 20 years' experience stretching across a wide range of media, including top magazines, global charities and publishers including HarperCollins, Hodder & Stoughton and Penguin Random House. Having worked in central London, she now continues to flourish as a creative amongst the Northern Hills, still loving paper, people and life to the full.

Foreword

The world is constantly changing. Today so many people, particularly the millennial generation, take in information and learn through visual imagery. Even I am on Instagram. This is why I'm so thrilled that *The Infographic Bible* now allows everyone, whether they have a faith or not, to engage with the drama and story of God's word in a new, exciting visual way.

The apostle Paul, whose letters make up a large portion of the New Testament, eschewed formal language to write in the vernacular of the street in order to bring the story of the early church to life for as many ordinary people as possible, and it is so exciting to see people like Karen using their God-given creativity to make the gospel accessible today.

Karen Sawrey was part of our congregation at Holy Trinity Brompton and on the staff here as a creative designer at a time when she experienced a relationship with Jesus in a new way. Karen has chosen this theme of restored relationship to tell the Bible's big picture narrative – a message that is so relevant today – through graphics in this book.

At HTB, we are passionate about seeing people from outside the church come to know Jesus. The best way we have found to introduce the Christian faith is through Alpha. If you would like to find out more about doing Alpha in a church, home, business or school near you, please visit alpha.org.

Through Alpha, and indeed through our own Leadership Conference, we have had the immense privilege of building relationships across the denominations and, in doing so, seeing those relationships restored. From Pentecostal to Roman Catholic, Baptist to Methodist, Orthodox to Episcopal, as we have got to know leaders and individuals, I have been struck by how true it is that what unites us is infinitely greater than what divides us. This book is a picture of this as it draws together contributions from individuals with a wide range of viewpoints and theology, yet united around one person: Jesus Christ, whose message is as relevant now as it was 2,000 years ago. It is my sincere hope that your journey through this book will point you to Him.

Nicky Gumbel
[VICAR OF HTB AND PIONEER OF ALPHA]

Introduction

We live in a world often described as a global village, in which we are constantly absorbing information. A global visual language is quickly becoming the currency of communication for this generation. Projects such as Noun and the use of emojis have grown exponentially for a reason – in fact Noun's research has shown that combining visuals with text improves communication and learning by 89 per cent*.

Jesus spoke in parables – creating images to help His audience understand and remember the essence of His message – and Paul chose to write in the street language of the day. *The Infographic Bible's* aim is to do both: to create a visual image, and then support that graphic with text that can be understood by anyone who picks up the book.

The Infographic Bible does not simply illustrate the biblical text. It doesn't cover every book or subject, nor is it a replacement for the Bible. Rather its aim is always to point back to it. The content concentrates on the Bible's big picture narrative, with subjects chosen to help drive that story forward. The main aim is to show that God's word can be approached, wrestled with, analysed and meditated on. The Bible is one of the key places we encounter God and His heart for a relationship with us, bringing nourishment and wholeness as we interact with it.

The Infographic Bible is the result of me and my team interacting with God's word. The more we meditate on the Bible, the more we learn about God, His character and His ways, impacting how we interpret the Bible, and as a result, how we see the world around us. Working on this project has undoubtedly changed some of my opinions; I've grown and learnt more about God's character and ways since beginning the project in 2013.

There are so many different theologies on the Bible, it would be impossible for me to reveal every one on each subject, and any attempt to do so would make it hard to lift this book off the coffee table. However, I have purposefully gathered a wide range of contributors from different theological backgrounds for this project, people who carry a heart for, and in some instances authority on, that subject. It is important to note that each contributor's view is uniquely linked to their data set and will often differ from other contributor's, or in fact, my own, view. Those different theologies are not something to be feared, but to be embraced and grappled with. A healthy maturity comes from this wrestling.

This book invites you to interact with God's life-giving word in a fun and relevant way inside these pages. No matter where you are in your journey with God, study, analyse, interact and create with it. It is an incredible gift extended to every single person – enjoy!

* The Noun Project, The Power of Visual Communication, https://www.slideshare.net/NounProject

How to read the book

You may choose to read a graphic in isolation and that's totally fine – freedom reigns, enjoy! Otherwise it can be helpful to zoom out to the Bible's big picture narrative, revealing an amazing relational journey between us and God. You can take a sneaky peek at that big picture narrative on page 206, where the journey has been broken down into eight stages from Genesis to Revelation. The contents page will also help you navigate the timeline of *The Infographic Bible*, showing you where the big picture stages are and what subjects have been chosen to give you further insight to that stage. Either side and in between the big picture narrative there are graphics about the Bible itself.

Each big picture stage has a colour assigned to it, and these are shown in the contents, on the stage starting spread, and on a small tab at the bottom left underneath the page numbers. The graphics about the Bible have a grey section start and tab. These tabs should help you navigate the book and know where in the big picture narrative each graphic sits.

Most graphics take up a double-page spread, but some span several pages or a single page. If you don't see a title on a particular page, then just flip back to the start of that graphic.

The graphics range from simple to complex. Simple ones can be grasped quickly, whereas in the more complex ones it will take time to digest the different levels of information. Look to see if the graphic has a key to help reveal and process the information.

Finally, remember the graphics take the leading role with the text playing the supporting cast in labelling the graphic. Writing these graphic labels has proven to be one of the greatest challenges of this project and this text is often quite small as a result. I had toyed with the idea of supplying a magnifying glass with this book, but I'm afraid the budget wouldn't stretch… but if you have one handy?

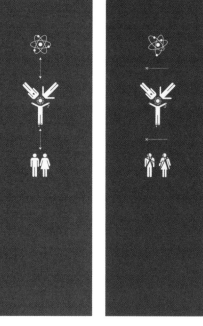
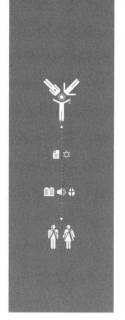

THE OLD TESTAMENT

Contents

ABOUT THE BIBLE ———o BIBLE'S BIG PICTURE NARRATIVE

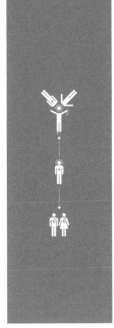

THE NEW TESTAMENT

STAGE 6 —————o   STAGE 7 —————o   STAGE 8 —————|

ABOUT THE BIBLE:
SETTING THE SCENE

see pp124-125

Formation of Holy Scripture

Who made the calls? *

THE NAMES OF THE OLD AND NEW TESTAMENT BOOKS ARRANGED IN ORDER, WITH...

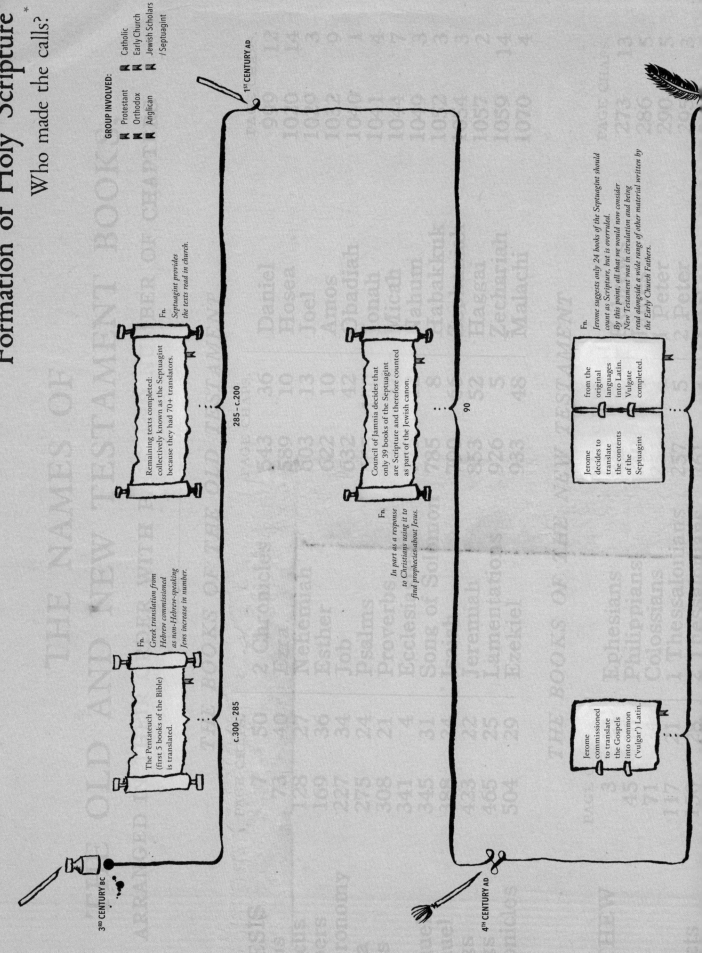

3RD CENTURY BC

c.300 – 285
The Pentateuch (first 5 books of the Bible) is translated.
Fn. Greek translation from Hebrew commissioned as non-Hebrew-speaking Jews increase in number.

285 – c.200
Remaining texts completed: collectively known as the Septuagint because they had 70+ translators.
Fn. Septuagint provides the texts read in church.

1ST CENTURY AD

90
Council of Jamnia decides that only 39 books of the Septuagint are Scripture and therefore counted as part of the Jewish canon.
Fn. In part as a response to Christians using it to find prophecies about Jesus.

4TH CENTURY AD

Jerome commissioned to translate the Gospels into common ('vulgar') Latin.

Jerome decides to translate the contents of the Septuagint from the original languages into Latin. Vulgate completed.
Fn. Jerome suggests only 24 books of the Septuagint should count as Scripture, but is overruled. By this point, all that we would now consider New Testament was in circulation and being read alongside a wide range of other material written by the Early Church Fathers.

THE BOOKS OF THE OLD TESTAMENT

Genesis
Exodus
Leviticus
Numbers
Deuteronomy
Joshua
Judges
Ruth
1 Samuel
2 Samuel
1 Kings
2 Kings
1 Chronicles
2 Chronicles
Ezra
Nehemiah
Esther
Job
Psalms
Proverbs
Ecclesiastes
Song of Solomon
Isaiah
Jeremiah
Lamentations
Ezekiel
Daniel
Hosea
Joel
Amos
Obadiah
Jonah
Micah
Nahum
Habakkuk
Haggai
Zechariah
Malachi

THE BOOKS OF THE NEW TESTAMENT

MATTHEW
Mark
...
Ephesians
Philippians
Colossians
1 Thessalonians
...
Peter
2 Peter

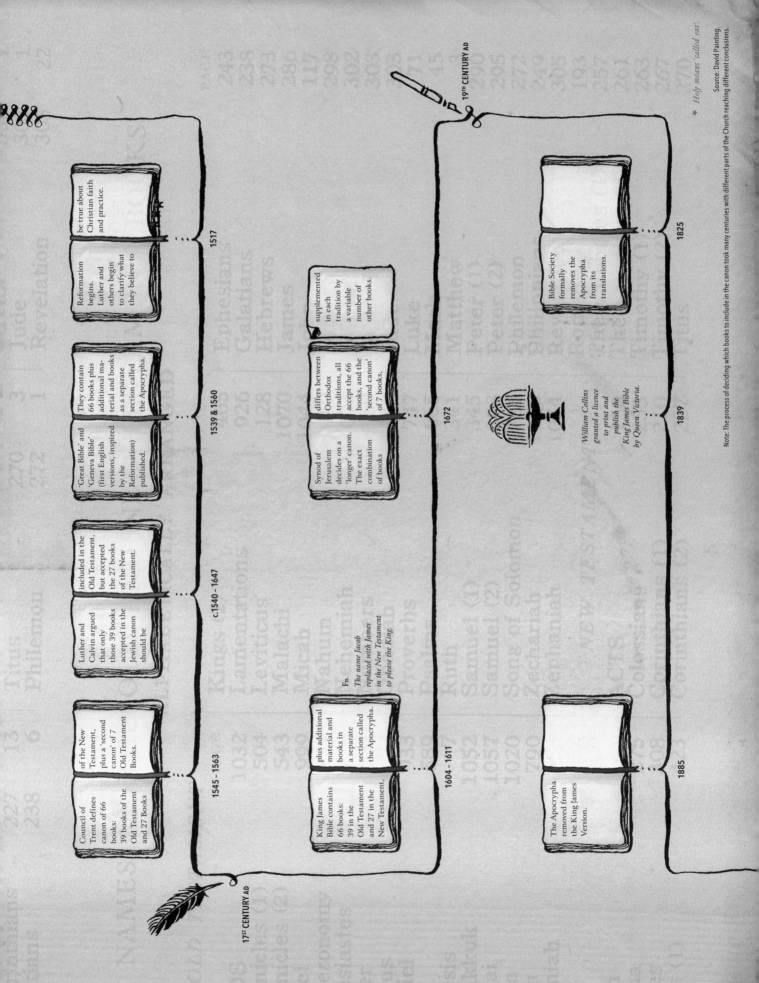

17TH CENTURY AD

19TH CENTURY AD

1545 – 1563 — Council of Trent defines canon of 66 books: 39 books of the Old Testament and 27 Books of the New Testament, plus a 'second canon' of 7 Old Testament Books.

c.1540 – 1647 — Luther and Calvin argued that only those 39 books accepted in the Jewish canon should be included in the Old Testament, but accepted the 27 books of the New Testament.

1539 & 1560 — 'Great Bible' and 'Geneva Bible' (first English versions, inspired by the Reformation) published. They contain 66 books plus additional material and books as a separate section called the Apocrypha.

1517 — Reformation begins. Luther and others begin to clarify what they believe to be true about Christian faith and practice.

1672 — Synod of Jerusalem decides on a 'longer' canon. The exact combination of books differs between Orthodox traditions, all accept the 66 books, and the 'second canon' of 7 books, supplemented in each tradition by a variable number of other books.

1604 – 1611 — King James Bible contains 66 books: 39 in the Old Testament and 27 in the New Testament, plus additional material and books in a separate section called the Apocrypha.

Fn... *The name Jacob replaced with James in the New Testament to please the King.*

1825 — Bible Society formally removes the Apocrypha from its translations.

1839 — *William Collins granted a licence to print and publish the King James Bible by Queen Victoria.*

1885 — The Apocrypha removed from the King James Version.

* *Holy means 'called out'.*

Note: The process of deciding which books to include in the canon took many centuries with different parts of the Church reaching different conclusions.

Source: David Painting.

Books of the Bible
Today's tally of chapter & verse

BOOK

Book Abb	BOOK NAME
Summary of content	No. of chapters = c / No. of verses = v

COUNTED AS CANONICAL OR AS HELPFUL TO BE READ BY:

- Protestant
- Orthodox
- Anglican
- Catholic
- Early Church
- Jewish Scholars / Septuagint

Old Testament

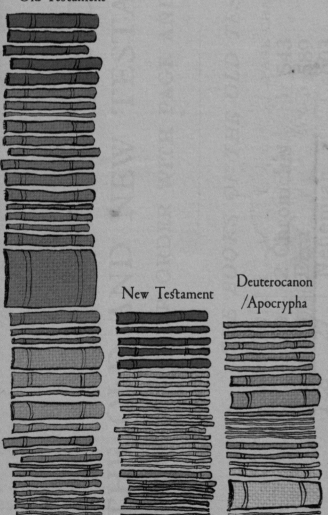

New Testament

Deuterocanon /Apocrypha

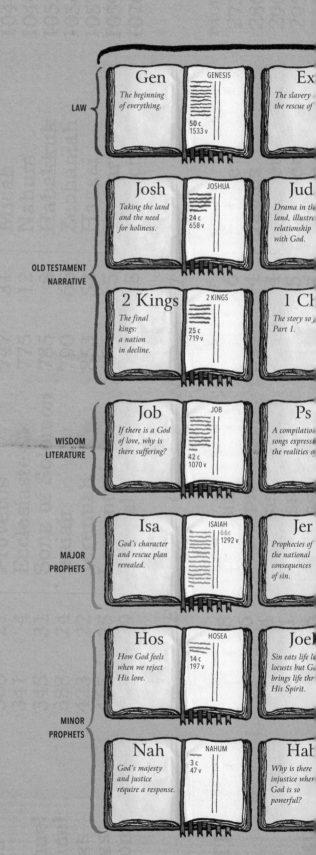

LAW

Gen
GENESIS
The beginning of everything.
50 c
1533 v

Ex
The slavery
the rescue of

OLD TESTAMENT NARRATIVE

Josh
JOSHUA
Taking the land and the need for holiness.
24 c
658 v

Jud
Drama in the land, illustra relationship with God.

2 Kings
2 KINGS
The final kings: a nation in decline.
25 c
719 v

1 Ch
The story so Part 1.

WISDOM LITERATURE

Job
JOB
If there is a God of love, why is there suffering?
42 c
1070 v

Ps
A compilatio songs expressi the realities o

MAJOR PROPHETS

Isa
ISAIAH
God's character and rescue plan revealed.
66 c
1292 v

Jer
Prophecies of the national consequences of sin.

MINOR PROPHETS

Hos
HOSEA
How God feels when we reject His love.
14 c
197 v

Joel
Sin eats life l locusts but G brings life thr His Spirit.

Nah
NAHUM
God's majesty and justice require a response.
3 c
47 v

Hab
Why is there injustice wher God is so powerful?

see pp22-23

Old Testament

Lev — LEVITICUS
How to relate to a holy God.
27 c
859 v

Num — NUMBERS
How to receive God's promise.
36 c
1288 v

Deut — DEUTERONOMY
How to live in relationship with God and others.
34 c
959 v

Ruth — RUTH
A story of faithfulness, courage and redemption
4 c
85 v

1 Sam — 1 SAMUEL
Choosing a man to be king instead of God.
31 c
810 v

2 Sam — 2 SAMUEL
Saul and David: the first kings.
24 c
695 v

1 Kings — 1 KINGS
The kingdom divided.
22 c
816 v

2 Chr — 2 CHRONICLES
The story so far – Part 2.
36 c
822 v

Ezra — EZRA
Return from exile; rebuilding the Temple
10 c
280 v

Neh — NEHEMIAH
Return from exile; rebuilding the walls.
13 c
406 v

Esth — ESTHER
An ordinary girl becomes queen and saves her people.
10 c
167 v

Prov — PROVERBS
Truth-filled sayings of wisdom.
31 c
915 v

Eccl — ECCLESIASTES
What is really important in life?
12 c
222 v

Song — SONG OF SONGS
An intimate insight into the joy of physical love.
8 c
117 v

Lam — LAMENTATIONS
A lament for the disasters befalling the nation.
5 c
154 v

Ezek — EZEKIEL
Prophecies of exile and national disgrace.
48 c
1273 v

Dan — DANIEL
Faith in God in the face of lethal opposition.
12 c
357 v

Am — AMOS
Prosperity breeds complacency.
9 c
146 v

Ob — OBADIAH
Warnings against pride; God is just.
1 c
21 v

Jon — JONAH
Mercy outweighs justice.
4 c
48 v

Mic — MICAH
Judgment and hope pointing people back to God.
7 c
105 v

Zeph — ZEPHANIAH
Israel had been exiled, yet Judah fails to repent.
3 c
53 v

Hag — HAGGAI
When God brings freedom, don't neglect responsibility.
2 c
38 v

Zech — ZECHARIAH
God works through history, preparing the coming Kingdom.
14 c
211 v

Mal — MALACHI
Promises of restoration through the coming King.
4 c
55 v

see pp22-23

BOOK

Book
Abb

BOOK NAME

Summary of content

| No. of chapters = c | No. of verses = v |

MATERIAL

Abb

MATERIAL NAME

Summary of content

| No. of chapters = c | No. of verses = v |

* v = Variations in numbering schemes make number of verses meaningless

COUNTED AS CANONICAL OR AS HELPFUL TO

- Protestant
- Orthodox
- Anglican
- Catholic
- Early Church
- Jewish Scholars / Sept

New Testament

NEW TESTAMENT NARRATIVE

Mt
MATTHEW
The Good News of Jesus by a Jew, for Jews.
28 c
1071 v

Mk
MARK
The Good News of Jesus by a young man.
16 c
678 v

Lk
LUKE
The Good News of Jesus written by a professional.
24 c
1151 v

Jn
JOHN
The Good News of Jesus retold and explained.
21 c
879 v

Act
What God d next. After goes back to He sends H Holy Spirit

PAULINE EPISTLES

Rom
ROMANS
God's plan for salvation explained.
16 c
433 v

1 Cor
1 CORINTHIANS
A letter about love and life in church.
16 c
437 v

2 Cor
2 CORINTHIANS
Second letter answering questions about morality and church.
13 c
257 v

Gal
GALATIANS
A letter to a church that was going off the rails.
6 c
149 v

Ep
A letter encouraging everyone to to one anoth

Phil
PHILIPPIANS
A letter outlining how Jesus gave up everything because of His love for us.
4 c
104 v

Col
COLOSSIANS
A letter opposing false teaching.
4 c
95 v

1 Thess
1 THESSALONIANS
A letter of personal encouragement to keep doing well.
5 c
89 v

2 Thess
2 THESSALONIANS
A letter discussing the return of Jesus.
3 c
47 v

1 Ti
A letter from to his God- encouraging as a leader.

2 Tim
2 TIMOTHY
A letter setting out the requirements for leaders and teachers.
4 c
83 v

Titus
TITUS
A letter instructing Titus on the role of those leading church.
3 c
46 v

Philem
PHILEMON
A letter to a friend whose slave had run away.
1 c
25 v

GENERAL EPISTLES

Heb
HEBREWS
A recounting of the whole Bible story.
13 c
303 v

Jas
JAMES
We are saved by faith, but faith must result in action.
5 c
108 v

1 Pet
1 PETER
Encouragement to a church facing opposition.
5 c
105 v

2 Pet
2 PETER
A corrective to wrong views about the second coming.
3 c
61 v

1 Jn
1 JOHN
The truth, love and light of God.
5 c
105 v

2 Jn
2 JOHN
Jesus came physically in person, not just as a spirit.
1 c
13 v

3 Jn
3 JOHN
A personal letter to Demetrius.
1 c
14 v

Jude
JUDE
Similar to 2Peter, correcting views about the second coming.
1 c
25 v

APOCALYPTIC EPISTLE

Rev
REVELATION
How it all ends, with a recreation of how God intended life with Him to be.
22 c
404 v

note: In some traditio

Deuterocanon/Apocrypha

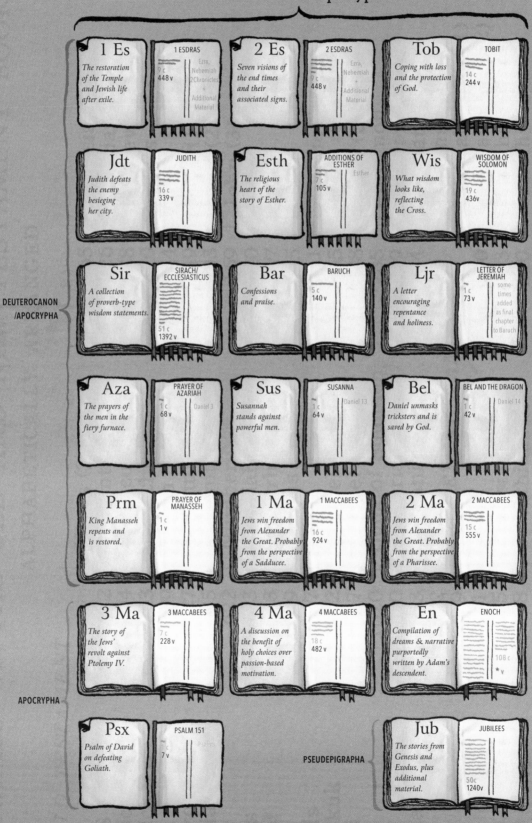

ACTS

PHESIANS

TIMOTHY

DEUTEROCANON /APOCRYPHA

1 Es
The restoration of the Temple and Jewish life after exile.

1 ESDRAS
9 c
448 v
Ezra, Nehemiah 2Chronicles + Additional Material

2 Es
Seven visions of the end times and their associated signs.

2 ESDRAS
9 c
448 v
Ezra, Nehemiah + Additional Material

Tob
Coping with loss and the protection of God.

TOBIT
14 c
244 v

Jdt
Judith defeats the enemy besieging her city.

JUDITH
16 c
339 v

Esth
The religious heart of the story of Esther.

ADDITIONS OF ESTHER
7 c
105 v
Esther

Wis
What wisdom looks like, reflecting the Cross.

WISDOM OF SOLOMON
19 c
436v

Sir
A collection of proverb-type wisdom statements.

SIRACH/ ECCLESIASTICUS
51 c
1392 v

Bar
Confessions and praise.

BARUCH
5 c
140 v

Ljr
A letter encouraging repentance and holiness.

LETTER OF JEREMIAH
1 c
73 v
sometimes added as final chapter to Baruch

Aza
The prayers of the men in the fiery furnace.

PRAYER OF AZARIAH
1 c
68 v
Daniel 3

Sus
Susannah stands against powerful men.

SUSANNA
1 c
64 v
Daniel 13

Bel
Daniel unmasks tricksters and is saved by God.

BEL AND THE DRAGON
1 c
42 v
Daniel 14

Prm
King Manasseh repents and is restored.

PRAYER OF MANASSEH
1 c
1 v

1 Ma
Jews win freedom from Alexander the Great. Probably from the perspective of a Sadducee.

1 MACCABEES
16 c
924 v

2 Ma
Jews win freedom from Alexander the Great. Probably from the perspective of a Pharissee.

2 MACCABEES
15 c
555 v

3 Ma
The story of the Jews' revolt against Ptolemy IV.

3 MACCABEES
7 c
228 v

4 Ma
A discussion on the benefit of holy choices over passion-based motivation.

4 MACCABEES
18 c
482 v

En
Compilation of dreams & narrative purportedly written by Adam's descendent.

ENOCH
108 c
* v

APOCRYPHA

Psx
Psalm of David on defeating Goliath.

PSALM 151
1 c
7 v
Psalms

PSEUDEPIGRAPHA

Jub
The stories from Genesis and Exodus, plus additional material.

JUBILEES
50 c
1240v

source: David Painting. The 66 Books of the Bible: size and genre (retrieved from www.blueletterbible.org//study/misc/66books.cfm).

rks form additions to canonical books; in others they are combined with books in the canon under different titles, e.g. 'Additions to Daniel', making it difficult to count how many books are Apocryphal. The books that comprise the Septuagint vary between manuscripts.

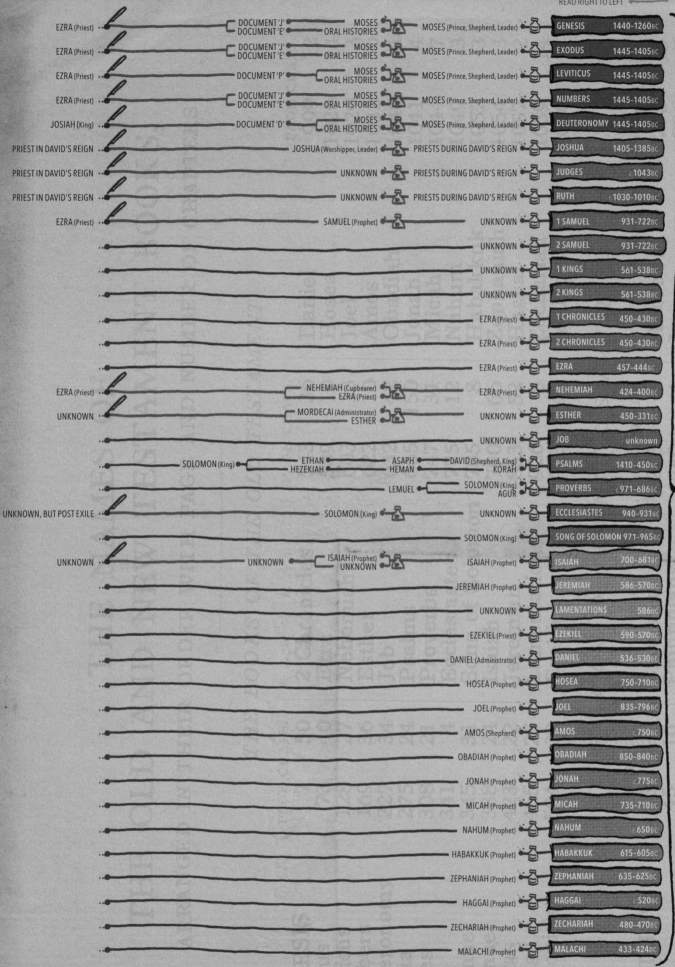

EZRA (Priest) — DOCUMENT 'J' / DOCUMENT 'E' — MOSES / ORAL HISTORIES — MOSES (Prince, Shepherd, Leader) — GENESIS 1440–1260 BC

EZRA (Priest) — DOCUMENT 'J' / DOCUMENT 'E' — MOSES / ORAL HISTORIES — MOSES (Prince, Shepherd, Leader) — EXODUS 1445–1405 BC

EZRA (Priest) — DOCUMENT 'P' — MOSES / ORAL HISTORIES — MOSES (Prince, Shepherd, Leader) — LEVITICUS 1445–1405 BC

EZRA (Priest) — DOCUMENT 'J' / DOCUMENT 'E' — MOSES / ORAL HISTORIES — MOSES (Prince, Shepherd, Leader) — NUMBERS 1445–1405 BC

JOSIAH (King) — DOCUMENT 'D' — MOSES / ORAL HISTORIES — MOSES (Prince, Shepherd, Leader) — DEUTERONOMY 1445–1405 BC

PRIEST IN DAVID'S REIGN — JOSHUA (Worshipper, Leader) — PRIESTS DURING DAVID'S REIGN — JOSHUA 1405–1385 BC

PRIEST IN DAVID'S REIGN — UNKNOWN — PRIESTS DURING DAVID'S REIGN — JUDGES c.1043 BC

PRIEST IN DAVID'S REIGN — UNKNOWN — PRIESTS DURING DAVID'S REIGN — RUTH c.1030–1010 BC

EZRA (Priest) — SAMUEL (Prophet) — UNKNOWN — 1 SAMUEL 931–722 BC

UNKNOWN — 2 SAMUEL 931–722 BC

UNKNOWN — 1 KINGS 561–538 BC

UNKNOWN — 2 KINGS 561–538 BC

EZRA (Priest) — 1 CHRONICLES 450–430 BC

EZRA (Priest) — 2 CHRONICLES 450–430 BC

EZRA (Priest) — EZRA 457–444 BC

EZRA (Priest) — NEHEMIAH (Cupbearer) / EZRA (Priest) — EZRA (Priest) — NEHEMIAH 424–400 BC

UNKNOWN — MORDECAI (Administrator) / ESTHER — UNKNOWN — ESTHER 450–331 BC

UNKNOWN — JOB unknown

SOLOMON (King) — ETHAN / HEZEKIAH — ASAPH / HEMAN — DAVID (Shepherd, King) / KORAH — PSALMS 1410–450 BC

LEMUEL — SOLOMON (King) / AGUR — PROVERBS c.971–686 BC

UNKNOWN, BUT POST EXILE — SOLOMON (King) — UNKNOWN — ECCLESIASTES 940–931 BC

SOLOMON (King) — SONG OF SOLOMON 971–965 BC

UNKNOWN — UNKNOWN — ISAIAH (Prophet) / UNKNOWN — ISAIAH (Prophet) — ISAIAH 700–681 BC

JEREMIAH (Prophet) — JEREMIAH 586–570 BC

UNKNOWN — LAMENTATIONS 586 BC

EZEKIEL (Priest) — EZEKIEL 590–570 BC

DANIEL (Administrator) — DANIEL 536–530 BC

HOSEA (Prophet) — HOSEA 750–710 BC

JOEL (Prophet) — JOEL 835–796 BC

AMOS (Shepherd) — AMOS c.750 BC

OBADIAH (Prophet) — OBADIAH 850–840 BC

JONAH (Prophet) — JONAH c.775 BC

MICAH (Prophet) — MICAH 735–710 BC

NAHUM (Prophet) — NAHUM c.650 BC

HABAKKUK (Prophet) — HABAKKUK 615–605 BC

ZEPHANIAH (Prophet) — ZEPHANIAH 635–625 BC

HAGGAI (Prophet) — HAGGAI c.520 BC

ZECHARIAH (Prophet) — ZECHARIAH 480–470 BC

MALACHI (Prophet) — MALACHI 433–424 BC

Old Testament

The Bible's Bibliography
Many voices: one message

BOOK — **GENERAL DATE**

VIEWPOINT A AUTHOR

VIEWPOINT B AUTHOR (IF DIFFERENT FROM A)

VIEWPOINT B COMPILER / EDITOR

→ READ LEFT TO RIGHT

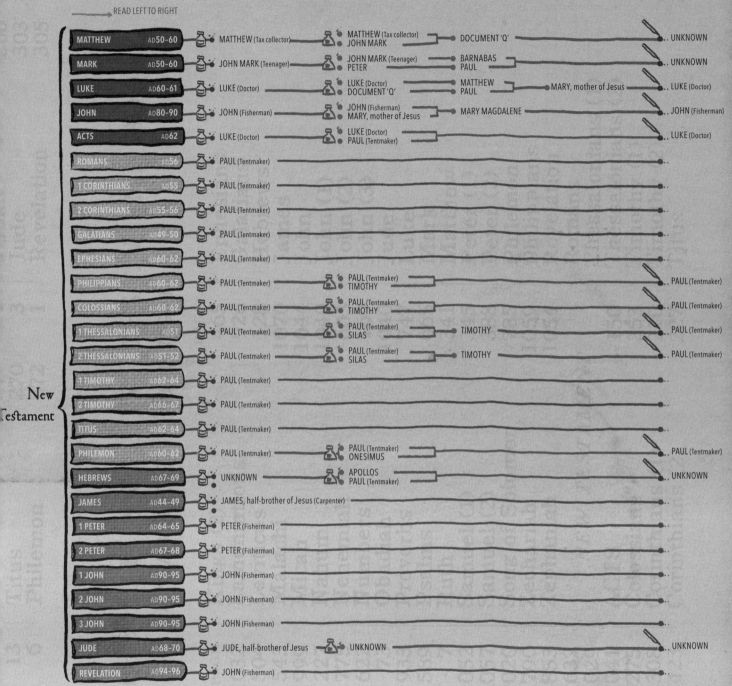

Book	Date	Viewpoint A Author	Viewpoint B Author			Viewpoint B Compiler/Editor
MATTHEW	AD 50–60	MATTHEW (Tax collector)	MATTHEW (Tax collector) / JOHN MARK	DOCUMENT 'Q'		UNKNOWN
MARK	AD 50–60	JOHN MARK (Teenager)	JOHN MARK (Teenager) / PETER	BARNABAS / PAUL		UNKNOWN
LUKE	AD 60–61	LUKE (Doctor)	LUKE (Doctor) / DOCUMENT 'Q'	MATTHEW / PAUL	MARY, mother of Jesus	LUKE (Doctor)
JOHN	AD 80–90	JOHN (Fisherman)	JOHN (Fisherman) / MARY, mother of Jesus	MARY MAGDALENE		JOHN (Fisherman)
ACTS	AD 62	LUKE (Doctor)	LUKE (Doctor) / PAUL (Tentmaker)			LUKE (Doctor)
ROMANS	AD 56	PAUL (Tentmaker)				
1 CORINTHIANS	AD 55	PAUL (Tentmaker)				
2 CORINTHIANS	AD 55–56	PAUL (Tentmaker)				
GALATIANS	AD 49–50	PAUL (Tentmaker)				
EPHESIANS	AD 60–62	PAUL (Tentmaker)				
PHILIPPIANS	AD 60–62	PAUL (Tentmaker)	PAUL (Tentmaker) / TIMOTHY			PAUL (Tentmaker)
COLOSSIANS	AD 60–62	PAUL (Tentmaker)	PAUL (Tentmaker) / TIMOTHY			PAUL (Tentmaker)
1 THESSALONIANS	AD 51	PAUL (Tentmaker)	PAUL (Tentmaker) / SILAS	TIMOTHY		PAUL (Tentmaker)
2 THESSALONIANS	AD 51–52	PAUL (Tentmaker)	PAUL (Tentmaker) / SILAS	TIMOTHY		PAUL (Tentmaker)
1 TIMOTHY	AD 62–64	PAUL (Tentmaker)				
2 TIMOTHY	AD 66–67	PAUL (Tentmaker)				
TITUS	AD 62–64	PAUL (Tentmaker)				
PHILEMON	AD 60–62	PAUL (Tentmaker)	PAUL (Tentmaker) / ONESIMUS			PAUL (Tentmaker)
HEBREWS	AD 67–69	UNKNOWN	APOLLOS / PAUL (Tentmaker)			UNKNOWN
JAMES	AD 44–49	JAMES, half-brother of Jesus (Carpenter)				
1 PETER	AD 64–65	PETER (Fisherman)				
2 PETER	AD 67–68	PETER (Fisherman)				
1 JOHN	AD 90–95	JOHN (Fisherman)				
2 JOHN	AD 90–95	JOHN (Fisherman)				
3 JOHN	AD 90–95	JOHN (Fisherman)				
JUDE	AD 68–70	JUDE, half-brother of Jesus	UNKNOWN			UNKNOWN
REVELATION	AD 94–96	JOHN (Fisherman)				

New Testament

The sources, compilers or writers of Scripture are the subjects of scholarly debate, as are the dates. This graphic also offers a multiple-contributors view (view point B) held by some scholars who believe that there were additional documentary sources for some of the books that have generally been attributed to a single author. For example, the 'Documentary hypothesis' suggests the first five books of the Bible were compiled at different times from a number of sources, though other theories would offer alternative explanations:

DOCUMENT 'J' = 'Yahwist': Possible source for the Torah, perhaps written in the Southern Kingdom (Judah). } – *Emphasises Moses as the rescuer for a people now in need, again, of rescue.*

DOCUMENT 'E' = 'Elohist': Possible source for the Torah, perhaps written in the Northern Kingdom (Israel).

DOCUMENT 'D' = 'Deuteronomist': Possible source for the Torah, discovered or compiled by King Josiah. – *For a nation in decline: emphasises the consequences of sin and the need for holiness.*

DOCUMENT 'P' = 'Priestly': Possible source for the Torah, perhaps written whilst in exile in Babylon. – *Emphasises the role of Aaron, the priest, and Temple life, to remind a people now remote from Jerusalem.*

Other possible source for the Synoptic Gospels:

DOCUMENT 'Q' = Possible compilation of the sayings of Jesus, used by Matthew and Luke.

source: View point B: David Painting. Viewpoint A and dates: derived from Blue Letter Bible. ESV Introductions. Blue Letter Bible. Web. 9 Mar, 2018. <https://www.blueletterbible.org/study/intros/esv_intros.cfm>.
note: Viewpoint B is just one of many other alternative viewpoints.

Viewpoint A	Author (Their background)	Author (Their background)	Viewpoint B
13	PAUL (Tentmaker)	PAUL (Tentmaker)	17
8	(UNKNOWN) (Unknown)	(UNKNOWN) (Unknown)	10
5	JOHN (Fisherman)	JOHN (Fisherman)	5
5	MOSES (Prince, Shepherd, Leader)	MOSES (Prince, Shepherd, Leader)	5
4	EZRA (Priest)	ORAL HISTORIES	5
3	PRIESTS DURING DAVID'S REIGN (Priest)	EZRA (Priest)	4
3	SOLOMON (King)	SOLOMON (King)	4
2	LUKE (Doctor)	TIMOTHY (Unknown)	4
2	PETER (Fisherman)	DOCUMENT 'E'	3
1	AGUR (Unknown)	DOCUMENT 'J'	3
1	AMOS (Shepherd)	PETER (Fisherman)	3
1	ASAPH (Worship leader)	DOCUMENT 'Q'	2
1	DANIEL (Administrator)	JOHN MARK (Teenager)	2
1	DAVID (Shepherd, King)	LUKE (Doctor)	2
1	ETHAN (Unknown)	MARY MOTHER OF JESUS	2
1	EZEKIEL (Priest)	MATTHEW (Tax collector)	2
1	HABAKKUK (Prophet)	SILAS (Unknown)	2
1	HAGGAI (Prophet)	AGUR (Unknown)	1
1	HEMAN (Unknown)	AMOS (Shepherd)	1
1	HEZEKIAH (Prophet)	APOLLOS (Unknown)	1
1	HOSEA (Prophet)	ASAPH (Worship leader)	1
1	ISAIAH (Prophet)	BARNABAS (Unknown)	1
1	JAMES, HALF-BROTHER OF JESUS (Carpenter)	DANIEL (Administrator)	1
1	JEREMIAH (Prophet)	DAVID (Shepherd, King)	1
1	JOEL (Prophet)	DOCUMENT 'D'	1
1	JOHN MARK (Teenager)	DOCUMENT 'P'	1
1	JONAH (Prophet)	ESTHER (Queen)	1

Authors' Contributions

How big a voice did each one have?

1 — HABAKKUK (Prophet)
1 — HAGGAI (Prophet)
1 — HEMAN (Unknown)
1 — HEZEKIAH (Prophet)
1 — HOSEA (Prophet)
1 — ISAIAH (Prophet)
1 — JAMES, HALF-BROTHER OF JESUS (Carpenter)
1 — JEREMIAH (Prophet)
1 — JOEL (Prophet)
1 — JONAH (Prophet)
1 — JOSHUA (Leader)
1 — KORAH (Unknown)
1 — LEMUEL (Unknown)
1 — MALACHI (Prophet)
1 — MARY MAGDALENE (Unknown)
1 — MICAH (Prophet)
1 — MORDECAI (Administrator)
1 — NAHUM (Prophet)
1 — NEHEMIAH (King's cupbearer)
1 — OBADIAH (Prophet)
1 — ONESIMUS (Slave)
1 — SAMUEL (Prophet)
1 — ZECHARIAH (Prophet)
1 — ZEPHANIAH (Prophet)

1 — LEMUEL (Unknown)
1 — MALACHI (Prophet)
1 — MATTHEW (Tax collector)
1 — MICAH (Prophet)
1 — NAHUM (Prophet)
1 — OBADIAH (Prophet)
1 — UNKNOWN, BUT POST EXILE
1 — ZECHARIAH (Prophet)
1 — ZEPHANIAH (Prophet)

0 — APOLLOS (Unknown)
0 — BARNABAS (Unknown)
0 — DOCUMENT 'D'
0 — DOCUMENT 'E'
0 — DOCUMENT 'J'
0 — DOCUMENT 'P'
0 — DOCUMENT 'Q'
0 — ESTHER (Queen)
0 — JOSHUA (Leader)
0 — MARY, MOTHER OF JESUS
0 — MARY MAGDALENE (Unknown)
0 — MORDECAI (Administrator)
0 — NEHEMIAH (King's cupbearer)
0 — ONESIMUS (Slave)
0 — ORAL HISTORIES
0 — SAMUEL (PROPHET)
0 — SILAS (Unknown)
0 — TIMOTHY (Unknown)

0 — JUDE, HALF-BROTHER OF JESUS (Unknown)
0 — PRIESTS DURING DAVID'S REIGN (Priest)
0 — UNKNOWN, BUT POST EXILE

source: View point B: David Painting. Viewpoint A and dates: derived from Blue Letter Bible. ESV Introductions. Blue Letter Bible. Web. 9 Mar, 2018. <https://www.blueletterbible.org/study/intros/esv_intros.cfm>.
note: Viewpoint B is just one of many other alternative viewpoints.

GOD IS LOVE
From beginning to end
1 JN 4:8

THE OLD TESTAMENT

STAGE 1

The Nature & Character of God
Who is like the Lord our God?

Over the centuries,
theologians have analysed
the Bible in attempts to
describe the indescribable.
Many books on systematic
theology use the method of
'dividing' God into two parts:
God's transcendent nature
and God's character.

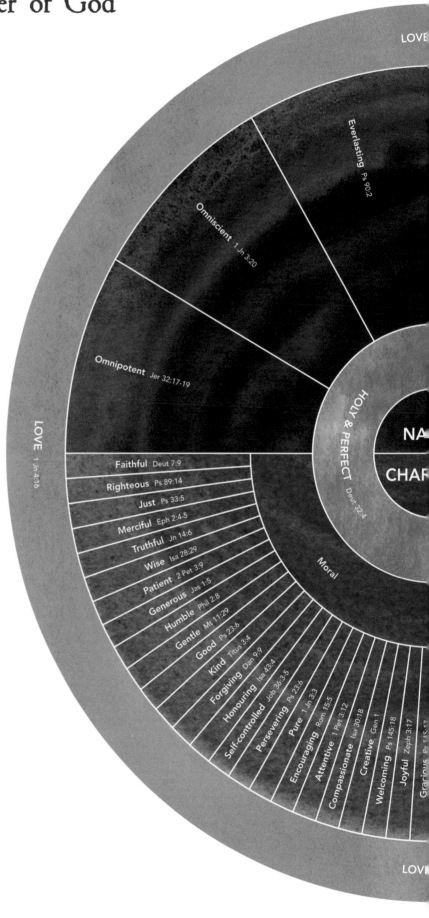

Everlasting Ps 90:2

Omniscient 1 Jn 3:20

Omnipotent Jer 32:17-19

LOVE 1 Jn 4:16

LOVE

LOVE

HOLY & PERFECT Deut 32:4

NA

CHAR

Moral

Faithful Deut 7:9

Righteous Ps 89:14

Just Ps 33:5

Merciful Eph 2:4-5

Truthful Jn 14:6

Wise Isa 28:29

Patient 2 Pet 3:9

Generous Jas 1:5

Humble Phil 2:8

Gentle Mt 11:29

Good Ps 23:6

Kind Titus 3:4

Forgiving Dan 9:9

Honouring Isa 43:4

Self-controlled Job 36:3-5

Persevering Ps 23:6

Pure 1 Jn 3:3

Encouraging Rom 15:5

Attentive 1 Pet 3:12

Compassionate Isa 30:18

Creative Gen 1

Welcoming Ps 145:18

Joyful Zeph 3:17

Gracious Ps 145:17

see pp132-133, 142 & 182-183

NATURE:

those things that
God is which we are not.

CHARACTER:

God's attributes that we
can also develop.

Omnipresent Ps 139:7-10

Infinite Rev 22:13

Triune Deut 6:4

LOVE 1 Jn 4:16

HOLY & PERFECT

Deut 32:3-4

Grief
Gen 6:5-6

Joy
Zeph 3:17

Compassion
Ps 145:9

Anger
Ps 30:5

Emotions

Personal

Will 2 Chr 7:14

Relational

Mind

Speech
Gen 1:3-5

Memory
Ps 105:8

Imagination
Job 38

Reasoning
Isa 1:18

Trinity

Father Rom 8:15

Son Jn 17:3

source: Dr K.L Robertson, Miriam Lowe.
Gen, Deut, 2 Chr, Job, Ps, Isa, Jer, Dan, Zeph, Mt, Jn, Rom, 2 Cor, Eph, Phil, Titus, Jas, 1 Pet, 2 Pet, 1 Jn, Rev
Alistair E. McGrath, *Christian Theology: An Introduction* (Blackwells: Oxford, 2001).
Elizabeth A. Johnson, *Quest for the Living God: Mapping Frontiers in the Theology of God* (Continuum: London, 2011).
Clark H. Pinnock, *Most Moved Mover: A Theology of God's Openness* (Paternoster Press: Carlisle, 2001).

note: Attempts to give definition and meaning to the attributes of God's nature will differ according to the theologies they draw on.
The attributes of God's character are more universally accepted. The data contributor and author have drawn on personal interpretation and choices when collating this data.

Names of God
An Old Testament 'role' call

El Shaddai · Adonai

The all-sufficient One who does not need therapy from humanity as the idols of the nations, the *sheddim*, are dependent on their worshippers.

Always used in the plural when referring to God; the singular implies a human lord.

YAH

El-Roi
El Olam
Jehovah-Jireh

The covenant name of God, also known as the Tetragrammaton. It comes from the verb to be, *havah*, The Self-Existent One.

God sees and provides. From *Jireh* – to see, or foresee, as a prophet.

Qanna
El Elyon
Attiq Yomin

Jehovah-Shammah
Jehovah-Rohi
Yahweh Hoseenu
Jehovah-Shalom

God wh... and whe... His pres...

Our pea... – the pe... person ... to God ...

Ha Shem

Jehovah-M'kaddesh

God, the Rock. Used five times in the *Song of Moses*.

Jehovah

Tsur

God, the commander of the angelic host and the armies of God.

028 | 029

see p142

lohim
WEH
-Sabaoth
Jehovah-Tsidkenu
El

God the Creator and Preserver, transcendent, mighty and strong.

God the Deliverer who fights for us and is victorious on the battlefield. From the word to glisten or lift up.

Jehovah-Nissi

Jehovah-Rophe

Ehyeh Asher Ehyeh

I AM that I AM. Name given to Moses at the burning bush.

From *Rophe* – to heal. Implies spiritual, emotional as well as physical healing. Can also be transliterated Rapha.

eness
le
onship

God our Righteousness. From *tsidek*, meaning straight, declared innocent, or balanced – as on weighing scales.

God who is mighty or strong. First used in connection with Melchizedek, the priest of the Most High God, this name is given to the promised Messiah in Isaiah 9:6-7.

F GOD, EPITHET (descriptive term), TITLE OF GOD   SIZE of text REFLECTS FREQUENCY OF USE

source: Dr Amy Orr-Ewing: Director of The Oxford Centre for Christian Apologetics. OXFORD CENTRE www.theocca.org. The Old Testament
note: This graphic represents the frequency of use of a selection of names, titles and epithets for God used in the Old Testament. The data is subjective and differs between sources.

NAME	MEANING	FIRST USE
ELOHIM	God	Gen 1:1
YAHWEH	The LORD	Gen 2:4
EL	God	Gen 14:18
EL ELYON	Most High God	Gen 14:19
ADONAI	Lord or Master	Gen 15:2
EL-ROI	The God who Sees	Gen 16:13
EL SHADDAI	God Almighty	Gen 17:5
EL OLAM	The Everlasting God	Gen 21:33
JEHOVAH-JIREH	The Lord will Provide	Gen 22:14
EHYEH ASHER EHYEH	I AM that I AM	Ex 3:14
JEHOVAH-ROPHE	The Lord who Heals	Ex 15:22-26
JEHOVAH-NISSI	The Lord my Banner	Ex 17:15
QANNA	The Jealous	Ex 20:5
JEHOVAH-M'KADDESH	The Lord Sanctifies	Ex 31:13
HA SHEM	The Name	Lev 24:16
TSUR	The Rock	Deut 32:4
JEHOVAH-SHALOM	The Lord is Peace	Judg 6:24
JEHOVAH-SABAOTH	The Lord of Hosts	1 Sam 1:3
JEHOVAH-ROHI	The Lord our Shepherd	Ps 23:1
YAHWEH HOSEENU	The Lord Creator	Ps 95:6
JEHOVAH-TSIDKENU	The Lord our Righteousness	Jer 23:5
JEHOVAH-SHAMMAH	The Lord is There	Ezek 48:35
ATTIQ YOMIN	Ancient of Days	Dan 7:9

CREATED
FOR RELATIONSHIP
To be loved

GEN 1:27-28

THE OLD TESTAMENT

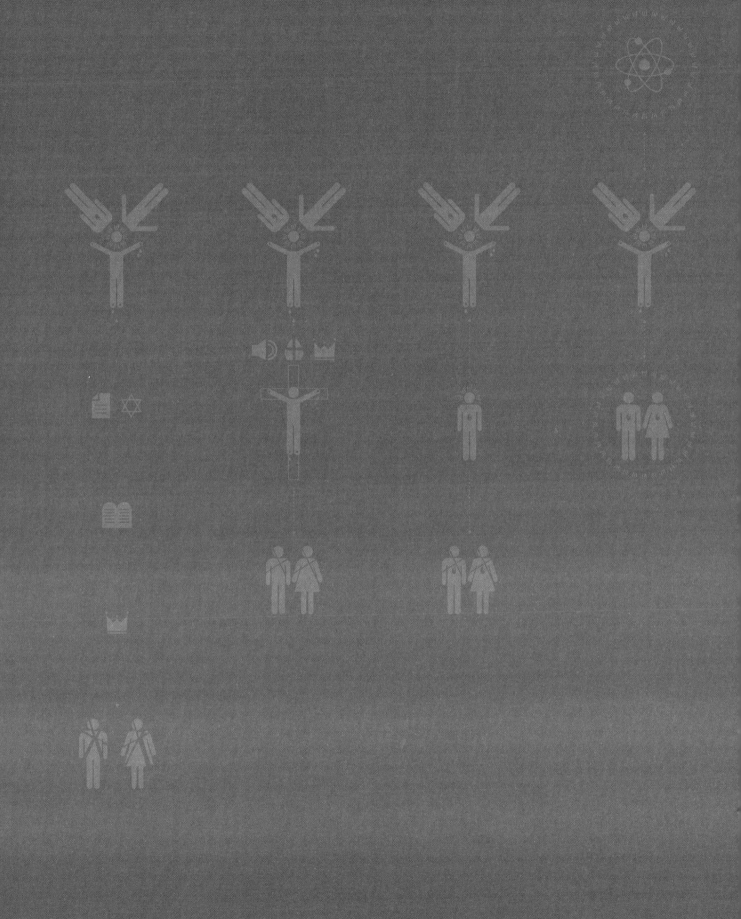

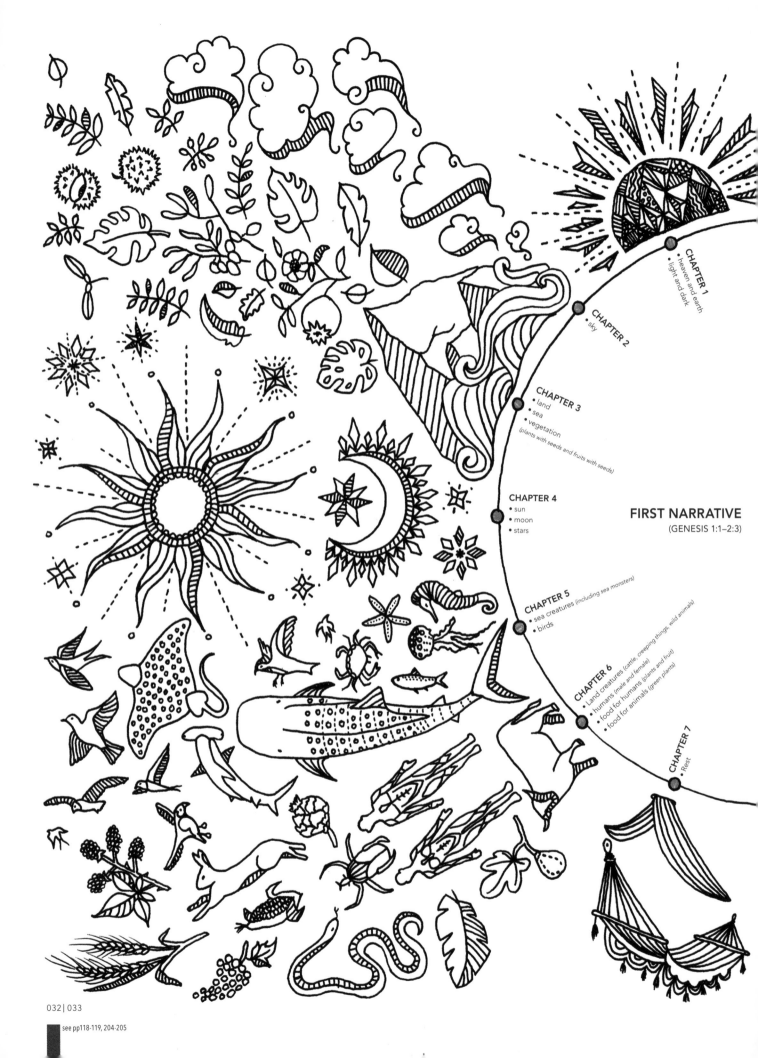

CHAPTER 1
• heaven and earth
• light and dark

CHAPTER 2
• sky

CHAPTER 3
• land
• sea
• vegetation
(plants with seeds and fruits with seeds)

CHAPTER 4
• sun
• moon
• stars

FIRST NARRATIVE
(GENESIS 1:1–2:3)

CHAPTER 5
• sea creatures (including sea monsters)
• birds

CHAPTER 6
• Land creatures (cattle, creeping things, wild animals)
• humans (male and female)
• food for humans (plants and fruit)
• food for animals (green plants)

CHAPTER 7
• Rest

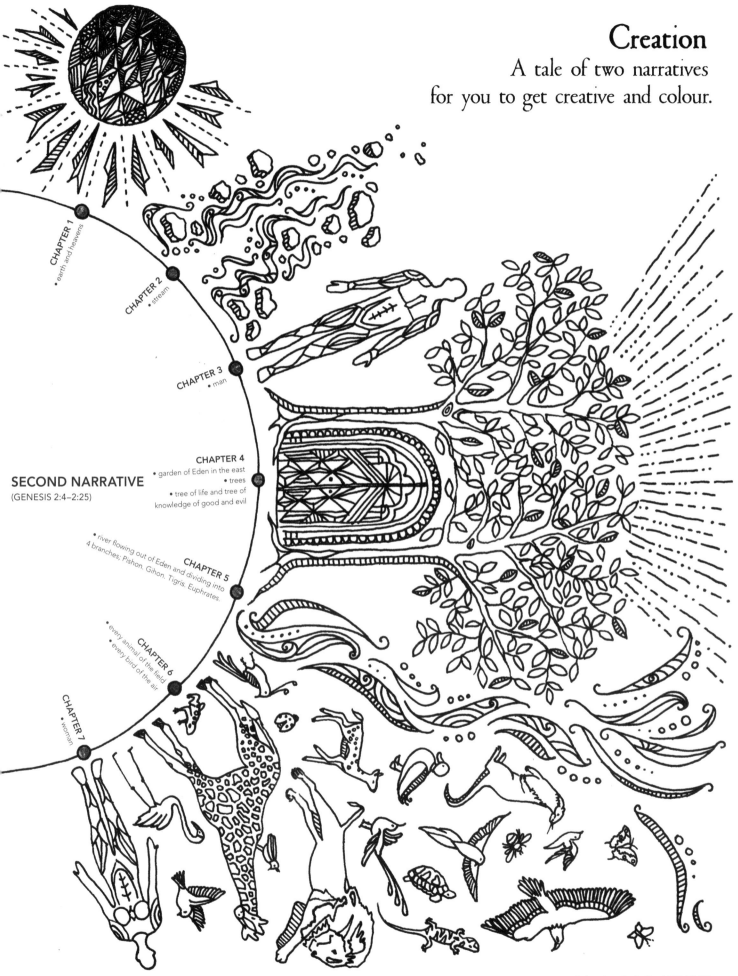

Creation

A tale of two narratives
for you to get creative and colour.

CHAPTER 1
• earth and heavens

CHAPTER 2
• stream

CHAPTER 3
• man

SECOND NARRATIVE
(GENESIS 2:4–2:25)

CHAPTER 4
• garden of Eden in the east
• trees
• tree of life and tree of
knowledge of good and evil

CHAPTER 5
• river flowing out of Eden and dividing into
4 branches; Pishon. Gihon. Tigris. Euphrates.

CHAPTER 6
• every animal of the field
• every bird of the air

CHAPTER 7
• woman

source: Professor James Crossley. Genesis 1:1-2:3, 2:4-25

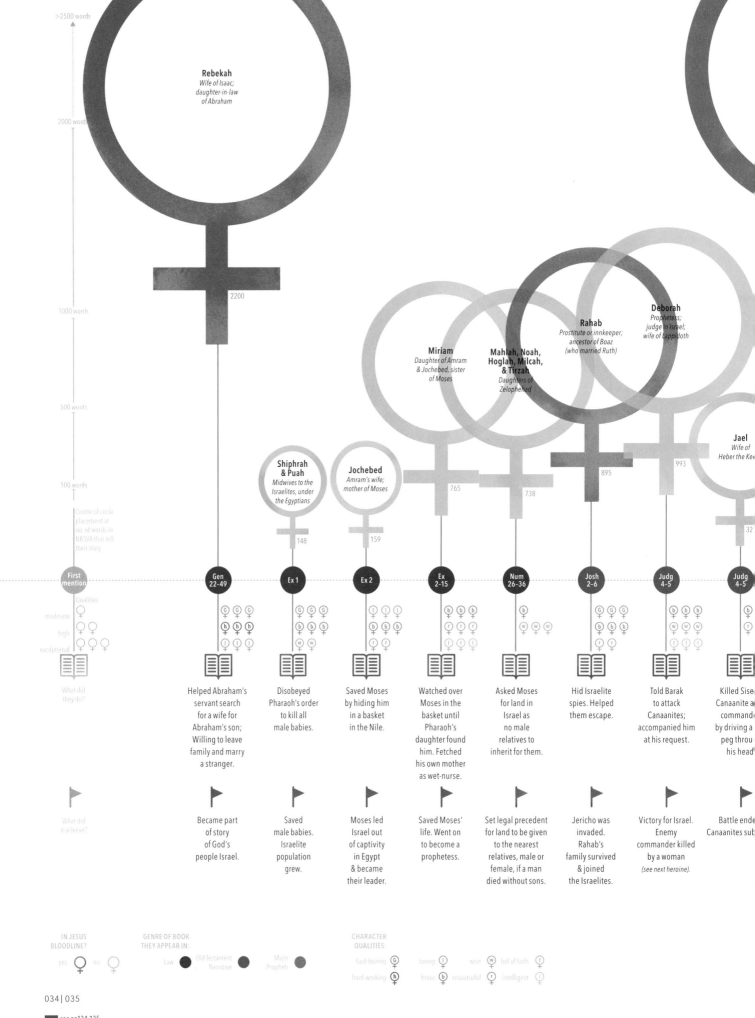

>2500 words

2000 words

Rebekah
*Wife of Isaac;
daughter-in-law
of Abraham*

1000 words

2200

500 words

Deborah
*Prophetess;
judge in Israel;
wife of Lappidoth*

Rahab
*Prostitute or innkeeper;
ancestor of Boaz
(who married Ruth)*

Miriam
*Daughter of Amram
& Jochebed, sister
of Moses*

**Mahlah, Noah,
Hoglah, Milcah,
& Tirzah**
*Daughters of
Zelophehad*

Jael
*Wife of
Heber the Ken...*

100 words

**Shiphrah
& Puah**
*Midwives to the
Israelites, under
the Egyptians*

Jochebed
*Amram's wife;
mother of Moses*

765

738

895

993

Centre of circle
placement at
no. of words in
NRSVA that tell
their story

148

159

32

First mention	Gen 22-49	Ex 1	Ex 2	Ex 2-15	Num 26-36	Josh 2-6	Judg 4-5	Judg 4-5

Qualities

moderate

high

exceptional

What did
they do?

| Helped Abraham's servant search for a wife for Abraham's son; Willing to leave family and marry a stranger. | Disobeyed Pharaoh's order to kill all male babies. | Saved Moses by hiding him in a basket in the Nile. | Watched over Moses in the basket until Pharaoh's daughter found him. Fetched his own mother as wet-nurse. | Asked Moses for land in Israel as no male relatives to inherit for them. | Hid Israelite spies. Helped them escape. | Told Barak to attack Canaanites; accompanied him at his request. | Killed Sise... Canaanite a... command... by driving a... peg throu... his head... |

What did
it achieve?

| | Became part of story of God's people Israel. | Saved male babies. Israelite population grew. | Moses led Israel out of captivity in Egypt & became their leader. | Saved Moses' life. Went on to become a prophetess. | Set legal precedent for land to be given to the nearest relatives, male or female, if a man died without sons. | Jericho was invaded. Rahab's family survived & joined the Israelites. | Victory for Israel. Enemy commander killed by a woman *(see next heroine).* | Battle ende... Canaanites su... |

**IN JESUS
BLOODLINE?**

yes ♀ no ♀

**GENRE OF BOOK
THEY APPEAR IN:**

Law ● Old Testament Narrative ● Major Prophets ●

**CHARACTER
QUALITIES:**

God-fearing ⓖ   loving ⓛ   wise ⓦ   full of faith ⓕ

hard-working ⓗ   brave ⓑ   resourceful ⓡ   intelligent ⓘ

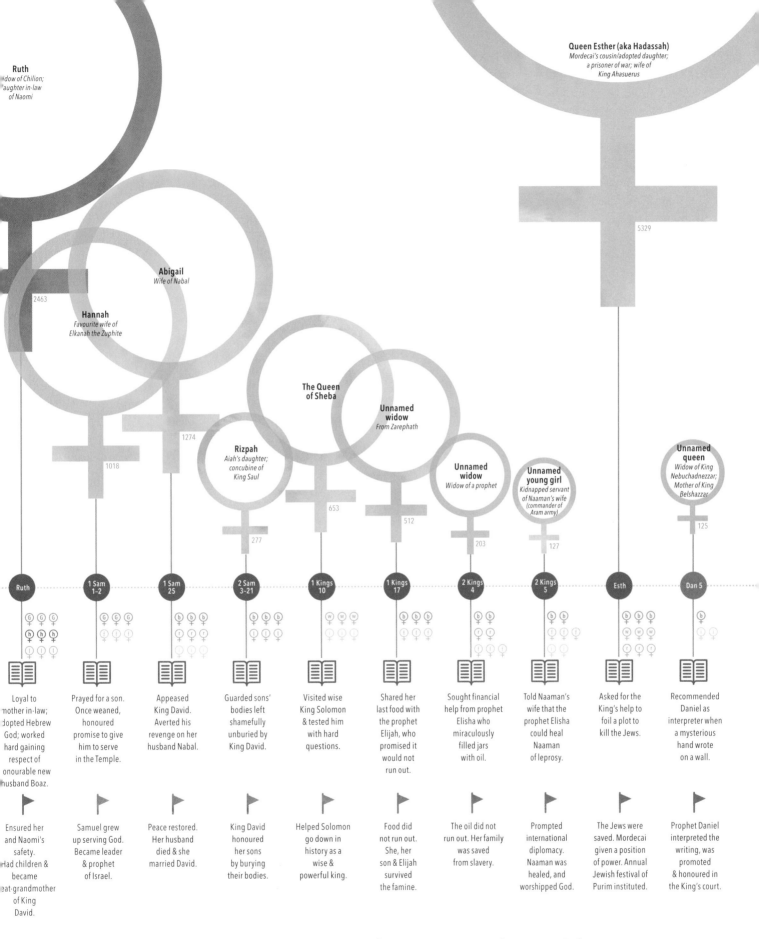

Ruth
Widow of Chilion; daughter in-law of Naomi

Queen Esther (aka Hadassah)
Mordecai's cousin/adopted daughter; a prisoner of war; wife of King Ahasuerus
5329

Abigail
Wife of Nabal
2463

Hannah
Favourite wife of Elkanah the Zuphite
1274

1018

The Queen of Sheba

Unnamed widow
From Zarephath

Rizpah
Aiah's daughter; concubine of King Saul
653

512

Unnamed widow
Widow of a prophet
277

Unnamed young girl
Kidnapped servant of Naaman's wife (commander of Aram army)
203

Unnamed queen
Widow of King Nebuchadnezzar; Mother of King Belshazzar
125

127

Ruth	1 Sam 1–2	1 Sam 25	2 Sam 3–21	1 Kings 10	1 Kings 17	2 Kings 4	2 Kings 5	Esth	Dan 5

Loyal to mother in-law; adopted Hebrew God; worked hard gaining respect of honourable new husband Boaz.

Prayed for a son. Once weaned, honoured promise to give him to serve in the Temple.

Appeased King David. Averted his revenge on her husband Nabal.

Guarded sons' bodies left shamefully unburied by King David.

Visited wise King Solomon & tested him with hard questions.

Shared her last food with the prophet Elijah, who promised it would not run out.

Sought financial help from prophet Elisha who miraculously filled jars with oil.

Told Naaman's wife that the prophet Elisha could heal Naaman of leprosy.

Asked for the King's help to foil a plot to kill the Jews.

Recommended Daniel as interpreter when a mysterious hand wrote on a wall.

Ensured her and Naomi's safety. Had children & became great-grandmother of King David.

Samuel grew up serving God. Became leader & prophet of Israel.

Peace restored. Her husband died & she married David.

King David honoured her sons by burying their bodies.

Helped Solomon go down in history as a wise & powerful king.

Food did not run out. She, her son & Elijah survived the famine.

The oil did not run out. Her family was saved from slavery.

Prompted international diplomacy. Naaman was healed, and worshipped God.

The Jews were saved. Mordecai given a position of power. Annual Jewish festival of Purim instituted.

Prophet Daniel interpreted the writing, was promoted & honoured in the King's court.

Despite the restrictive culture in which they lived, there were women with the wisdom and initiative to use what power they had to change their world. By rising to their challenges, they not only lived out God's wider purposes but changed human history.

Women of Influence in the Old Testament
Wisdom, initiative and opportunity

source: Ruth M. Bancewicz, with thanks to Dr Hilary Marlow, Faraday Institute for Science and Religion. Gen, Ex, Num, Deut, Josh, Judg, Ruth, 1 Sam, 2 Sam, 1 Kings, 2 Kings, 1 Chr, 2 Chr, Esth, Dan, Mic, Lk, Heb, Jas. *All About Jesus: The Single Story from Matthew, Mark, Luke and John*, compiled by Roger Quy (Authentic, 2007). note: The data contributor and author have drawn on personal interpretation and choices when collating this data.

One of God's people. Queen to a
foreign king. Saved God's people
through diplomatic genius.
54

BAAL

Supreme sky god of Canaan and
Phoenicia mocked by Elijah at Mount
Carmel for non-response to his own
prophets.
55

REUBEN

Jacob's son. Joseph's brother.
One of the 12 tribes of Israel.
Persuaded his brothers not to kill
Joseph in jealousy.
55

ELIJAH

Ordered rain to stop for 3.5 years.
Enemy of King Ahab. Taken
away in a chariot of fire and
never died.
66

DANIEL

Exiled with God's people.
Refused to worship foreign kings.
Miraculously saved from
lions' den.
71

JEHOSHAPHAT

A rare good king of God's people
(Judah). Brought social reform.
Made peace with God's people
in North (Israel).
75

JEROBOAM I

Evil king of God's people (Israel).
Led the people away from God
to worship two golden calves.
82

AHAB

An evil king of God's people
(Israel). Married evil pagan
queen Jezebel. Enemy of Elijah.
82

ESAU

Son of Isaac.
Brother of Jacob. Hunter.
Founder of the country Edom.
88

ABSALOM

Son of King David.
Started rebellion against David.
Caught in an oak tree and killed by Joab.
92

ISAAC

Son of Abraham.
Miracle baby of God's promise.
Saved by God from being a human
sacrifice requested by God.
105

JONATHAN

Son of King Saul.
Best friends with King David.
Helped David escape from Saul.
106

SAMUEL

Miracle baby dedicated to God.
Heard God's voice as a child.
Anointed first two kings (Saul and David)
of God's people.
118

HEZEKIAH

Good king of God's people (Judah).
Reinstated Temple worship.
Defied Assyrian invaders.
119

JOAB

Nephew of King David.
Killed the rebellious Absalom.
131

JEREMIAH

'Weeping prophet'.
Called by God as prophet before birth.
Laments disobedience of God's people.
Saw destruction of Jerusalem.
134

PHARAOH

King of Egypt. Oppressed all God's
people in slavery. Enemy to Moses.
Hardened his heart towards God
during plagues.
162

JOSEPH

Son of Jacob. Judah's brother.
Wore a technicolour coat.
Governed Egypt and God's people
through a famine.
169

JOSHUA

Moses' assistant and successor.
Led God's people into Promised Land.
Circled and destroyed walls of Jericho.
200

KING /QUEEN

SON OF KING

PATRIARCH

WIFE & MOTHER
OF A PATRIARCH

SON OF A PATRIARCH

LEADER OF
GOD'S PEOPLE

COMMANDER OF
DAVID'S ARMY

PRIEST

PROPHET

A FALSE GOD

see pp136-137

est.
would grow.

219

226

and Judah).
rth.

268

333

SAUL

Called to be 1st human king of all
God's people (Israel and Judah).
Became David's father-in-law.
Attempted to kill David.

334

MOSES

Led God's people out of slavery in Egypt.
Received ten commandments from God.

716

DAVID

Good king of all God's people (Israel and Judah).
'A man after God's own heart'.
Shepherd. Killed giant Goliath.

930

Most-mentioned Characters in the Old Testament
Each playing their part

source: Dr Stuart C. Weir. Old Testament.

**RELATIONSHIP
BROKEN**
People choose separation

GEN 3:14-19

THE OLD TESTAMENT

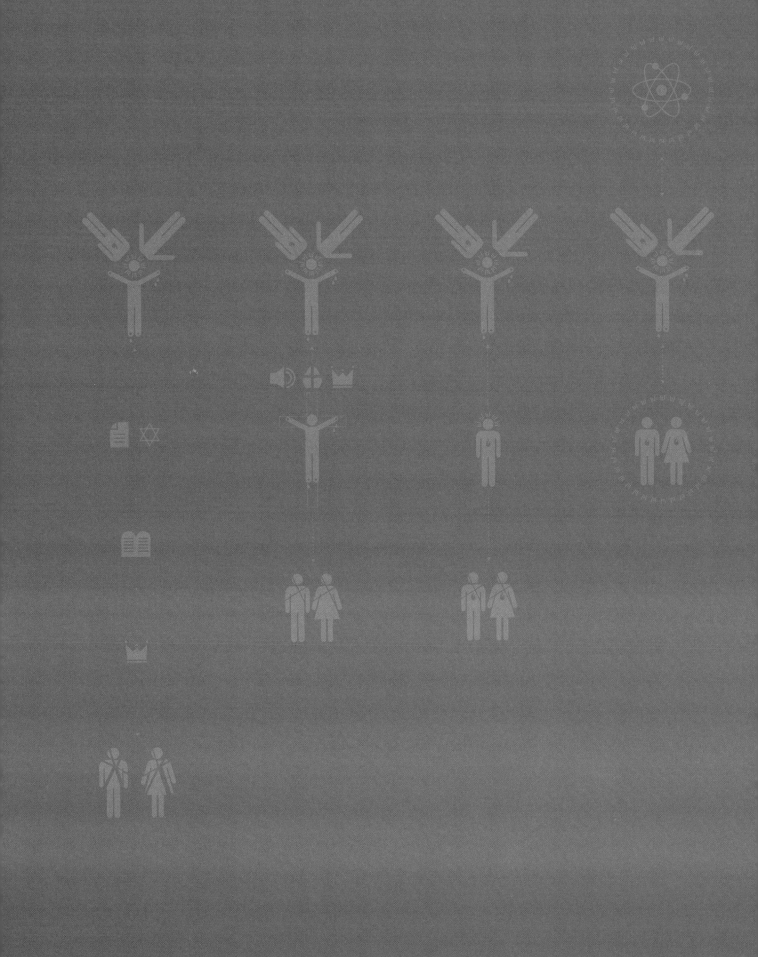

The Fall Explained
Love does not insist on its own way

Relationship
with God

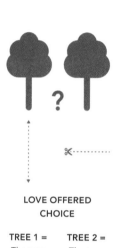

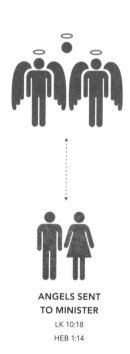

**CREATED IN
GOD'S IMAGE**

God is love

GEN 1:26

**LOVE OFFERED
CHOICE**

TREE 1 =
The tree
that
brings life

(The tree of life)

TREE 2 =
The tree
that brings
death

*(The tree of
the knowledge
of good
and evil)*

GEN 2:9

1 COR 13:4-7

**ANGELS SENT
TO MINISTER**

LK 10:18

HEB 1:14

see pp106-107, 110-111

GOD CHOSE

GEN 6:5-8

✗ **1.** To Destroy?
(possible by His nature)

OR

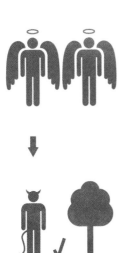

✗ — — — — — —

**SATAN CHOSE, THEN
TEMPTED MANKIND**

To be like God
in ways that were
never intended

GEN 3:1-5

WE CHOSE

The Father of Lies
instead of
the Father of Light

GEN 3:6-7

✗ **2.** To Ignore?
(possible by His nature)

OR

✓ **3.** To Redeem!
*(possible by His character
& nature)*

source: David Painting. Gen 1–6, Lk 10, Heb 1, 1 Cor 13.

note: The data contributor and author have drawn on personal interpretation when collating this data and dividing it into steps for the purposes of this graphic. There are other interpretations of the purpose of angels and the timing of Satan's fall from heaven.

see pp76-79

The Fall Out

How Old Testament language describes an increasingly broken world

After the Fall, the use of positive words decreases as the use of negative words progressively increases. To demonstrate this, negative words that represent 'brokenness' have been counted and subtracted from the total words, with the result then charted as a percentage of the verses in that period.

TOTAL FALL IN PERCENTAGE OF POSITIVE & NEUTRAL WORDS PER BIBLE SECTION:

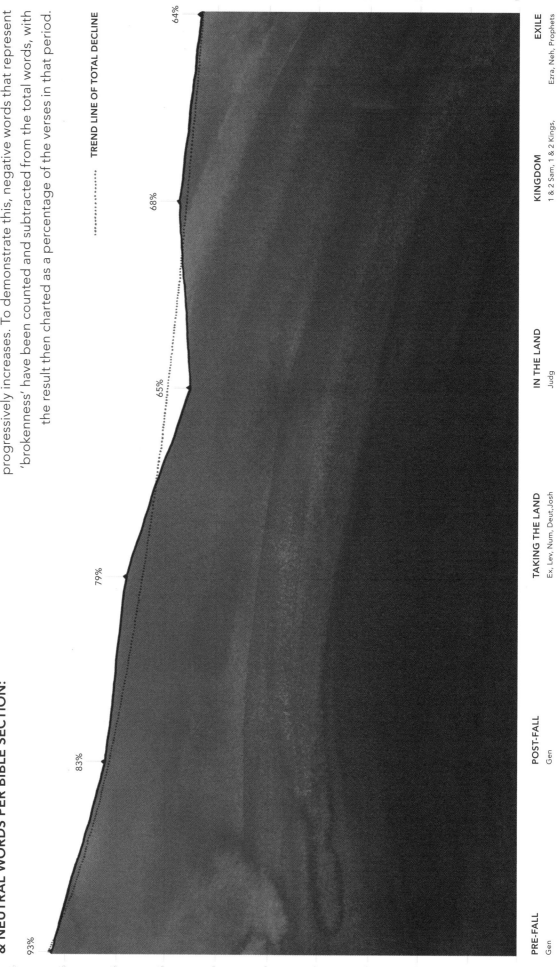

TREND LINE OF TOTAL DECLINE

93%

83%

79%

65%

68%

64%

PRE-FALL	POST-FALL	TAKING THE LAND	IN THE LAND	KINGDOM	EXILE
Gen	Gen	Ex, Lev, Num, Deut, Josh	Judg	1 & 2 Sam, 1 & 2 Kings, 1 & 2 Chr	Ezra, Neh, Prophets

TREND LINES FOR EACH WORD USED:

PRE-FALL	POST-FALL	TAKING THE LAND	IN THE LAND	KINGDOM	EXILE
Gen	Gen	Ex, Lev, Num, Deut, Josh	Judg	1 & 2 Sam, 1 & 2 Kings, 1 & 2 Chr	Ezra, Neh, Prophets

WORDS USED IN THE DATA:

Kill	Battle	Anger	War	Hate	Murder
Death	Die	Destroy	Destruction	Oppress	Mourn
Grieve	Grief	Despair	Sorry/sorrow	Punish	Burden
Injustice	Slavery	Sin	Evil	Wicked	Curse

source: David Painting. The Old Testament.

note: Words selected by the contributor are intended to be a representative, but not exclusive, list of words that might relate to the effects of the Fall.

The First Family Tree

Humanity takes its first steps on a new earth … twice

■ = Length of life (age at death) known
▢ = Length of life unknown
👥 = had other sons and daughters

■ = Male line of Abraham
■ = Male
■ = Female

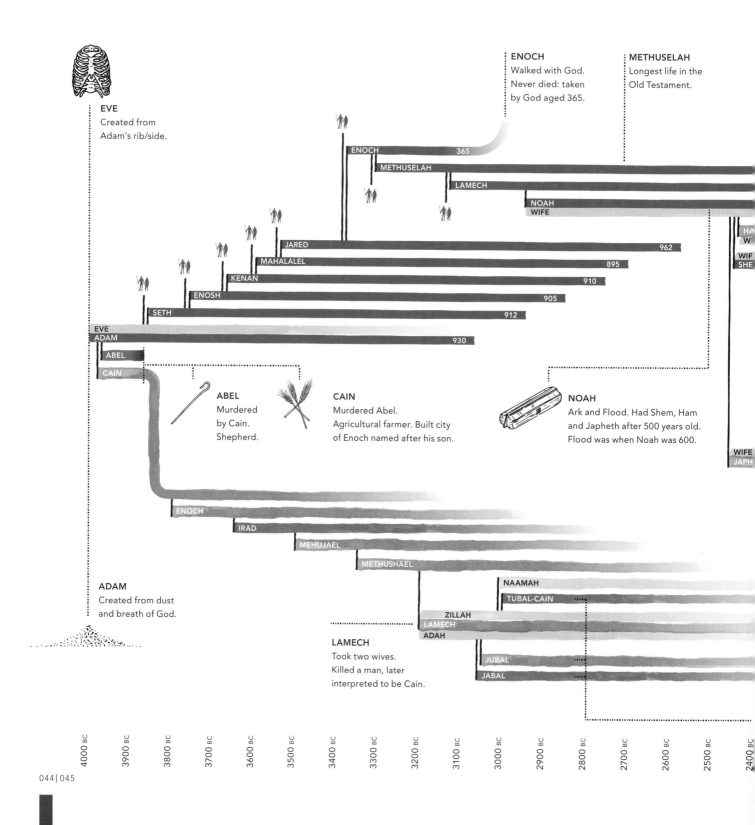

ENOCH
Walked with God.
Never died: taken
by God aged 365.

METHUSELAH
Longest life in the
Old Testament.

EVE
Created from
Adam's rib/side.

ENOCH — 365
METHUSELAH
LAMECH
NOAH
WIFE
JARED — 962
MAHALALEL — 895
KENAN — 910
ENOSH — 905
SETH — 912
EVE
ADAM — 930
ABEL
CAIN
HA
W
WIF
SHE

ABEL
Murdered
by Cain.
Shepherd.

CAIN
Murdered Abel.
Agricultural farmer. Built city
of Enoch named after his son.

NOAH
Ark and Flood. Had Shem, Ham
and Japheth after 500 years old.
Flood was when Noah was 600.

WIFE
JAPH

ENOCH
IRAD
MEHUJAEL
METHUSHAEL

NAAMAH
TUBAL-CAIN
ZILLAH
LAMECH
ADAH

ADAM
Created from dust
and breath of God.

JUBAL
JABAL

LAMECH
Took two wives.
Killed a man, later
interpreted to be Cain.

4000 BC 3900 BC 3800 BC 3700 BC 3600 BC 3500 BC 3400 BC 3300 BC 3200 BC 3100 BC 3000 BC 2900 BC 2800 BC 2700 BC 2600 BC 2500 BC 2400 BC

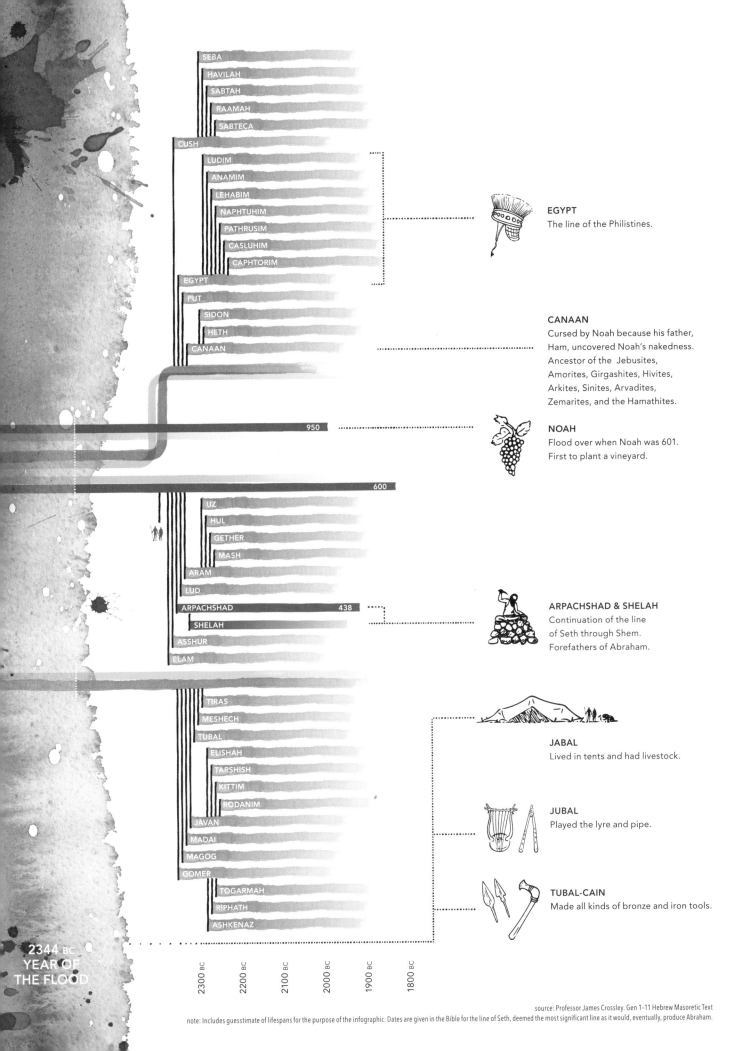

SEBA
HAVILAH
SABTAH
RAAMAH
SABTECA
CUSH
LUDIM
ANAMIM
LEHABIM
NAPHTUHIM
PATHRUSIM
CASLUHIM
CAPHTORIM
EGYPT
PUT
SIDON
HETH
CANAAN

EGYPT
The line of the Philistines.

CANAAN
Cursed by Noah because his father,
Ham, uncovered Noah's nakedness.
Ancestor of the Jebusites,
Amorites, Girgashites, Hivites,
Arkites, Sinites, Arvadites,
Zemarites, and the Hamathites.

950

NOAH
Flood over when Noah was 601.
First to plant a vineyard.

600

UZ
HUL
GETHER
MASH
ARAM
LUD
ARPACHSHAD   438
SHELAH
ASSHUR
ELAM

ARPACHSHAD & SHELAH
Continuation of the line
of Seth through Shem.
Forefathers of Abraham.

TIRAS
MESHECH
TUBAL
ELISHAH
TARSHISH
KITTIM
RODANIM
JAVAN
MADAI
MAGOG
GOMER
TOGARMAH
RIPHATH
ASHKENAZ

JABAL
Lived in tents and had livestock.

JUBAL
Played the lyre and pipe.

TUBAL-CAIN
Made all kinds of bronze and iron tools.

**2344 BC
YEAR OF
THE FLOOD**

2300 BC   2200 BC   2100 BC   2000 BC   1900 BC   1800 BC

source: Professor James Crossley. Gen 1–11 Hebrew Masoretic Text
note: Includes guesstimate of lifespans for the purpose of the infographic. Dates are given in the Bible for the line of Seth, deemed the most significant line as it would, eventually, produce Abraham.

Noah's Ark
A blueprint for life – take two

CONSTRUCTION

The Hebrew for 'ark' is *têba*, a word meaning 'box'. The 'gopher wood' used in its construction is unknown but is usually translated as cypress, a timber known to be resistant to rot. It was coated with pitch inside and out.

COST OF BUILDING IN TODAY'S MONEY
£1044 per m² (£97 per ft²) or £9.3 million

DISPLACEMENT
c. 20 million kg (20,000 tons)

INTERIOR CAPACITY
39,644 m³ (1.4 million ft³)

APPROXIMATE TOTAL DECK AREA
8,891 m² (95,700 ft²)

1 cubit = 0.45 metres

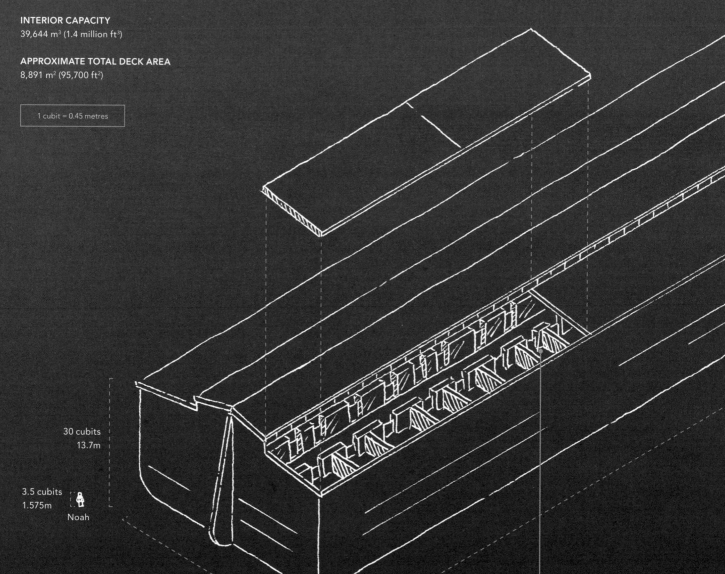

30 cubits
13.7m

3.5 cubits
1.575m
Noah

50 cubits
23m

Make rooms inside.
Gen 6:14

see pp40-41, 42-43, 166-167

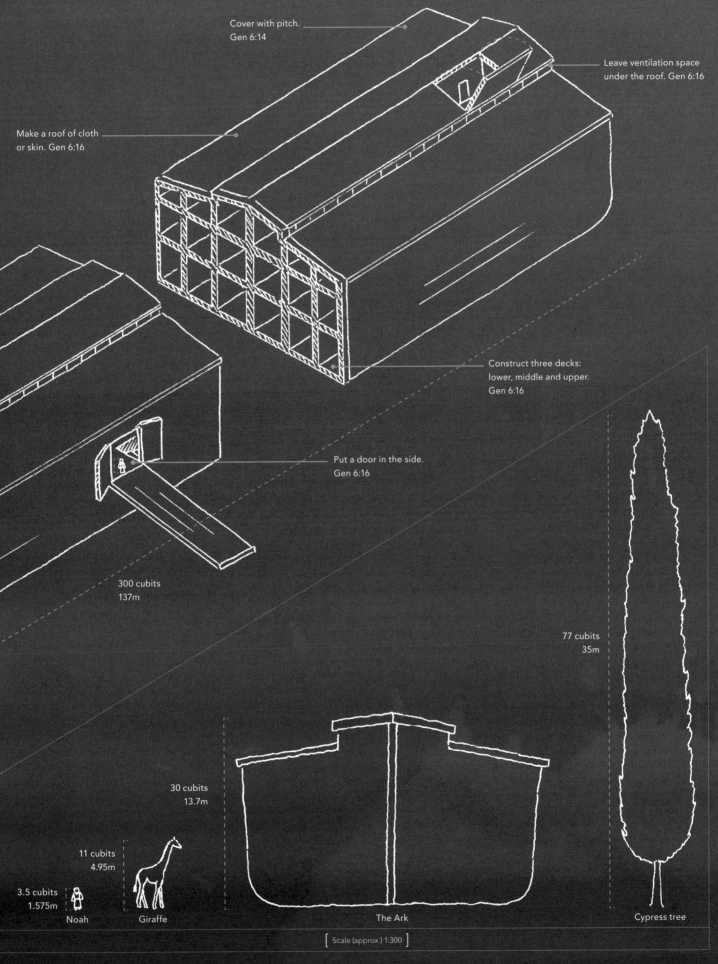

Cover with pitch.
Gen 6:14

Leave ventilation space
under the roof. Gen 6:16

Make a roof of cloth
or skin. Gen 6:16

Construct three decks:
lower, middle and upper.
Gen 6:16

Put a door in the side.
Gen 6:16

300 cubits
137m

77 cubits
35m

30 cubits
13.7m

11 cubits
4.95m

3.5 cubits
1.575m

Noah

Giraffe

The Ark

Cypress tree

[Scale (approx.) 1:300]

source: Nick Page. Genesis 6:9–9:29.
Source for Noah, giraffe & cypress tree height: Wikipedia.org

A RESCUE PLAN
God calls Israel

GEN 12:1-3

THE OLD TESTAMENT

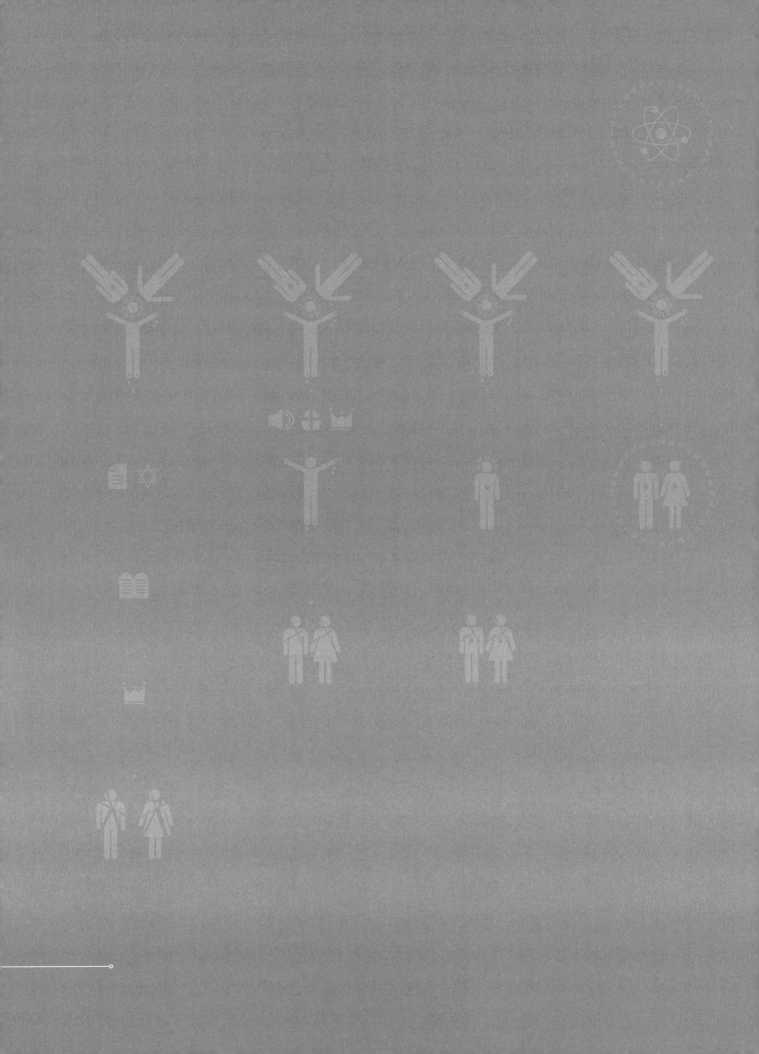

Abraham
Unpacking the promise made by God

WHAT IS
THE PROMISE OF BLESSING

WHY A COVENANT?
God longs to restore relationship between all people and himself.

WITH WHOM?
It begins with Abraham (whose name means 'father of many') who was a shepherd from Ur.
He was married to Sarah, but remained childless for many years. His first child, Ishmael, was born
to his servant Hagar as they tried to resolve their childlessness on their own. Isaac, a son promised
by God, was eventually born to Abraham and Sarah in their old age.

WHY WAS HE CHOSEN?
God sees and chooses Abraham as his man to receive the covenant. Abraham has faith because
he is chosen by God.

WHAT IS THE COVENANT?
A gracious declaration and promise to Abraham, his descendants and the generations to come.
A relational promise that will bring flourishing and wholeness in life, centred around God.
This is taken over into the New Testament by the church who become the children of Abraham.

WHAT IS THE GOAL OF THE COVENANT?
To create a people that passionately entrust their lives, are bound up to God and are fulfilled
by Jesus Christ. To bring people of all nations into God's blessing.

WHAT ARE THE BENEFITS OF THE COVENANT?
The kingdom of God – God's rule and reign in our lives. To know and be known by God. To find
our meaning and purpose in Him and to glorify Him in all that we are and do. To be blessed as we
are a blessing to others.

HOW DOES JESUS AFFECT THE COVENANT?
Jesus brings the blessing through His death and resurrection – we can enjoy some of the blessing
now while we await the fullness of the blessing in the future kingdom to come.

WHEN WILL THE COVENANT BE FULFILLED?
When the new heaven and the new earth come into being, when everyone becomes part of God's
family. When relationship between man and God is restored.

see pp214-215

GOD REMINDS US OF HIS PROMISE THROUGHOUT THE BIG PICTURE

GEN 12:2-3 — 'I will make of you a great nation, and I will bless you, and make your name great, so that you will be a blessing. I will bless those who bless you, and the one who curses you I will curse; and in you all the families of the earth shall be blessed.'

GEN 15:5 — He brought him outside and said, 'Look towards heaven and count the stars, if you are able to count them.' Then he said to him, 'So shall your descendants be.'

GEN 18:17-18 — The Lord said, 'Shall I hide from Abraham what I am about to do, seeing that Abraham shall become a great and mighty nation, and all the nations of the earth shall be blessed in him?'

GEN 22:17-18 — 'I will indeed bless you, and I will make your offspring as numerous as the stars of heaven and as the sand that is on the seashore. And your offspring shall possess the gate of their enemies, and by your offspring shall all the nations of the earth gain blessing for themselves, because you have obeyed my voice.'

GEN 26:4 — 'I will make your offspring as numerous as the stars of heaven, and will give to your offspring all these lands; and all the nations of the earth shall gain blessing for themselves through your offspring.'

GEN 27:29 — 'Let peoples serve you, and nations bow down to you. Be lord over your brothers, and may your mother's sons bow down to you. Cursed be everyone who curses you, and blessed be everyone who blesses you!'

GEN 28:3 — 'May God Almighty bless you and make you fruitful and numerous, that you may become a company of peoples.'

GEN 28:14 — 'And your offspring shall be like the dust of the earth, and you shall spread abroad to the west and to the east and to the north and to the south; and all the families of the earth shall be blessed in you and in your offspring.'

GEN 30:27 — But Laban said to him, 'If you will allow me to say so, I have learned by divination that the Lord has blessed me because of you.'

GEN 39:5 — From the time that he made him overseer in his house and over all that he had, the Lord blessed the Egyptian's house for Joseph's sake; the blessing of the Lord was on all that he had, in house and field.

GEN 47:7 — Then Joseph brought in his father Jacob, and presented him before Pharaoh, and Jacob blessed Pharaoh.

NUM 24:9 — 'He crouched, he lay down like a lion, and like a lioness; who will rouse him up? Blessed is everyone who blesses you, and cursed is everyone who curses you.'

DEUT 9:5 — 'It is not because of your righteousness or the uprightness of your heart that you are going in to occupy their land; but because of the wickedness of those nations that the Lord your God is dispossessing them before you, in order to fulfil the promise that the Lord made on oath to your ancestors, to Abraham, to Isaac, and to Jacob.

PS 72:17 — May his name endure for ever, his fame continue as long as the sun. May all nations be blessed in him; may they pronounce him happy.

PS 105:8-11 — He is mindful of his covenant for ever, of the word that he commanded, for a thousand generations, the covenant that he made with Abraham, his sworn promise to Isaac, which he confirmed to Jacob as a statute, to Israel as an everlasting covenant, saying, 'To you I will give the land of Canaan as your portion for an inheritance.'

ISA 19:24-25 — On that day Israel will be the third with Egypt and Assyria, a blessing in the midst of the earth, whom the Lord of hosts has blessed, saying, 'Blessed be Egypt my people, and Assyria the work of my hands, and Israel my heritage.'

JER 4:2 — And if you swear, 'As the Lord lives!' in truth, in justice, and in uprightness, then nations shall be blessed by him, and by him they shall boast.

ZECH 8:13 — Just as you have been a cursing among the nations, O house of Judah and house of Israel, so I will save you and you shall be a blessing. Do not be afraid, but let your hands be strong.

LK 1:48 — 'For he has looked with favour on the lowliness of his servant. Surely, from now on all generations will call me blessed.'

LK 1:54-55 — 'He has helped his servant Israel, in remembrance of his mercy, according to the promise he made to our ancestors, to Abraham and to his descendants for ever.'

ACTS 3:25-26 — 'You are the descendants of the prophets and of the covenant that God gave to your ancestors, saying to Abraham, "And in your descendants all the families of the earth shall be blessed." When God raised up his servant, he sent him first to you, to bless you by turning each of you from your wicked ways.'

GAL 3:9 — For this reason, those who believe are blessed with Abraham who believed.

GAL 3:16 — Now the promises were made to Abraham and to his offspring; it does not say, 'And to offsprings', as of many; but it says, 'And to your offspring', that is, to one person, who is Christ.

EPH 1:3 — Blessed be the God and Father of our Lord Jesus Christ, who has blessed us in Christ with every spiritual blessing in the heavenly places.

1 PET 3:9 — Do not repay evil for evil or abuse for abuse; but, on the contrary, repay with a blessing. It is for this that you were called – that you might inherit a blessing.

REV 21:3 — And I heard a loud voice from the throne saying, 'See, the home of God is among mortals. He will dwell with them; they will be his peoples, and God himself will be with them.'

A RESCUE PLAN — THE PLAN REJECTED — STARTING OVER — RELATIONSHIP RESTORED

source: What Is the Promise: Revd Dr Graham R. Houston, Rhoda Fearon and Dr Stuart C. Weir.
God Reminds Us: Dr Stuart C. Weir. Gen, Num, Deut, Ps, Isa, Jer, Zech, Lk, Acts, Gal, Eph, 1 Pet, Rev. Richard Bauckham, *Bible and Mission: Christian Witness in a Postmodern World* (Paternoster: Carlisle, 2003).
note: The data contributor and author have drawn on personal choices when collating the data used to reveal what the Blessing is and where we are reminded of it in Scripture.

The Land Is Promised

But the departure delayed ... by about 500 years

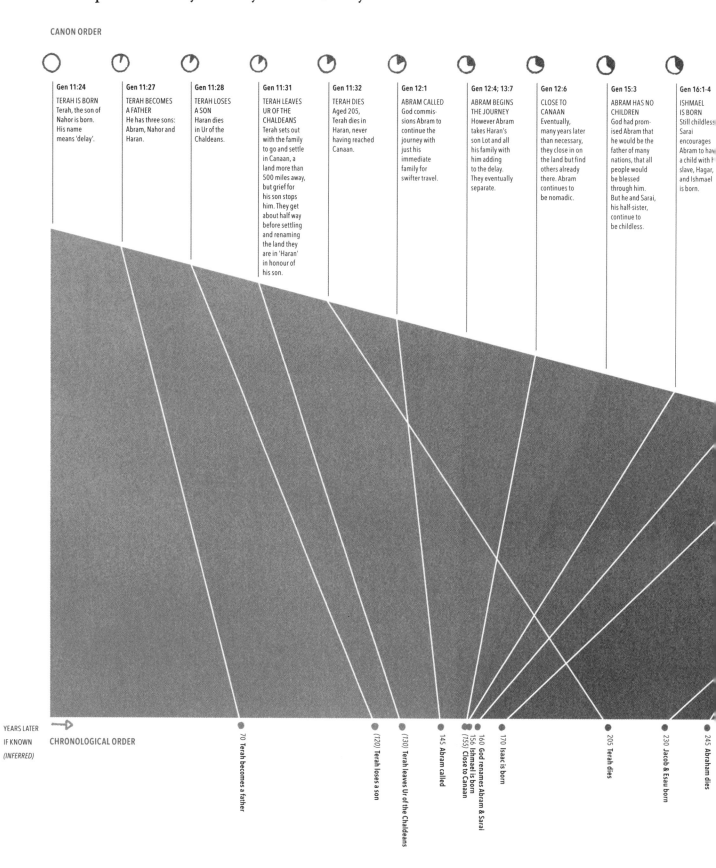

Gen 11:24

TERAH IS BORN
Terah, the son of
Nahor is born.
His name
means 'delay'.

Gen 11:27

TERAH BECOMES
A FATHER
He has three sons:
Abram, Nahor and
Haran.

Gen 11:28

TERAH LOSES
A SON
Haran dies
in Ur of the
Chaldeans.

Gen 11:31

TERAH LEAVES
UR OF THE
CHALDEANS
Terah sets out
with the family
to go and settle
in Canaan, a
land more than
500 miles away,
but grief for
his son stops
him. They get
about half way
before settling
and renaming
the land they
are in 'Haran'
in honour of
his son.

Gen 11:32

TERAH DIES
Aged 205,
Terah dies in
Haran, never
having reached
Canaan.

Gen 12:1

ABRAM CALLED
God commis-
sions Abram to
continue the
journey with
just his
immediate
family for
swifter travel.

Gen 12:4; 13:7

ABRAM BEGINS
THE JOURNEY
However Abram
takes Haran's
son Lot and all
his family with
him adding
to the delay.
They eventually
separate.

Gen 12:6

CLOSE TO
CANAAN
Eventually,
many years later
they close in on
the land but find
others already
there. Abram
continues to
be nomadic.

Gen 15:3

ABRAM HAS NO
CHILDREN
God had prom-
ised Abram that
he would be the
father of many
nations, that all
people would
be blessed
through him.
But he and Sarai,
his half-sister,
continue to
be childless.

Gen 16:1-4

ISHMAEL
IS BORN
Still childless
Sarai
encourages
Abram to have
a child with h
slave, Hagar,
and Ishmael
is born.

YEARS LATER
IF KNOWN
(INFERRED)

CHRONOLOGICAL ORDER

70 **Terah becomes a father**

(120) **Terah loses a son**

(130) **Terah leaves Ur of the Chaldeans**

145 **Abram called**

160 **God renames Abram & Sarai**
156 **Ishmael is born**
(155) **Close to Canaan**

170 **Isaac is born**

205 **Terah dies**

230 **Jacob & Esau born**

245 **Abraham dies**

see pp74-75, 104-105

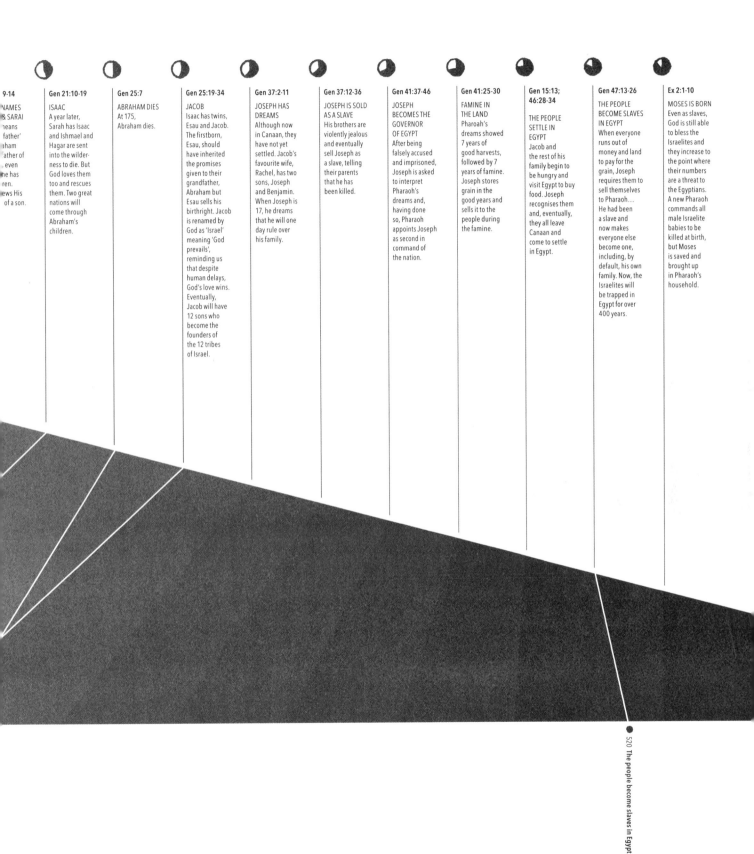

9-14

NAMES
& SARAI
means
father'
aham
ather of
even
he has
ren.
ews His
of a son.

Gen 21:10-19

ISAAC
A year later,
Sarah has Isaac
and Ishmael and
Hagar are sent
into the wilder-
ness to die. But
God loves them
too and rescues
them. Two great
nations will
come through
Abraham's
children.

Gen 25:7

ABRAHAM DIES
At 175,
Abraham dies.

Gen 25:19-34

JACOB
Isaac has twins,
Esau and Jacob.
The firstborn,
Esau, should
have inherited
the promises
given to their
grandfather,
Abraham but
Esau sells his
birthright. Jacob
is renamed by
God as 'Israel'
meaning 'God
prevails',
reminding us
that despite
human delays,
God's love wins.
Eventually,
Jacob will have
12 sons who
become the
founders of
the 12 tribes
of Israel.

Gen 37:2-11

JOSEPH HAS
DREAMS
Although now
in Canaan, they
have not yet
settled. Jacob's
favourite wife,
Rachel, has two
sons, Joseph
and Benjamin.
When Joseph is
17, he dreams
that he will one
day rule over
his family.

Gen 37:12-36

JOSEPH IS SOLD
AS A SLAVE
His brothers are
violently jealous
and eventually
sell Joseph as
a slave, telling
their parents
that he has
been killed.

Gen 41:37-46

JOSEPH
BECOMES THE
GOVERNOR
OF EGYPT
After being
falsely accused
and imprisoned,
Joseph is asked
to interpret
Pharaoh's
dreams and,
having done
so, Pharaoh
appoints Joseph
as second in
command of
the nation.

Gen 41:25-30

FAMINE IN
THE LAND
Pharoah's
dreams showed
7 years of
good harvests,
followed by 7
years of famine.
Joseph stores
grain in the
good years and
sells it to the
people during
the famine.

**Gen 15:13;
46:28-34**

THE PEOPLE
SETTLE IN
EGYPT
Jacob and
the rest of his
family begin to
be hungry and
visit Egypt to buy
food. Joseph
recognises them
and, eventually,
they all leave
Canaan and
come to settle
in Egypt.

Gen 47:13-26

THE PEOPLE
BECOME SLAVES
IN EGYPT
When everyone
runs out of
money and land
to pay for the
grain, Joseph
requires them to
sell themselves
to Pharaoh…
He had been
a slave and
now makes
everyone else
become one,
including, by
default, his own
family. Now, the
Israelites will
be trapped in
Egypt for over
400 years.

Ex 2:1-10

MOSES IS BORN
Even as slaves,
God is still able
to bless the
Israelites and
they increase to
the point where
their numbers
are a threat to
the Egyptians.
A new Pharaoh
commands all
male Israelite
babies to be
killed at birth,
but Moses
is saved and
brought up
in Pharaoh's
household.

520 The people become slaves in Egypt

source: David Painting. Gen, Ex, Num, Deut, Josh.
note: The contributor and author have drawn on personal opinions when choosing events to illustrate the journey. The timings shown are based on internal evidence and best estimates.

Plagues on Egypt The hardening of Pharaoh's heart

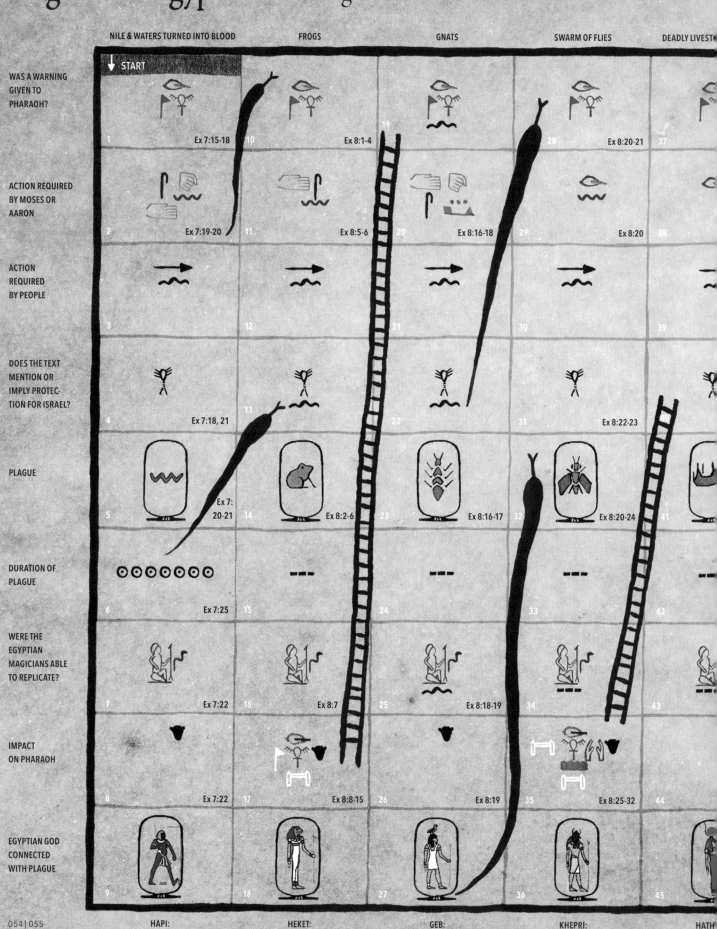

	NILE & WATERS TURNED INTO BLOOD	FROGS	GNATS	SWARM OF FLIES	DEADLY LIVEST⬤
WAS A WARNING GIVEN TO PHARAOH?	Ex 7:15-18	Ex 8:1-4		Ex 8:20-21	
ACTION REQUIRED BY MOSES OR AARON	Ex 7:19-20	Ex 8:5-6	Ex 8:16-18	Ex 8:20	
ACTION REQUIRED BY PEOPLE					
DOES THE TEXT MENTION OR IMPLY PROTECTION FOR ISRAEL?	Ex 7:18, 21			Ex 8:22-23	
PLAGUE	Ex 7: 20-21	Ex 8:2-6	Ex 8:16-17	Ex 8:20-24	
DURATION OF PLAGUE	Ex 7:25				
WERE THE EGYPTIAN MAGICIANS ABLE TO REPLICATE?	Ex 7:22	Ex 8:7	Ex 8:18-19		
IMPACT ON PHARAOH	Ex 7:22	Ex 8:8-15	Ex 8:19	Ex 8:25-32	
EGYPTIAN GOD CONNECTED WITH PLAGUE	**HAPI:** Nile god	**HEKET:** Goddess of childbirth, depicted as a frog	**GEB:** God of the earth and vegetation, father of snakes	**KHEPRI:** God of creation and sun, associated with scarab beetle	**HATH⬤** Mother and s⬤ depicted

With the help of the key and the instructions overleaf, follow the gruesome story of the plagues of Egypt.
Start at the top left hand corner and follow the numbered squares. Discover the gods connected to each plague and join in the drama.

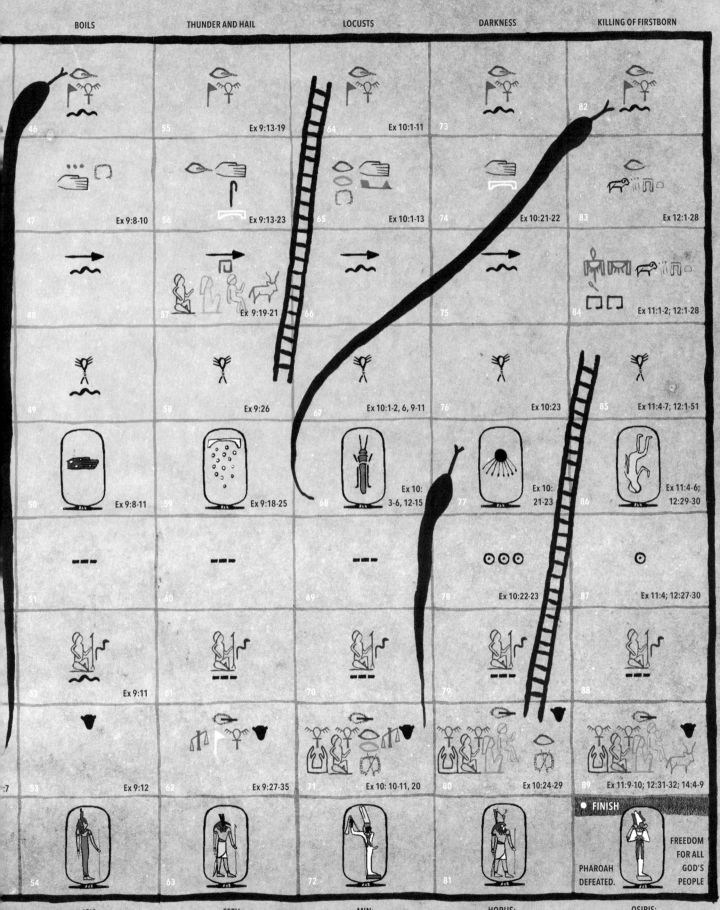

BOILS · THUNDER AND HAIL · LOCUSTS · DARKNESS · KILLING OF FIRSTBORN

ISIS:
Goddess of life and
associated with healing

SETH:
Depicted in
wind and storms

MIN:
God of fertility
and vegetation

HORUS:
Associated
with the sun

OSIRIS:
Personal god of Pharoah
and judge of the dead

Play along

Experience the journey through plagues to freedom.

GET READY:

Settle down with a pre-dinner drink, and play along before you eat your Passover meal overleaf.

Firstly, use the key to decipher the hieroglyphs on the board and reveal the Israelites' journey out of Egypt to freedom.

Then cut out and stick together the board pieces on the opposite page. Choose your character and follow them through the petrifying plagues. Feel their frustrations and triumphs as each plays their part in this epic adventure.

PLAY:

Roll the dice, and move the number of spaces indicated. If you stop at the foot of a ladder you can climb to the top, but if you halt on the head of a snake, you must slide all the way down to the tip of the tail.

The first player to exit Egypt is the winner!

Go and enjoy the Passover meal of freedom.

P.S. If you chose to be Moses you made a good choice! God chose Moses to lead and so you get to make the first move and be the first to roll the dice.

SEE PREVIOUS PAGE FOR BOARD

Play along rules source: Karen Sawrey. Duncan Drury.
note: Rules of play have been created for purposes of this graphic.

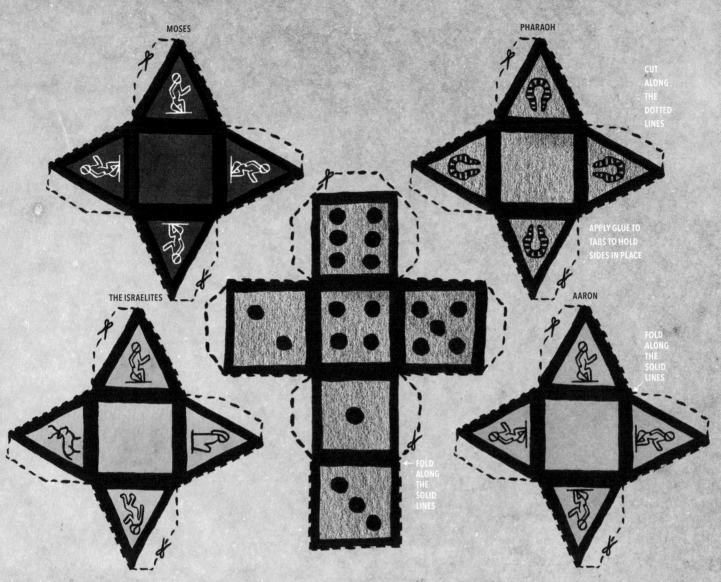

MOSES

PHARAOH

CUT ALONG THE DOTTED LINES

APPLY GLUE TO TABS TO HOLD SIDES IN PLACE

THE ISRAELITES

AARON

FOLD ALONG THE SOLID LINES

FOLD ALONG THE SOLID LINES

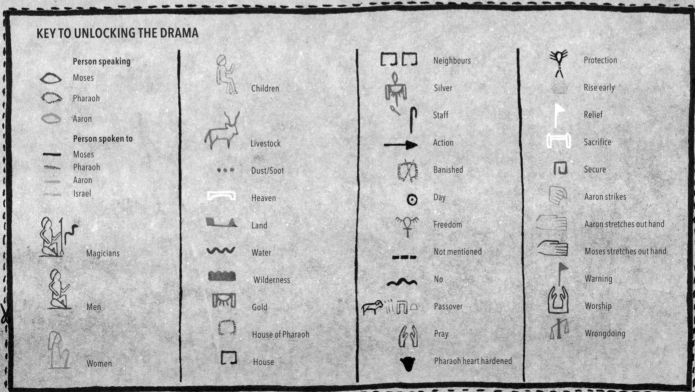

KEY TO UNLOCKING THE DRAMA

Person speaking
Moses
Pharaoh
Aaron

Person spoken to
Moses
Pharaoh
Aaron
Israel

Magicians

Men

Women

Children

Livestock

Dust/Soot

Heaven

Land

Water

Wilderness

Gold

House of Pharaoh

House

Neighbours

Silver

Staff

Action

Banished

Day

Freedom

Not mentioned

No

Passover

Pray

Pharaoh heart hardened

Protection

Rise early

Relief

Sacrifice

Secure

Aaron strikes

Aaron stretches out hand

Moses stretches out hand

Warning

Worship

Wrongdoing

source: Professor James Crossley. Exodus 7–12 (Hebrew Masoretic Text)
note: Precise links between Egyptian gods and the plagues are not always certain and are used here for purposes of comparison.

for 'First Passover' see pp158-159

Beginner's Guide to the First Passover
Step by step guide to your first Passover meal

STEPS:

PREPARATION

METHOD

TO SERVE

INGREDIENTS:

LAMB OR KID
1 x unblemished, year-old male with unbroken bones.

UNLEAVENED BREAD
½ cup of water; 2 cups of flour.

BITTER HERBS
We suggest horseradish and romaine lettuce.

HYSSOP
1 x bunch.

SERVES: Serves a family or household.
ETIQUETTE: Eat in a hurry to enhance the thrill of escaping from Pharaoh.
DRESS CODE: Girded loins, sandals and staff.

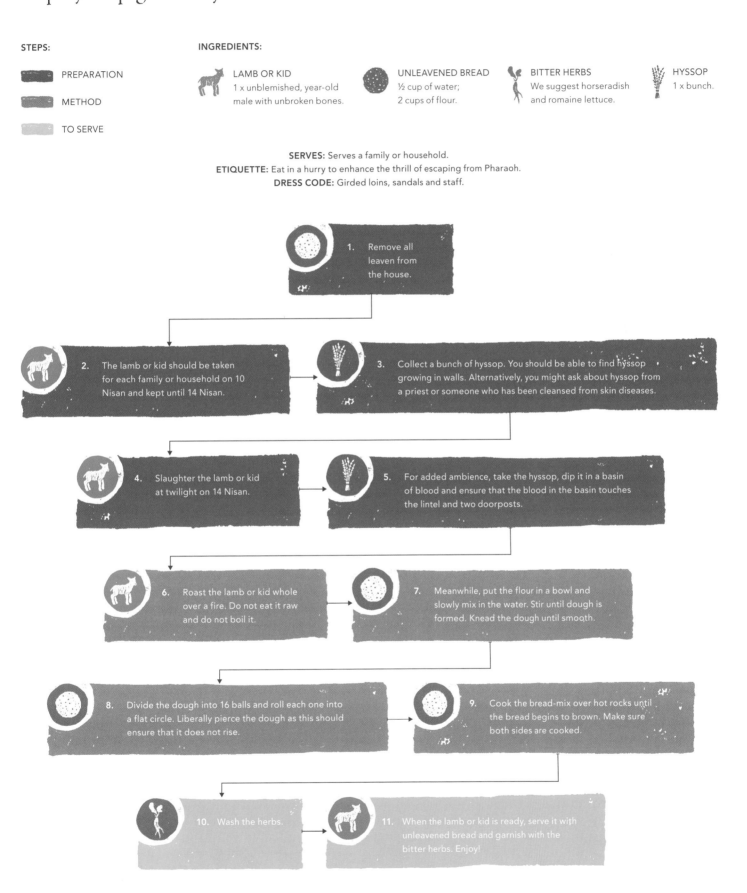

1. Remove all leaven from the house.

2. The lamb or kid should be taken for each family or household on 10 Nisan and kept until 14 Nisan.

3. Collect a bunch of hyssop. You should be able to find hyssop growing in walls. Alternatively, you might ask about hyssop from a priest or someone who has been cleansed from skin diseases.

4. Slaughter the lamb or kid at twilight on 14 Nisan.

5. For added ambience, take the hyssop, dip it in a basin of blood and ensure that the blood in the basin touches the lintel and two doorposts.

6. Roast the lamb or kid whole over a fire. Do not eat it raw and do not boil it.

7. Meanwhile, put the flour in a bowl and slowly mix in the water. Stir until dough is formed. Knead the dough until smooth.

8. Divide the dough into 16 balls and roll each one into a flat circle. Liberally pierce the dough as this should ensure that it does not rise.

9. Cook the bread-mix over hot rocks until the bread begins to brown. Make sure both sides are cooked.

10. Wash the herbs.

11. When the lamb or kid is ready, serve it with unleavened bread and garnish with the bitter herbs. Enjoy!

source: Professor James Crossley. Ex 12; Num 9; Deut 16
note: Additional details sourced from Jewish traditions

Moses born into genocide.

Pharaoh orders the death of all Israelite baby boys. Moses' mother saves him by hiding him at home for 3 months and then in a basket on the river Nile.

EX 1:22; 2:1-3, ACTS 7:20, HEB 11:23

Moses rescued from the Nile.

Moses discovered by Pharaoh's daughter who disobeys her father's decree to rescue him. Moses' sister sees the rescue and offers to bring her mother to nurse him.

EX 2:5,9

Moses adopted by Pharaoh's daughter.

Pharaoh's daughter moves him to the palace and adopts him as her son. She names him Moses because he was drawn out of the water. He becomes learned in all the wisdom of Egypt, mighty in word and deed.

EX 2:10, ACTS 7:21-22

Moses visits his people.

Aged 40, Moses leaves the palace and goes out to his people. Observing an Egyptian beating an Israelite, he is angry and deliberately kills and buries the Egyptian. Pharaoh hears about it and attempts to kill Moses.

EX 2:11-15, ACTS 7:23-25

Moses flees Egypt and marries Zipporah.

Arriving as a stranger in Midian he meets Jethro's daughters at a well and helps them. One of the daughters, Zipporah, becomes his wife. They have 2 sons, Gershom and Eliezer.

EX 2:16-22; 18:3-4

Moses becomes a shepherd.

Moses moves from royal householder to shepherd when given the flock of his father-in-law to tend at Mount Horeb.

EX 3:1-2

God introduces Himself to Moses at the burning bush.

God miraculously shows His power as the Angel of the Lord appears to Moses and calls him to partner God in leading His people to freedom.

EX 3:1-4:17, ACTS 7:30-34

Moses doubts himself.

God reminds doubtful Moses that His power is at work, not Moses' ability. Aaron is made spokesperson for Moses.

EX 3:1-4:17

Moses returns to Egypt.

With Jethro's blessing, Moses returns to Egypt after 40 years accompanied by his family and carrying the staff of God. Moses and Aaron are reunited. God's rescue plan is shared with the Israelite leaders.

EX 4:18-28

Moses doubts himself again.

Moses doubts himself as God's choice. God affirms Moses and His commitment to free His people.

EX 6:2-8, 10:12, 28:30; 7:1-5

Moses speaks to Pharaoh. Requests freedom.

Moses asks that God's people be freed but Pharaoh refuses. Egyptian brutality to the Israelites increases, breaking their spirits and stopping them from hearing Moses' message of hope.

EX 4:29-5:21

Moses requests freedom again.

Aged 80, Moses goes before Pharaoh who demands that Moses perform a miracle. When Aaron throws down his staff it becomes a snake. The Egyptian magicians perform the same miracle but Aaron's staff swallows them all.

EX 7:8-13

Moses struggles with the burden of leading.

The people begin to complain about wanting meat to eat. 70 elders appointed and anointed by God to assist Moses.

NUM 11:11-30

Moses' leadership is questioned by others.

Moses' leadership is challenged by Miriam and Aaron. Moses prays for Miriam's healing. God trusts Moses with his people, speaking with him face to face. Moses is unlike anyone else.

NUM 12:1-11

Moses sends twelve spies into the Land of Promise.

Reports from 10 of 12 spies cause fear and the people rebel against Moses. Moses pleads for them. God says those lacking in faith would not see the Land of Promise but Caleb and his children will inherit it.

NUM 13:1-33; 14:1-35

Moses and Aaron's leadership questioned again by others.

Korah leads rebellion against Moses' leadership, claiming Moses has misled the people. Those guilty of rebelling die. The people rebel again and a plague breaks out in the camp. Moses pleads to save the people.

NUM 16:1-50

Moses gives further guidelines for living.

Moses receives and compiles the instructions and laws that would shape the nation of Israel.

DEUT 1-31

Moses asks God to allow him to enter the Land of Promise.

Moses' request to enter the Land of Promise is refused because he had not trusted God at Meribah.

DEUT 3:23-27, NUM 27:12-15

Moses leads God's people towards the Land of Promise.

Moses brings order to the people, leads them in victory, addresses false worship and establishes places of refuge. He encourages God and people, writing down this journey.

NUM 21-36

Moses' lack of trust denies him entry to the Land of Promise.

The people are thirsty at Meribah. God instructs Moses to command the rock to release water. Instead, Moses strikes the rock twice in anger. Water flows but Moses had not listened to God's voice.

NUM 20:1-13

Moses' final days with the people.

Moses composes his last song. Moses gives his final blessing to the people.

DEUT 32-33

Moses sees the Land of Promise and dies aged 120.

Moses climbs Mount Nebo and sees the land promised to Abraham, Isaac and Jacob. Moses dies and is buried in the land of Moab. His grave is for ever hidden from human sight. Moses is mourned for 30 days.

DEUT 34:1-8

Moses declared unequalled and the most humble man on earth.

Never since has there been a prophet like Moses who displayed the mighty acts and power of God in Egypt and to his people. He was known by God and met Him face to face.

NUM 12:3, DEUT 34:10-12

Moses finally enters the Promised Land.

Lack of trust stopped Moses entering the Land of Promise with his people. Through Jesus, he finally gets to stand on the Promised Land.

MT 17:1-8, MK 9:2-8, LK 9:28-35

The Ten Commandments, take two.

God renews his commitment and replaces the tablets of stone, promising to work wonders.
EX 34:1-28

Moses oversees the construction of the Tabernacle.

God gives instructions for the dimensions, materials and contents of the Tabernacle. God comes and meets with His people.
EX 35:4-40:38

Moses gives God's instruction for living.

God instructs Moses on moral, civil and ritual laws for health and wellbeing, encouraging growth in relationship between one another and God.
LEV 1-27

Moses continues to order a nation.

Moses acts as priest at dedication of Aaron and his sons. Moses numbers the people. The second Passover happens. Instruction continues on laws.
NUM 1-10

Moses pursues the person of God, not just performance.

God and Moses establish an intimate relationship. Moses pleads for God's presence to lead him and sets up a tent in the camp to meet with God.
EX 33:7-23; PS 103:7

Moses intercedes for God's people.

Moses returns to find the people worshipping golden statues. Angry at the people's choices he destroys the statues and breaks the stone tablets. Many die as a result of these choices.
EX 32:1-35

The Ten Commandments. Moses spends 40 days and nights in God's presence.

Moses receives 2 tablets of stone. Through God's instruction, Moses begins to shape a nation with moral, civil, and ritual laws. Moses receives the Tabernacle blueprint
EX 20:1-31:18

Moses prepares the people. God reaffirms His commitment.

God instructs Moses to dedicate the people in preparation for meeting with Him. He promises that if they follow His voice, they will be His treasured possession.
EX 19:1-3:25

Moses: Prince, Prophet & Priest

The miraculous opening of the Red Sea

God performs miracles; the plagues begin.

God's power and miraculous signs show that God has sent Moses. Moses' earlier doubts dissipate but Pharaoh hardens his heart.
EX 7:14-8:15

Moses gives instructions for the first Passover.

God gives instruction for the Passover. All generations are to celebrate it and remember when God passed over their houses and spared their lives.
EX 12:1-28

The final plague.

All firstborn across the land die. Pharaoh seems to agree to the release of the people, ending 430 years of slavery.
EX 11:1-10; 12:29-42

The plagues continue and increase.

Pharaoh's magicians acknowledge the power of God and the Egyptians think highly of Moses. Pharaoh hardens his heart and refuses to let the Israelites go.
EX 8:16-10:29

Moses' family is reunited.

Jethro brings Moses' wife and sons to him. Jethro encourages Moses to delegate leadership to others. Moses organises a judiciary.
EX 18:1-26

Moses leads in the wilderness.

God does the miraculous and provides victory, food and water in different ways. God begins to test and prove his people.
EX 15-17

God miraculously opens the Red Sea.

God's people cross on dry land but the pursuing Egyptians are swallowed by the returning waters. God's people are in awe and put their trust in God and Moses.
EX 14:15-31

Trapped at the Red Sea, Moses stands in faith.

God's people leave Egypt led by Moses. The cloud directs by day and the pillar of fire by night. With the Egyptians in pursuit and the Red Sea in front of them, Moses calls the people to stand firm and watch how God will deliver them.
EX 14:1-14

source: Miriam Lowe. Ex, Lev, Num, Deut, Ps, Mt, Mk, Lk, Acts, Heb.

note: The contributor and author have drawn on personal opinions when choosing events to illustrate highlights of Moses' life.

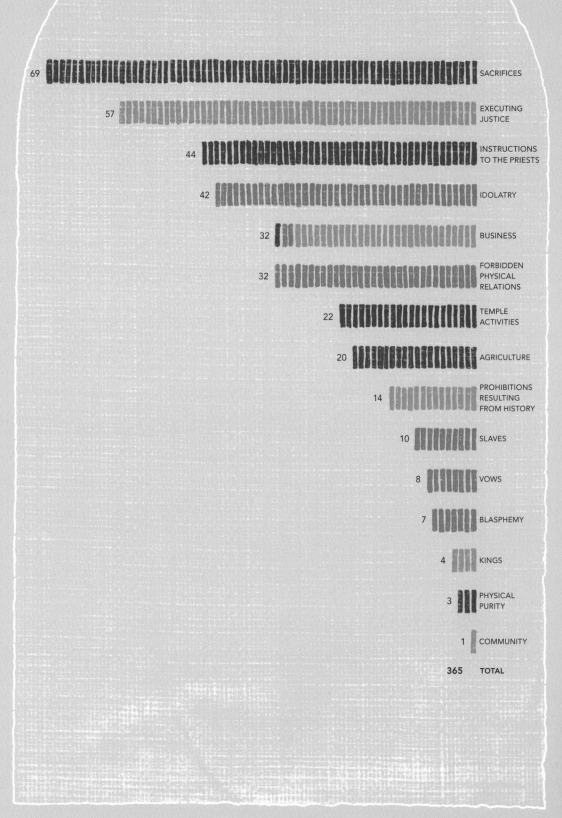

You shall not...

Therefore the law was our tutor to bring us to Christ, that we might be justified by faith.

GALATIANS 3:24 [NKJV]

CIVIL LAW: Takes specific situations and uses eternal principles to say 'if this, then that'.

MORAL LAW: Absolute truths about right and wrong, often stated without any consequences.

RITUAL LAW: How to live. Often set out for different groups (such as priests or monarchs, or people in general).

69	SACRIFICES
57	EXECUTING JUSTICE
44	INSTRUCTIONS TO THE PRIESTS
42	IDOLATRY
32	BUSINESS
32	FORBIDDEN PHYSICAL RELATIONS
22	TEMPLE ACTIVITIES
20	AGRICULTURE
14	PROHIBITIONS RESULTING FROM HISTORY
10	SLAVES
8	VOWS
7	BLASPHEMY
4	KINGS
3	PHYSICAL PURITY
1	COMMUNITY
365	**TOTAL**

The Law
The 'shalls' v the 'shall nots'
– how do they stack up?

You shall...

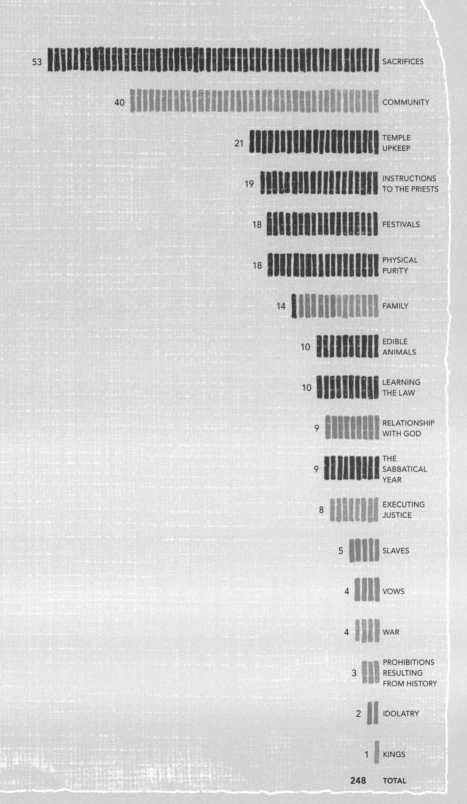

53 — SACRIFICES

40 — COMMUNITY

21 — TEMPLE UPKEEP

19 — INSTRUCTIONS TO THE PRIESTS

18 — FESTIVALS

18 — PHYSICAL PURITY

14 — FAMILY

10 — EDIBLE ANIMALS

10 — LEARNING THE LAW

9 — RELATIONSHIP WITH GOD

9 — THE SABBATICAL YEAR

8 — EXECUTING JUSTICE

5 — SLAVES

4 — VOWS

4 — WAR

3 — PROHIBITIONS RESULTING FROM HISTORY

2 — IDOLATRY

1 — KINGS

248 — TOTAL

source: David Painting. Gen, Ex, Lev, Deut, Num.
note: The data contributor and author have drawn on personal opinions when creating the categories.

Camp of Israel
Tribes in and around God's presence

NUMBER OF MALE WARRIORS
AGE 20 AND OVER:

1000   100

12 NAPHTALI
53400 MEN

11 ASHER
41500 MEN

10 DAN
62700 MEN

WEST
108100 MEN

LEVI, MERARI

LEVI, GERSHONITES

Tabernacle

LEVI, KOHATHITES

9 BENJAMIN
35400 MEN

8 MANASSEH
32200 MEN

7 EPHRAIM
40500 MEN

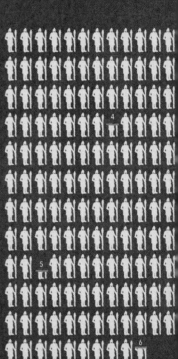

SOUTH
151450 MEN

NO|
157600

JUDAH
74600 MEN

1

ISSACHAR
54400 MEN

2

ZEBULUN
57400

3

EAST
186400 MEN

JBEN
600 MEN

MEON
300 MEN

D
550

source: Yolanda Oosthuizen. Num 2-3, Ezek 1, Rev 4.
note: According to rabbinical tradition (not the Bible), each of the four camps of Israel bore one of the four faces of the Cherubim on its standard.

Clean & Unclean Animals looking through the lens of Levitical law

REASON ANIMAL
CAN BE EATEN

Divided hooves; cloven feet; chews the cud

Enjoy!

CLEAN

UNCLEAN

Don't touch
with a
bargepole!

REASON ANIMAL
CANNOT BE EATEN

Undivided hooves; non-cloven feet; does not chew the cud

Moves on belly; moves on all fours; many feet

ANIMAL TYPE   ● Land animal   ● Creature that moves along the ground   ● Quadruped   ● Insect   ● Bird   ● Water creature

● Winged; walks on all fours; leaps on jointed legs   ● Fowl or game; non-scavenger; not bird of prey   ● Fins; scales

ks on four paws   ● Winged   ● Scavenger or bird of prey   ● No fins; no scales

source: Professor James Crossley. Lev 11 and Deut 14 (Hebrew Masoretic Text), additional Jewish interpretations
note: The carcass of any clean animal not ritually killed becomes unclean. Selection of animal examples chosen for graphic purposes only.

The Ark & Tabernacle
God dwells and journeys with His people

HEBREW FOR TABERNACLE / DWELLING PLACE:
ohel = a dwelling place for people Gen 4:20
miqdas/mishcahn = from shahcan 'to dwell'.
God dwells among us in Tabernacle Ex 26:1

GREEK FOR TABERNACLE / DWELLING PLACE:
skenoo = Jesus dwells among us in person as man and God Jn 1:14
naos = Holy Spirit dwells in us 1 Cor 3:16

1 cubit = 0.45 metres

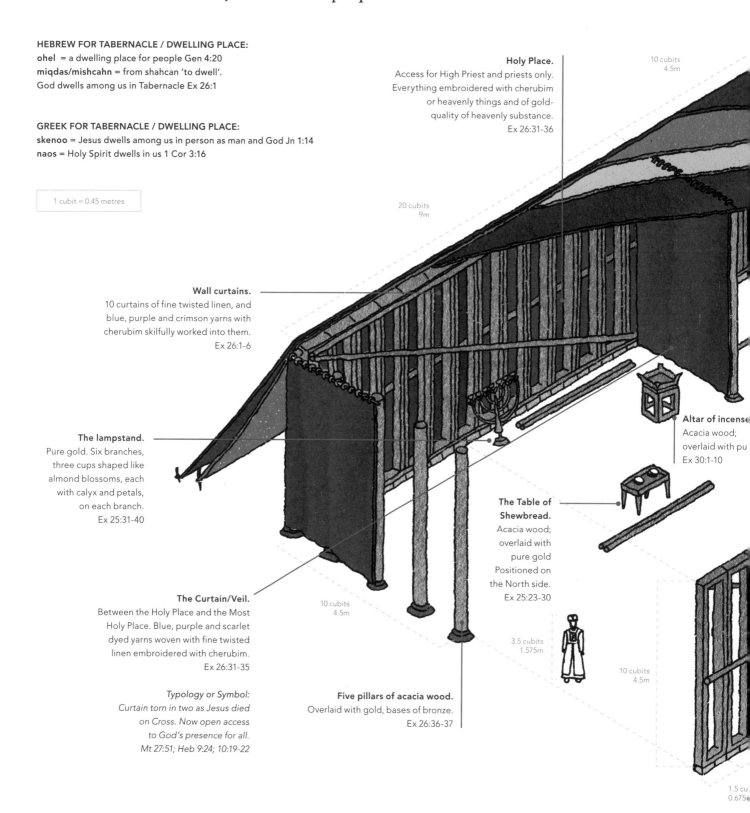

Holy Place.
Access for High Priest and priests only.
Everything embroidered with cherubim
or heavenly things and of gold-
quality of heavenly substance.
Ex 26:31-36

10 cubits
4.5m

20 cubits
9m

Wall curtains.
10 curtains of fine twisted linen, and
blue, purple and crimson yarns with
cherubim skilfully worked into them.
Ex 26:1-6

Altar of incense
Acacia wood;
overlaid with pu
Ex 30:1-10

The lampstand.
Pure gold. Six branches,
three cups shaped like
almond blossoms, each
with calyx and petals,
on each branch.
Ex 25:31-40

**The Table of
Shewbread.**
Acacia wood;
overlaid with
pure gold
Positioned on
the North side.
Ex 25:23-30

The Curtain/Veil.
Between the Holy Place and the Most
Holy Place. Blue, purple and scarlet
dyed yarns woven with fine twisted
linen embroidered with cherubim.
Ex 26:31-35

*Typology or Symbol:
Curtain torn in two as Jesus died
on Cross. Now open access
to God's presence for all.
Mt 27:51; Heb 9:24; 10:19-22*

Five pillars of acacia wood.
Overlaid with gold, bases of bronze.
Ex 26:36-37

10 cubits
4.5m

3.5 cubits
1.575m

10 cubits
4.5m

1.5 cu
0.675

see pp91-93, 164-165, 166-167

Curtain walls.
Fine twisted linen.
Ex 38:9-17

100 cubits
45m

Bronze basin.
Ex 30:17-21; 38:8

The Bronze Altar.
Ex 27:1-8; 38:1-7

50 cubits
22.5m

[Scale (approx.) 1:1000]

Most Holy Place.
High Priest to enter only once a year.
The whole room was gold, with cherubim all
around, and contained the Ark with its Mercy Seat.
Ex 40:34-38

Fine goatskin leather. Ex 26:14

Tanned rams' skins. Ex 26:14

Goats' hair cloth. Ex 26:7-13

**Fine twisted white linen
embroidered in blue,
scarlet, purple and gold.**
Ex 26:1-6

Mercy Seat.
Solid gold cherubim at the two ends,
with faces facing each other. The 'seat'
of God's Presence where the cloud and
pillar of fire rested, unless the people
of Israel were journeying. Blood
sprinkled here once a year.
Ex 25:17-22

Ark of the Covenant.
Acacia wooden chest overlaid
with pure gold. Contains two
stone tablets of the testimony,
golden urn holding manna and
Aaron's staff that budded.
Ex 25:10-22, 16:33; 37:1-9;
Num 17; Deut 31:26

**20 upright
frames.** Acacia
wood and gold.
Ex 26:15-30

The middle bar.
Halfway up the
frames, shall pass
through from end
to end.
Ex 26:15-30

40 bases of silver.
Ex 26:15-30

30 cubits
13.5m

35 cubits
15.75m

10 cubits
4.5m

3.5 cubits
1.575m

Aaron

The Tabernacle

Alternative Temple Porch
as most often illustrated

[Scale (approx.) 1:300]

source: Yolanda Oosthuizen and Miriam Lowe. Gen, Ex, Lev, Num, Deut, Mt, Jn, Rom, Heb, 1 Pet, Rev. ohel, miqdas/mishcahn, *Strong's Hebrew Lexicon.* Patrick Fairburn, *Typology of Scripture: Vol. 2* (Kregel Publications: Grand Rapids,1989) Thomas Newberry, *Types of the Tabernacle,* (Database copyright 2007 Word search Corp.) note: Typology and symbolism drawn from both Jewish tradition and the personal opinion of the contributors and author.

WHAT IT MEANT TO GOD:

The sacrifice prompted the Lord to speak to Balaam and caused him to bless Israel instead of cursing them

A pleasing fragrance

An act of serious pleading worth responding to

Remembrance of the sin

Not mentioned

Forgiveness

The mother is made clean

TYPE OF SACRIFICE:

- Grain offering
- Sin offering
- Burnt offering
- Offerings of well-being
- Guilt offering
- Sin offering if poor
- Burnt offering if poor

WHAT TO SACRIFICE:

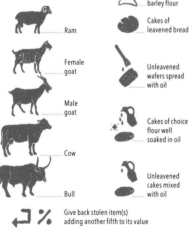

- Turtle dove
- Pigeon
- Sucking lamb
- Lamb in its first year
- Male lamb 1 year old
- Ram
- Female goat
- Male goat
- Cow
- Bull

- Drink-offering
- 2/10 of an ephah of choice flour and oil
- 1/10 of an ephah of barley flour
- Cakes of leavened bread
- Unleavened wafers spread with oil
- Cakes of choice flour well soaked in oil
- Unleavened cakes mixed with oil

Give back stolen item(s) adding another fifth to its value

FOR WHOM:

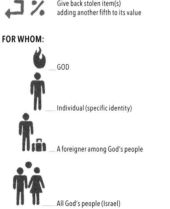

- GOD
- Individual (specific identity)
- A foreigner among God's people
- All God's people (Israel)

IF POOR

or

—— OR ——

or

or

Withholding a worker's wages until morning.

LEV 19:13, 22

Nurturing hatred for a family member.

LEV 19:17, 22

Making clothing out of two different materials.

LEV 19:19, 22

After a man has had sex with a female slave.

LEV 19:20-22

After a theft has been committed.

LEV 6:1-7

Ritual cleansing for a woman after childbirth.

LEV 12:6-8

Ritual cleansing for a woman after her period.

LEV 15:25-30

see pp166-167, 200-201

Sacrificial System
A selection of how worship, purity and sin worked

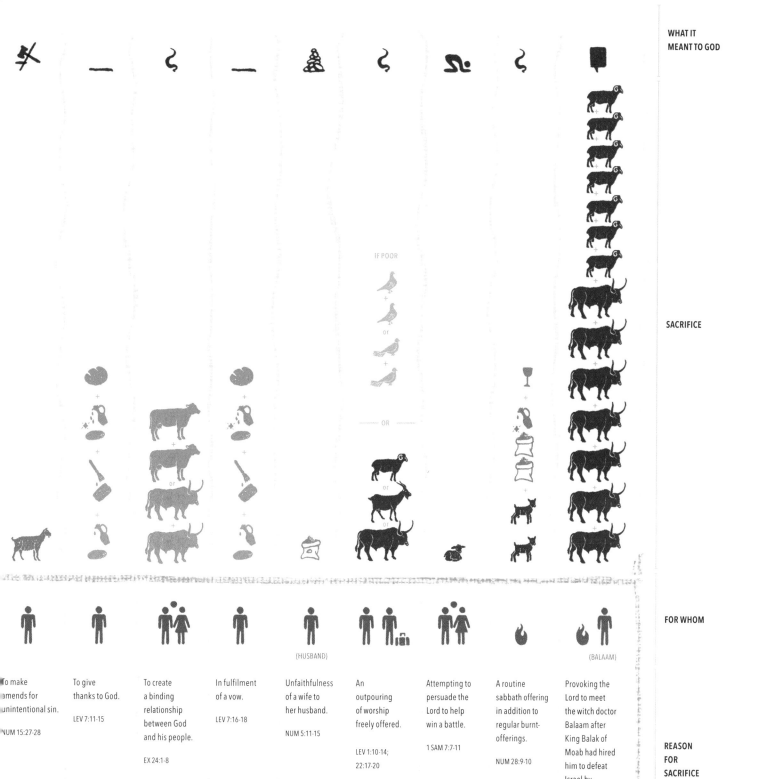

WHAT IT MEANT TO GOD

IF POOR

— OR —

SACRIFICE

FOR WHOM

(HUSBAND)

(BALAAM)

To make amends for unintentional sin.

NUM 15:27-28

To give thanks to God.

LEV 7:11-15

To create a binding relationship between God and his people.

EX 24:1-8

In fulfilment of a vow.

LEV 7:16-18

Unfaithfulness of a wife to her husband.

NUM 5:11-15

An outpouring of worship freely offered.

LEV 1:10-14; 22:17-20

Attempting to persuade the Lord to help win a battle.

1 SAM 7:7-11

A routine sabbath offering in addition to regular burnt-offerings.

NUM 28:9-10

Provoking the Lord to meet the witch doctor Balaam after King Balak of Moab had hired him to defeat Israel by cursing them.

NUM 22:41–23:6

REASON FOR SACRIFICE

source: Dr Stuart C. Weir. Ex, Lev, Num, 1 Sam.
R.K. Harrison, *Leviticus* (Tyndale Old Testament Commentaries) (IVP: Leicester, 1980), *NIV Zondervan Study Bible* (Zondervan: Nashville, 2016)

The Day of Atonement
Squeaky clean from head to toe

STEPS FOR
ATONEMENT

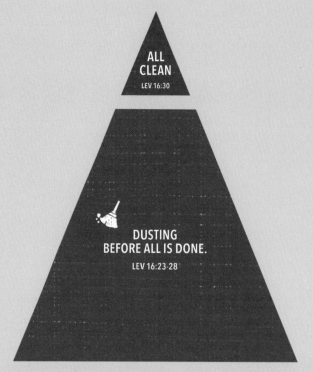

**ALL
CLEAN**
LEV 16:30

**DUSTING
BEFORE ALL IS DONE.**
LEV 16:23-28

**GETTING THE TABERNACLE
AND ALL GOD'S PEOPLE CLEAN.**
LEV 16:15-22

GETTING THE LEVITES CLEAN.
LEV 16:5-14

GETTING THE PRIEST CLEAN.
LEV 16:15-22

 GOD'S PEOPLE TAKE REST.
LEV 16:29

See pp166-167, 200-201

*'For on this day atonement shall be made for you, to cleanse you;
from all your sins you shall be clean before the Lord.'*

(LEV 16:30)

PERSON

All God's people ●
The priest ■
Extra priests chosen to help ▲ ▲

DETAILS OF STEPS

27 All have a clean slate before God.

26 Wash clothes and have a bath.

24 Release the second goat. Wash clothes and have a bath.

25 Burn the skin, flesh and dung of the animals offered as sin offerings.

20 Go into the Holy Place, take off the special clothes, leaving them there.

21 Take a bath and put normal clothes back on.

22 Make a personal burnt offering, and one for all for God's people.

23 Put fat of the sin offering on the altar to make smoke.

15 Slaughter the first goat as a sin offering for all God's people.

16 Sprinkle some blood on the front and beside the Mercy Seat seven times.

17 Put some of the bull's and goat's blood on the horns of the altar.

18 Take the second goat and tell it the sins of all God's people (they remain on the goat's head).

19 Send the second goat away into the desert with all God's people's sin.

7 Slaughter a bull as a personal sin offering and for the priesthood.

8 Take two male goats and put them at the front door of the Tabernacle.

9 Cast lots* to assign a role to each goat.

10 The first goat is given to God as a sin offering.

11 The second goat is presented alive to God as Azazel/scapegoat. **

12 Present the bull sin offering for himself and the priesthood.

13 Take some coals from the altar, add incense. Go into the Most Holy Place and put on the fire to make a cloud around the Mercy Seat.

14 Sprinkle some bull's blood on the front and beside the Mercy Seat seven times.

2 Go into the Holy Place.

3 Bring in a young bull for a sin offering.

4 Bring in a ram for a burnt offering.

5 Take a bath in water.

6 Put on special linen; underwear, tunic, sash and turban.

1 All except the priests to rest for the day.

*Casting lots was a way of finding out what God wanted when difficult decisions had to be made.
** 'Azazel' is a synonym for 'a scapegoat'

source: Dr Stuart C. Weir, Lev 16:1-34
note: The cleansing process has been divided into steps by the contributor and author for the purposes of this graphic but the order of tasks within each step follows the text.

Getting to the Land of Promise
By the scenic route

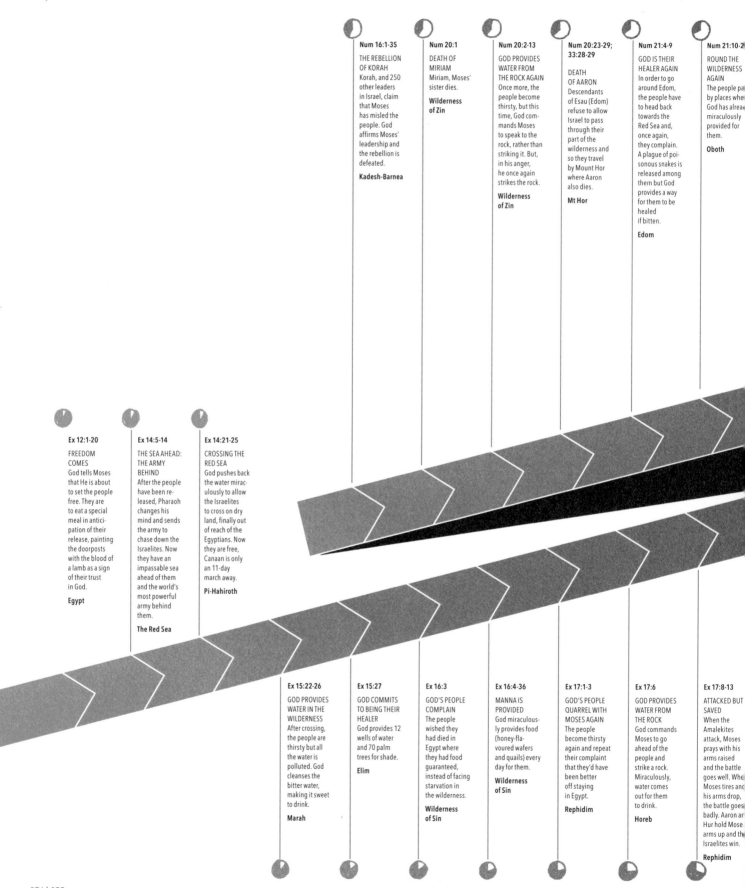

Num 16:1-35

THE REBELLION OF KORAH
Korah, and 250 other leaders in Israel, claim that Moses has misled the people. God affirms Moses' leadership and the rebellion is defeated.

Kadesh-Barnea

Num 20:1

DEATH OF MIRIAM
Miriam, Moses' sister dies.

Wilderness of Zin

Num 20:2-13

GOD PROVIDES WATER FROM THE ROCK AGAIN
Once more, the people become thirsty, but this time, God commands Moses to speak to the rock, rather than striking it. But, in his anger, he once again strikes the rock.

Wilderness of Zin

Num 20:23-29; 33:28-29

DEATH OF AARON
Descendants of Esau (Edom) refuse to allow Israel to pass through their part of the wilderness and so they travel by Mount Hor where Aaron also dies.

Mt Hor

Num 21:4-9

GOD IS THEIR HEALER AGAIN
In order to go around Edom, the people have to head back towards the Red Sea and, once again, they complain. A plague of poisonous snakes is released among them but God provides a way for them to be healed if bitten.

Edom

Num 21:10-2

ROUND THE WILDERNESS AGAIN
The people pa by places whe God has alrea miraculously provided for them.

Oboth

Ex 12:1-20

FREEDOM COMES
God tells Moses that He is about to set the people free. They are to eat a special meal in anticipation of their release, painting the doorposts with the blood of a lamb as a sign of their trust in God.

Egypt

Ex 14:5-14

THE SEA AHEAD: THE ARMY BEHIND
After the people have been released, Pharaoh changes his mind and sends the army to chase down the Israelites. Now they have an impassable sea ahead of them and the world's most powerful army behind them.

The Red Sea

Ex 14:21-25

CROSSING THE RED SEA
God pushes back the water miraculously to allow the Israelites to cross on dry land, finally out of reach of the Egyptians. Now they are free, Canaan is only an 11-day march away.

Pi-Hahiroth

Ex 15:22-26

GOD PROVIDES WATER IN THE WILDERNESS
After crossing, the people are thirsty but all the water is polluted. God cleanses the bitter water, making it sweet to drink.

Marah

Ex 15:27

GOD COMMITS TO BEING THEIR HEALER
God provides 12 wells of water and 70 palm trees for shade.

Elim

Ex 16:3

GOD'S PEOPLE COMPLAIN
The people wished they had died in Egypt where they had food guaranteed, instead of facing starvation in the wilderness.

Wilderness of Sin

Ex 16:4-36

MANNA IS PROVIDED
God miraculously provides food (honey-flavoured wafers and quails) every day for them.

Wilderness of Sin

Ex 17:1-3

GOD'S PEOPLE QUARREL WITH MOSES AGAIN
The people become thirsty again and repeat their complaint that they'd have been better off staying in Egypt.

Rephidim

Ex 17:6

GOD PROVIDES WATER FROM THE ROCK
God commands Moses to go ahead of the people and strike a rock. Miraculously, water comes out for them to drink.

Horeb

Ex 17:8-13

ATTACKED BUT SAVED
When the Amalekites attack, Moses prays with his arms raised and the battle goes well. Whe Moses tires and his arms drop, the battle goes badly. Aaron ar Hur hold Mose arms up and th Israelites win.

Rephidim

see pp52-53, 204-205

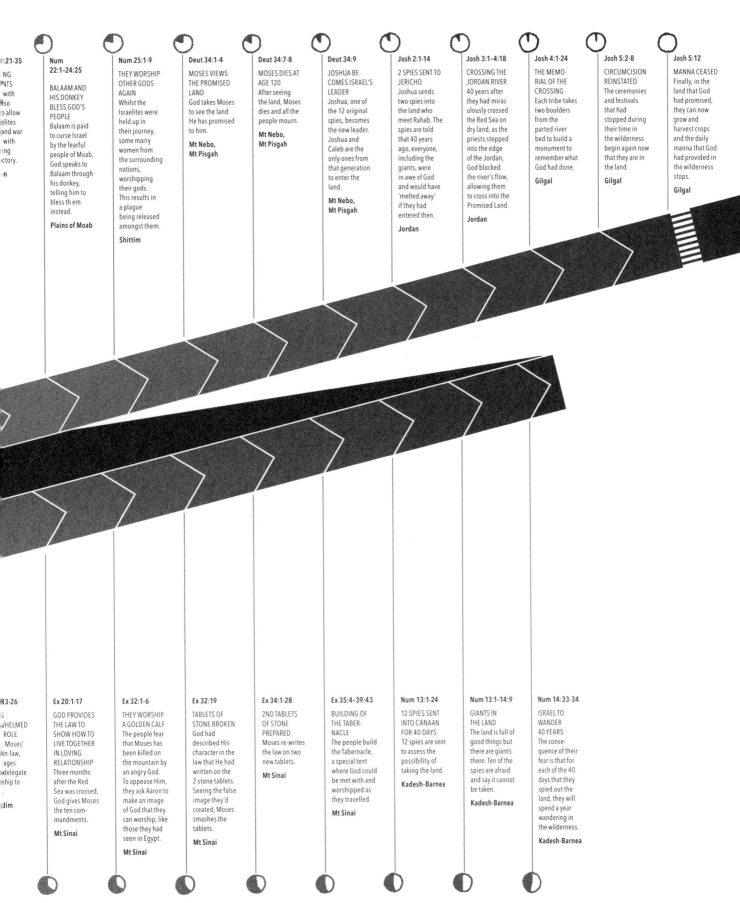

:21-35
NG
NTS
with
so
allow
elites
and war
with
ng
ctory.
n

Num 22:1-24:25

BALAAM AND HIS DONKEY BLESS GOD'S PEOPLE
Balaam is paid to curse Israel by the fearful people of Moab. God speaks to Balaam through his donkey, telling him to bless them instead.

Plains of Moab

Num 25:1-9

THEY WORSHIP OTHER GODS AGAIN
Whilst the Israelites were held up in their journey, some marry women from the surrounding nations, worshipping their gods. This results in a plague being released amongst them.

Shittim

Deut 34:1-4

MOSES VIEWS THE PROMISED LAND
God takes Moses to see the land He has promised to him.

Mt Nebo, Mt Pisgah

Deut 34:7-8

MOSES DIES AT AGE 120
After seeing the land, Moses dies and all the people mourn.

Mt Nebo, Mt Pisgah

Deut 34:9

JOSHUA BECOMES ISRAEL'S LEADER
Joshua, one of the 12 original spies, becomes the new leader. Joshua and Caleb are the only ones from that generation to enter the land.

Mt Nebo, Mt Pisgah

Josh 2:1-14

2 SPIES SENT TO JERICHO
Joshua sends two spies into the land who meet Rahab. The spies are told that 40 years ago, everyone, including the giants, were in awe of God and would have 'melted away' if they had entered then.

Jordan

Josh 3:1–4:18

CROSSING THE JORDAN RIVER
40 years after they had miraculously crossed the Red Sea on dry land, as the priests stepped into the edge of the Jordan, God blocked the river's flow, allowing them to cross into the Promised Land.

Jordan

Josh 4:1-24

THE MEMORIAL OF THE CROSSING
Each tribe takes two boulders from the parted river bed to build a monument to remember what God had done.

Gilgal

Josh 5:2-8

CIRCUMCISION REINSTATED
The ceremonies and festivals that had stopped during their time in the wilderness begin again now that they are in the land.

Gilgal

Josh 5:12

MANNA CEASED
Finally, in the land that God had promised, they can now grow and harvest crops and the daily manna that God had provided in the wilderness stops.

Gilgal

13-26
S
WHELMED
ROLE
Moses'
in-law,
ages
delegate
ship to
dim

Ex 20:1-17

GOD PROVIDES THE LAW TO SHOW HOW TO LIVE TOGETHER IN LOVING RELATIONSHIP
Three months after the Red Sea was crossed, God gives Moses the ten commandments.

Mt Sinai

Ex 32:1-6

THEY WORSHIP A GOLDEN CALF
The people fear that Moses has been killed on the mountain by an angry God. To appease Him, they ask Aaron to make an image of God that they can worship, like those they had seen in Egypt.

Mt Sinai

Ex 32:19

TABLETS OF STONE BROKEN
God had described His character in the law that He had written on the 2 stone tablets. Seeing the false image they'd created, Moses smashes the tablets.

Mt Sinai

Ex 34:1-28

2ND TABLETS OF STONE PREPARED
Moses re-writes the law on two new tablets.

Mt Sinai

Ex 35:4–39:43

BUILDING OF THE TABERNACLE
The people build the Tabernacle, a special tent where God could be met with and worshipped as they travelled.

Mt Sinai

Num 13:1-24

12 SPIES SENT INTO CANAAN FOR 40 DAYS
12 spies are sent to assess the possibility of taking the land.

Kadesh-Barnea

Num 13:1-14:9

GIANTS IN THE LAND
The land is full of good things but there are giants there. Ten of the spies are afraid and say it cannot be taken.

Kadesh-Barnea

Num 14:33-34

ISRAEL TO WANDER 40 YEARS
The consequence of their fear is that for each of the 40 days that they spied out the land, they will spend a year wandering in the wilderness.

Kadesh-Barnea

source: David Painting. Gen, Ex, Num, Deut, Josh.
note: The contributor and author have drawn on personal opinions when choosing events to illustrate the journey.

Judges
Rhythms of life
with and without God

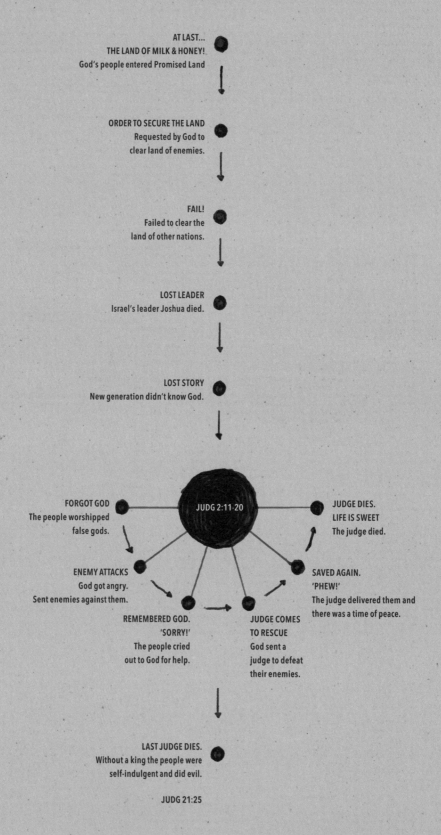

OVERVIEW:

AT LAST...
THE LAND OF MILK & HONEY!
God's people entered Promised Land

ORDER TO SECURE THE LAND
Requested by God to
clear land of enemies.

FAIL!
Failed to clear the
land of other nations.

LOST LEADER
Israel's leader Joshua died.

LOST STORY
New generation didn't know God.

FORGOT GOD
The people worshipped
false gods.

JUDG 2:11-20

JUDGE DIES.
LIFE IS SWEET
The judge died.

ENEMY ATTACKS
God got angry.
Sent enemies against them.

SAVED AGAIN.
'PHEW!'
The judge delivered them and
there was a time of peace.

REMEMBERED GOD.
'SORRY!'
The people cried
out to God for help.

JUDGE COMES
TO RESCUE
God sent a
judge to defeat
their enemies.

LAST JUDGE DIES.
Without a king the people were
self-indulgent and did evil.

JUDG 21:25

see pp42-43, 182-183

THE SPECIFICS OF EACH JUDGE:

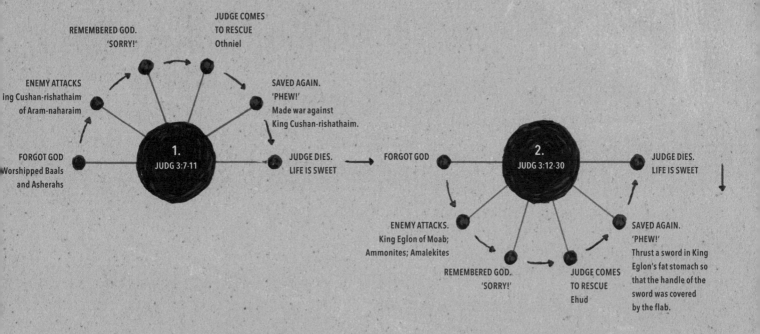

1.
JUDG 3:7-11

FORGOT GOD
Worshipped Baals and Asherahs

ENEMY ATTACKS
ing Cushan-rishathaim of Aram-naharaim

REMEMBERED GOD.
'SORRY!'

JUDGE COMES
TO RESCUE
Othniel

SAVED AGAIN.
'PHEW!'
Made war against King Cushan-rishathaim.

JUDGE DIES.
LIFE IS SWEET

2.
JUDG 3:12-30

FORGOT GOD

ENEMY ATTACKS.
King Eglon of Moab; Ammonites; Amalekites

REMEMBERED GOD.
'SORRY!'

JUDGE COMES
TO RESCUE
Ehud

SAVED AGAIN.
'PHEW!'
Thrust a sword in King Eglon's fat stomach so that the handle of the sword was covered by the flab.

JUDGE DIES.
LIFE IS SWEET

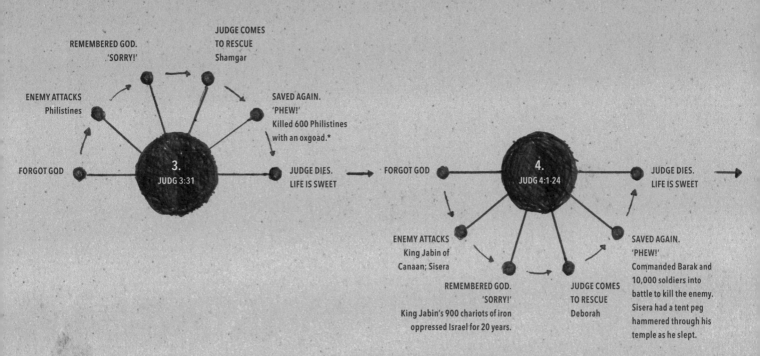

3.
JUDG 3:31

FORGOT GOD

ENEMY ATTACKS
Philistines

REMEMBERED GOD.
'SORRY!'

JUDGE COMES
TO RESCUE
Shamgar

SAVED AGAIN.
'PHEW!'
Killed 600 Philistines with an oxgoad.*

JUDGE DIES.
LIFE IS SWEET

4.
JUDG 4:1-24

FORGOT GOD

ENEMY ATTACKS
King Jabin of Canaan; Sisera

REMEMBERED GOD.
'SORRY!'
King Jabin's 900 chariots of iron oppressed Israel for 20 years.

JUDGE COMES
TO RESCUE
Deborah

SAVED AGAIN.
'PHEW!'
Commanded Barak and 10,000 soldiers into battle to kill the enemy. Sisera had a tent peg hammered through his temple as he slept.

JUDGE DIES.
LIFE IS SWEET

* a wooden tool, approximately eight feet long, fitted with an iron spike or point at one end, which was used to spur oxen as they pulled a plough or cart.

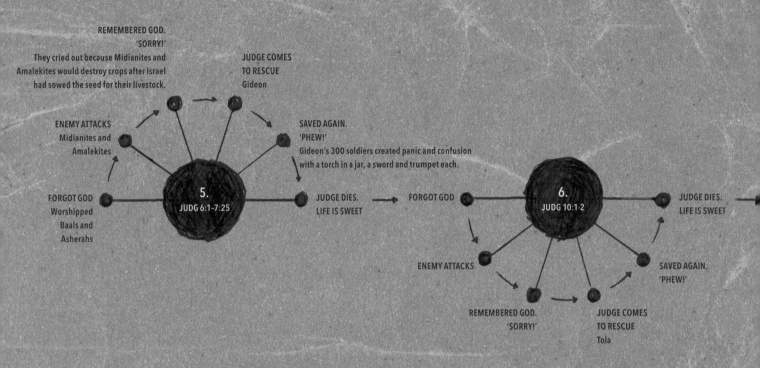

REMEMBERED GOD.
'SORRY!'
They cried out because Midianites and
Amalekites would destroy crops after Israel
had sowed the seed for their livestock.

JUDGE COMES
TO RESCUE
Gideon

ENEMY ATTACKS
Midianites and
Amalekites

SAVED AGAIN.
'PHEW!'
Gideon's 300 soldiers created panic and confusion
with a torch in a jar, a sword and trumpet each.

FORGOT GOD
Worshipped
Baals and
Asherahs

5.
JUDG 6:1-7:25

JUDGE DIES.
LIFE IS SWEET

FORGOT GOD

6.
JUDG 10:1-2

JUDGE DIES.
LIFE IS SWEET

ENEMY ATTACKS

SAVED AGAIN.
'PHEW!'

REMEMBERED GOD.
'SORRY!'

JUDGE COMES
TO RESCUE
Tola

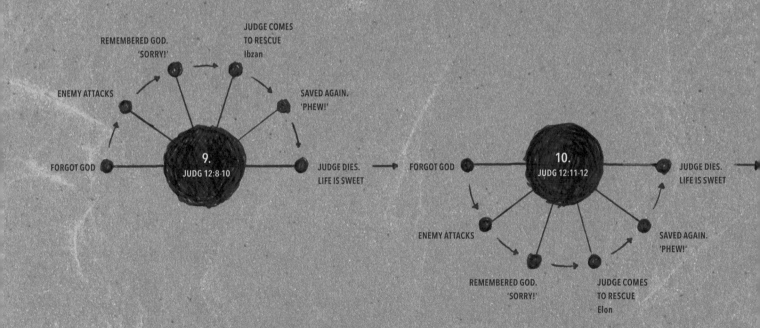

REMEMBERED GOD.
'SORRY!'

JUDGE COMES
TO RESCUE
Ibzan

ENEMY ATTACKS

SAVED AGAIN.
'PHEW!'

FORGOT GOD

9.
JUDG 12:8-10

JUDGE DIES.
LIFE IS SWEET

FORGOT GOD

10.
JUDG 12:11-12

JUDGE DIES.
LIFE IS SWEET

ENEMY ATTACKS

SAVED AGAIN.
'PHEW!'

REMEMBERED GOD.
'SORRY!'

JUDGE COMES
TO RESCUE
Elon

see pp.42-43, 182-183

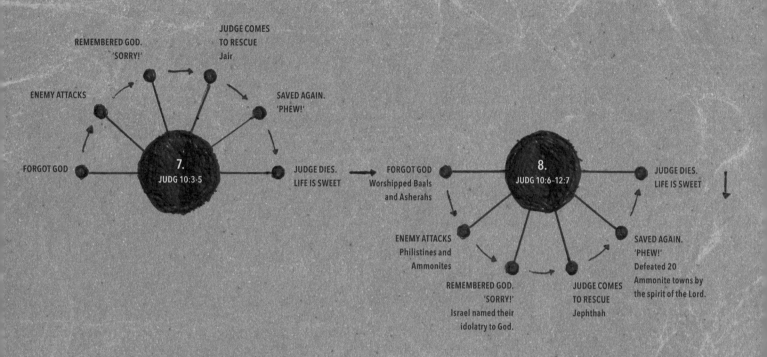

7.
JUDG 10:3-5

REMEMBERED GOD.
'SORRY!'

JUDGE COMES
TO RESCUE
Jair

ENEMY ATTACKS

SAVED AGAIN.
'PHEW!'

FORGOT GOD

JUDGE DIES.
LIFE IS SWEET

8.
JUDG 10:6-12:7

FORGOT GOD
Worshipped Baals
and Asherahs

JUDGE DIES.
LIFE IS SWEET

ENEMY ATTACKS
Philistines and
Ammonites

SAVED AGAIN.
'PHEW!'
Defeated 20
Ammonite towns by
the spirit of the Lord.

REMEMBERED GOD.
'SORRY!'
Israel named their
idolatry to God.

JUDGE COMES
TO RESCUE
Jephthah

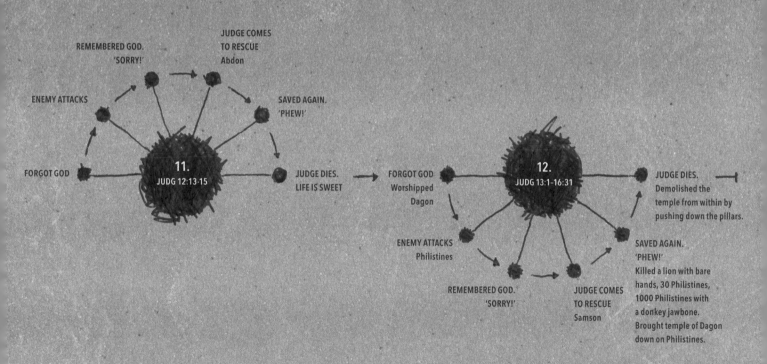

11.
JUDG 12:13-15

REMEMBERED GOD.
'SORRY!'

JUDGE COMES
TO RESCUE
Abdon

ENEMY ATTACKS

SAVED AGAIN.
'PHEW!'

FORGOT GOD

JUDGE DIES.
LIFE IS SWEET

12.
JUDG 13:1-16:31

FORGOT GOD
Worshipped
Dagon

JUDGE DIES.
Demolished the
temple from within by
pushing down the pillars.

ENEMY ATTACKS
Philistines

SAVED AGAIN.
'PHEW!'
Killed a lion with bare
hands, 30 Philistines,
1000 Philistines with
a donkey jawbone.
Brought temple of Dagon
down on Philistines.

REMEMBERED GOD.
'SORRY!'

JUDGE COMES
TO RESCUE
Samson

source: Dr Stuart C. Weir, Judges 3–4, 6, 10, 12–13

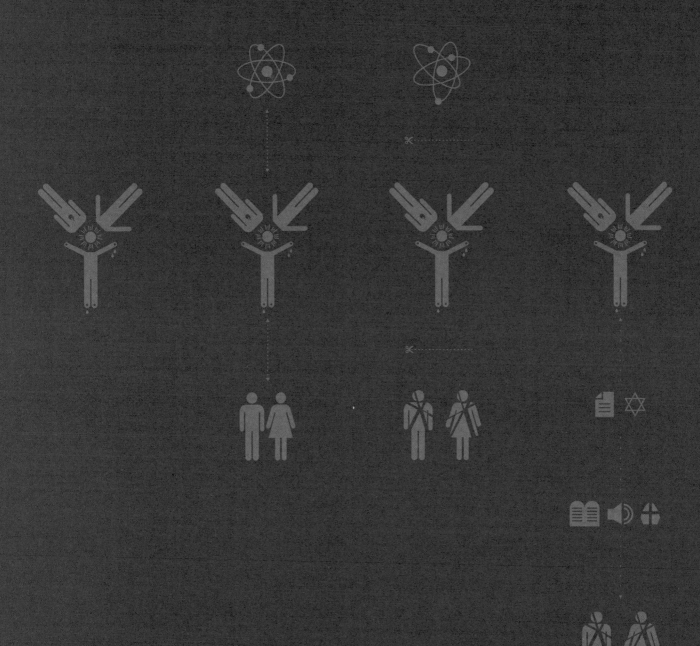

THE OLD TESTAMENT

THE PLAN REJECTED

People choose a king

1 SAM 8:5-7

The Lord
said to
Samuel,

*'Listen to
the voice
of the people
in all
that they
say to you;
for they
have not
rejected you,
but they
have rejected
me from
being king
over them.
Just as they
have done to
me, from the
day I brought
them up out
of Egypt to
this day,
forsaking me
and serving
other gods,
so also they
are doing
to you.
Now then,
listen to
their voice;
only you shall
solemnly
warn them,
and show
them the ways
of the king
who shall reign
over them.'*

(1 SAM 8:7-9)

GOD

Samuel
reported
all the
words of
the Lord to
the people
who were
asking
for a king.
He said

*'These will
be the ways
of the king
who will reign
over you:*

(1 SAM 8:10-11)

Samuel

'The people
refused to listen to the
voice of Samuel; they said,

"No!
*but we are determined
to have a king over us, so that
we also may be like other nations,
and that our king may govern us
and go out before us and
fight our battles."'*

(1 SAM 8:19-20)

THE PEOPLE

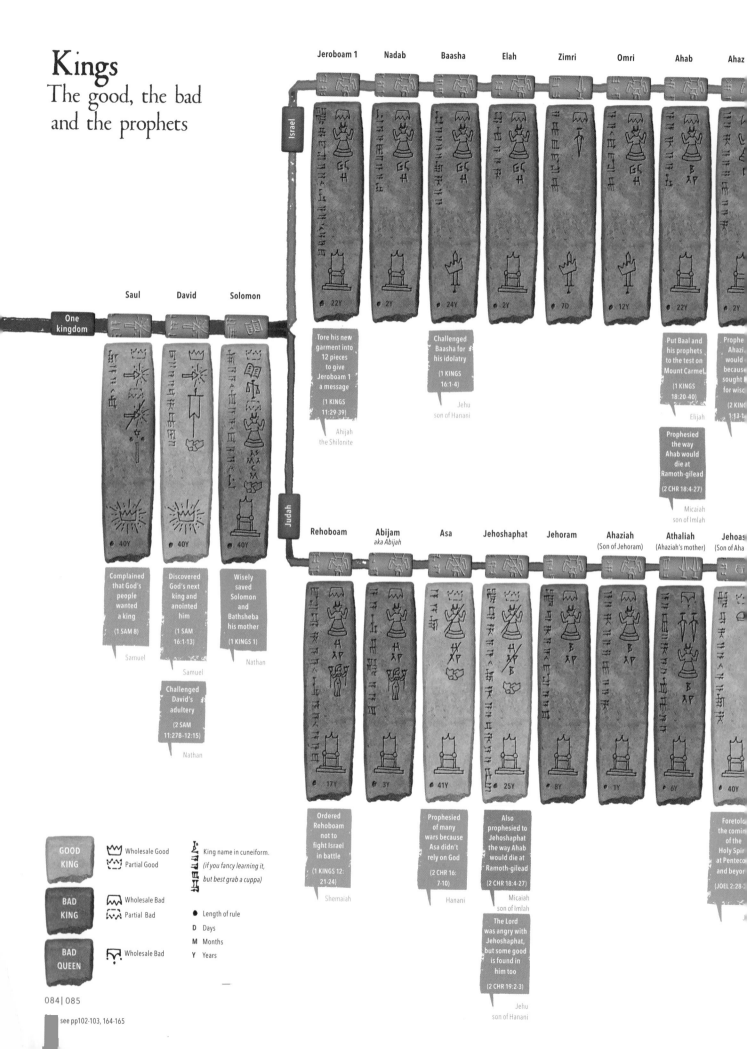

Kings
The good, the bad and the prophets

Jeroboam 1 · **Nadab** · **Baasha** · **Elah** · **Zimri** · **Omri** · **Ahab** · **Ahaz**

Israel

Jeroboam 1	Nadab	Baasha	Elah	Zimri	Omri	Ahab	Ahaz
22Y	2Y	24Y	2Y	7D	12Y	22Y	2Y

Saul · **David** · **Solomon**

One kingdom

Saul	David	Solomon
40Y	40Y	40Y

Judah

Tore his new garment into 12 pieces to give Jeroboam 1 a message
(1 KINGS 11:29-39)
Ahijah the Shilonite

Challenged Baasha for his idolatry
(1 KINGS 16:1-4)
Jehu son of Hanani

Put Baal and his prophets to the test on Mount Carmel
(1 KINGS 18:20-40)
Elijah

Prophe... Ahazi... would... because... sought... for wisc...
(2 KING... 1:13-1...)

Prophesied the way Ahab would die at Ramoth-gilead
(2 CHR 18:4-27)
Micaiah son of Imlah

Complained that God's people wanted a king
(1 SAM 8)
Samuel

Discovered God's next king and anointed him
(1 SAM 16:1-13)
Samuel

Challenged David's adultery
(2 SAM 11:27B-12:15)
Nathan

Wisely saved Solomon and Bathsheba his mother
(1 KINGS 1)
Nathan

Rehoboam · **Abijam** *aka Abijah* · **Asa** · **Jehoshaphat** · **Jehoram** · **Ahaziah** (Son of Jehoram) · **Athaliah** (Ahaziah's mother) · **Jehoas...** (Son of Aha...)

Rehoboam	Abijam	Asa	Jehoshaphat	Jehoram	Ahaziah	Athaliah	Jehoas...
17Y	3Y	41Y	25Y	8Y	1Y	6Y	40Y

Ordered Rehoboam not to fight Israel in battle
(1 KINGS 12:21-24)
Shemaiah

Prophesied of many wars because Asa didn't rely on God
(2 CHR 16:7-10)
Hanani

Also prophesied to Jehoshaphat the way Ahab would die at Ramoth-gilead
(2 CHR 18:4-27)
Micaiah son of Imlah

The Lord was angry with Jehoshaphat, but some good is found in him too
(2 CHR 19:2-3)
Jehu son of Hanani

Foretold the coming of the Holy Spir... at Penteco... and beyon...
(JOEL 2:28...)

Legend

GOOD KING — ⌢ Wholesale Good · ⌢ Partial Good

BAD KING — ⌢ Wholesale Bad · ⌢ Partial Bad

BAD QUEEN — ⌢ Wholesale Bad

King name in cuneiform. *(if you fancy learning it, but best grab a cuppa)*

● Length of rule
D Days
M Months
Y Years

see pp102-103, 164-165

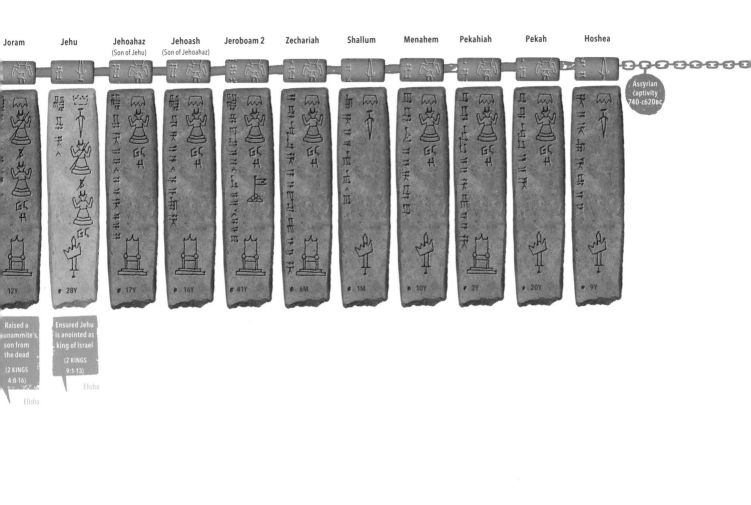

Joram · 12Y

Raised a Shunammite's son from the dead (2 KINGS 4:8-16)

Elisha

Jehu · 28Y

Ensured Jehu is anointed as king of Israel (2 KINGS 9:1-13)

Elisha

Jehoahaz (Son of Jehu) · 17Y

Jehoash (Son of Jehoahaz) · 16Y

Jeroboam 2 · 41Y

Zechariah · 6M

Shallum · 1M

Menahem · 10Y

Pekahiah · 2Y

Pekah · 20Y

Hoshea · 9Y

Assyrian captivity 740-c620BC

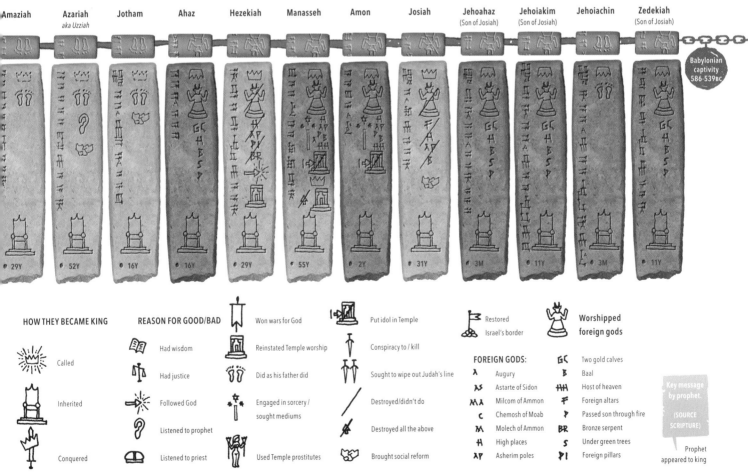

Amaziah · 29Y

Azariah *aka Uzziah* · 52Y

Jotham · 16Y

Ahaz · 16Y

Hezekiah · 29Y

Manasseh · 55Y

Amon · 2Y

Josiah · 31Y

Jehoahaz (Son of Josiah) · 3M

Jehoiakim (Son of Josiah) · 11Y

Jehoiachin · 3M

Zedekiah (Son of Josiah) · 11Y

Babylonian captivity 586-539BC

HOW THEY BECAME KING
Called
Inherited
Conquered

REASON FOR GOOD/BAD
Had wisdom
Had justice
Followed God
Listened to prophet
Listened to priest

Won wars for God
Reinstated Temple worship
Did as his father did
Engaged in sorcery / sought mediums
Used Temple prostitutes

Put idol in Temple
Conspiracy to / kill
Sought to wipe out Judah's line
Destroyed/didn't do
Destroyed all the above
Brought social reform

Restored Israel's border

FOREIGN GODS:
λ Augury
ΑS Astarte of Sidon
ΜΛ Milcom of Ammon
C Chemosh of Moab
Μ Molech of Ammon
Ⴇ High places
ΛΥ Asherim poles

Worshipped foreign gods

GC Two gold calves
B Baal
ΗΗ Host of heaven
Ϝ Foreign altars
Ϸ Passed son through fire
BR Bronze serpent
S Under green trees
ϷI Foreign pillars

Key message by prophet.
(SOURCE SCRIPTURE)

Prophet appeared to king

source: Dr Stuart C. Weir. 1 & 2 Sam, 1 & 2 Kings, 1 & 2 Chr.

1. SAMUEL ANOINTS DAVID AS KING OF ISRAEL

The young shepherd boy, David, is anointed by Samuel the prophet as future king of all God's people. The Spirit of God falls on David.
1 SAM 16:1-13

2. DAVID BECOMES KING SAUL'S ARMOUR-BEARER

King Saul is currently king of all God's people but is tormented by an evil spirit. Whenever David plays the lyre, the evil spirit departs.
1 SAM 16:14-23

3. DAVID KILLS GOLIATH

David puts himself forward to fight the giant Goliath, without armour. He kills him with a single sling shot.
1 SAM 17

9

4. JONATHAN MAKES A COVENANT WITH DAVID

The beginning of a powerful friendship between David and Saul's son, Jonathan.
1 SAM 18:1-9

5. KING SAUL TRIES TO KILL DAVID

Saul is afraid of David because God is with him. He tries to kill him.
1 SAM 18:10-16

6. DAVID MARRIES PRINCESS MICHAL

Michal is King Saul's daughter.
1 SAM 18:17-30

13. DAVID MARRIES AHINOAM

Ahinoam is from Jezreel.
1 SAM 25:43

14. DAVID CAPTURES KING SAUL AGAIN AND THEN SPARES HIS LIFE

Saul recognises David's voice and realises the mercy shown to him again.
1 SAM 26

15. DAVID STRENGTHENS HIMSELF IN GOD

David's family have been raided and taken captive, so David strengthens himself in God before rescuing his family and recovering the plunder.
1 SAM 30

16. DAVID ANOINTED & CROWNED KING OF JUDAH

King Saul is dead. David is led by God to the people and made king of Judah.
2 SAM 2

17. KING DAVID'S FIRST SONS ARE BORN

Born to David
with Ahinoam: Amnon.
With Abigail: Chileab.
With Maacah: Absalom.
With Haggith: Adonijah.
With Abital: Shephatiah.
With Eglah:Ithream.
2 SAM 3

22. KING DAVID COMMITS ADULTERY WITH BATHSHEBA

David is attracted to a young woman bathing and ends up committing adultery with her.
2 SAM 11:1-13

23. KING DAVID HAS URIAH KILLED

After committing adultery with his wife, David arranges for Uriah to be killed.
2 SAM 11:14-27

24. NATHAN THE PROPHET CONDEMNS KING DAVID

God sends Nathan to David. Nathan reminds David of all that God has done for him. David confesses that he's sinned.
2 SAM 12:1-15

32 **33**
51 **103**

25. BATHSHEBA'S CHILD DIES

David and Bathsheba's child becomes sick, so David fasts for the child. Seven days later the child dies. David responds by worshipping God in the midst of pain.
2 SAM 12:15B-23

26. SOLOMON IS BORN

Solomon is born after the death of David and Bathsheba's first child.
2 SAM 12:24-25

30. KING DAVID FLEES JERUSALEM

David ascends the Mount of Olives, weeping as he leaves.
2 SAM 15:13-31

3

31. KING DAVID HEARS OF ABSALOM'S DEATH

David mourns for his son Absalom 'Would that I had died instead of you…'
2 SAM 18:19-33

34. SOLOMON SUCCEEDS DAVID AS KING

When David is very old, Solomon is chosen to be the next king.
1 KINGS 1:28-53

36. DAVID DIES

David was buried in the city of David after reigning for 40 years (7 years in Hebron, 33 years in Jerusalem △).
1 KINGS 2:10-11;
1 CHR 29:26-30

 Psalm relating to the event

△ David reigns for 33 years over the combined kingdom

see pp112-113, 140-141, 164-165

7. JONATHAN PLEADS ON DAVID'S BEHALF

Saul speaks to Jonathan about killing David but Jonathan protects David from his father.

1 SAM 19:1-7

11

8. DAVID ESCAPES FROM KING SAUL

Michal helps David to escape from Saul (when an evil spirit comes over him).

1 SAM 19:9-17

59

9. DAVID HIDES IN THE CAVE AT ADULLAM

Everyone who is in distress, in debt or discontented gathers to David while he is hiding in the cave.

1 SAM 22:1-5

142

10. DAVID AVOIDS KING SAUL IN THE WILDERNESS

David evades an attack by Saul, after Jonathan confirms his father knows that one day David will be king of God's people.

1 SAM 23:15-29

11. DAVID CAPTURES KING SAUL AND THEN SPARES HIS LIFE

Saul is struck by the mercy shown: 'Now I know that you surely will be king' says Saul. 1 SAM 24

57

12. DAVID MARRIES ABIGAIL

Nabal has a conflict with David. David goes on to marry Nabal's widow, Abigail, shortly after he dies.

1 SAM 25:39-42

18. DAVID ANOINTED & CROWNED KING OF ALL GOD'S PEOPLE

The elders of Israel come to David at Hebron to anoint him as king of Israel and therefore king of all God's people.

2 SAM 5:1-5; 1 CHR 11:1-3

19. JERUSALEM MADE THE CAPITAL

David develops Jerusalem and calls it the city of David.

2 SAM 5:6-16; 1 CHR 11:4-9

20. KING DAVID BRINGS THE ARK TO JERUSALEM

David dances freely before the Lord as the Ark of the Covenant arrives in Jerusalem.

2 SAM 6; 1 CHR 15

68

21. GOD MAKES A COVENANT WITH KING DAVID

God promises never to take his steadfast love from David.

2 SAM 7:1-17; 1 CHR 17

27. KING DAVID DEFEATS THE AMMONITES' ARMY

David gathers everyone to go to Rabbah where they take the city, and all the others belonging to the Ammonites.

2 SAM 12:26-31

28. KING DAVID FORGIVES HIS SON, ABSALOM

David's son, Amnon, deceives his brother and lies with his wife. In retaliation Absalom kills Amnon. David now forgives Absalom for this.

2 SAM 14:25-33

29. KING ABSALOM USURPS THE THRONE FROM HIS FATHER, DAVID

Absalom gathers chariots, horses and men and sends secret messengers throughout Israel to all God's people that Absalom has become king.

2 SAM 15:1-12

32. KING DAVID RECALLED TO JERUSALEM

King David's nephew, Amasa, sways the heart of all the people of Judah who invite David to return as their king.

2 SAM 19:8-18

33. GOD'S JUDGEMENT ON KING DAVID'S AFFAIR WITH BATHSHEBA

King David asks God to take away his guilt after his foolish act. Judgement comes when God sends a plague to his people for three days: 70,000 died.

2 SAM 24:10-17

35. DAVID'S FINAL INSTRUCTION TO SOLOMON

David instructs Solomon to build the Temple. He tells him to 'Be strong and courageous, and keep the charge of the Lord your God ... so that you may prosper in all that you do.'

1 KINGS 2:1-9; 1 CHR 29:1-25

37. THE GENEALOGY OF JESUS

David listed in the genealogy to Jesus.

MT 1:6

King David

Shepherd, warrior, worshipper: a man after God's own heart

source: Revd Dr Graham R. Houston and Rhoda Fearon. 1 Sam, 2 Sam, 1 Kings, 1 Chr, Mt. Source for Psalms: 'Probable occasion when each psalm was composed.' Retrieved from https://www.blueletterbible.org/study/parallel/paral18.cfm

note: The data contributor and author have drawn on personal opinions when collating parts of this data.

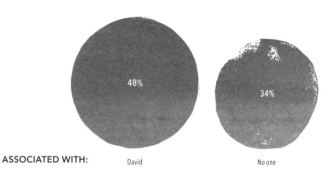

ASSOCIATED WITH:

48%	34%	7%	6%	2%	1%	1%	1%
David	No one	Asaph	The Korahites	Solomon	The Korahites and Heman the Ezrahite	Ethan the Ezrahite	Moses

Ps 56
When the Philistines seized David in Gath

Ps 30
A song at the dedication of the Temple

Ps 18
Addressed to God after God delivered David from his enemies and from Saul

Ps 51
When Nathan came to David after his liaison with Bathsheba

Ps 57
When David fled from Saul, in the cave

Ps 34
When David feigned madness before Abimelech

Ps 59
When Saul ordered his house to be watched in order to kill David

Ps 3
When David fled from Absalom

Ps 63
When David was in the Wilderness of Judah

LENGTH IN VERSES

PSALM

1 2 3 4 5 6 7 8 9 10 11 12 13 14 15 16 17 18 19 20 21 22 23 24 25 26 27 28 29 30 31 32 33 34 35 36 37 38 39 40 41 42 43 44 45 46 47 48 49 50 51 52 53 54 55 56 57 58 59 60 61 62 63 64 65 66 67 68 69 70

BOOK

One

Two

PSALM TYPE BY COLOUR

Praising...
the power of God
other

Plea for ...
Deliverance from enemies
other

miscellaneous
Trust in God's protection
other

ASSOCIATED WITH

David
No one
Asaph
Korahites
Solomon
Korahites and Heman
Ethan the Ezrahite
Moses

see pp112-113

The Psalms
How long?

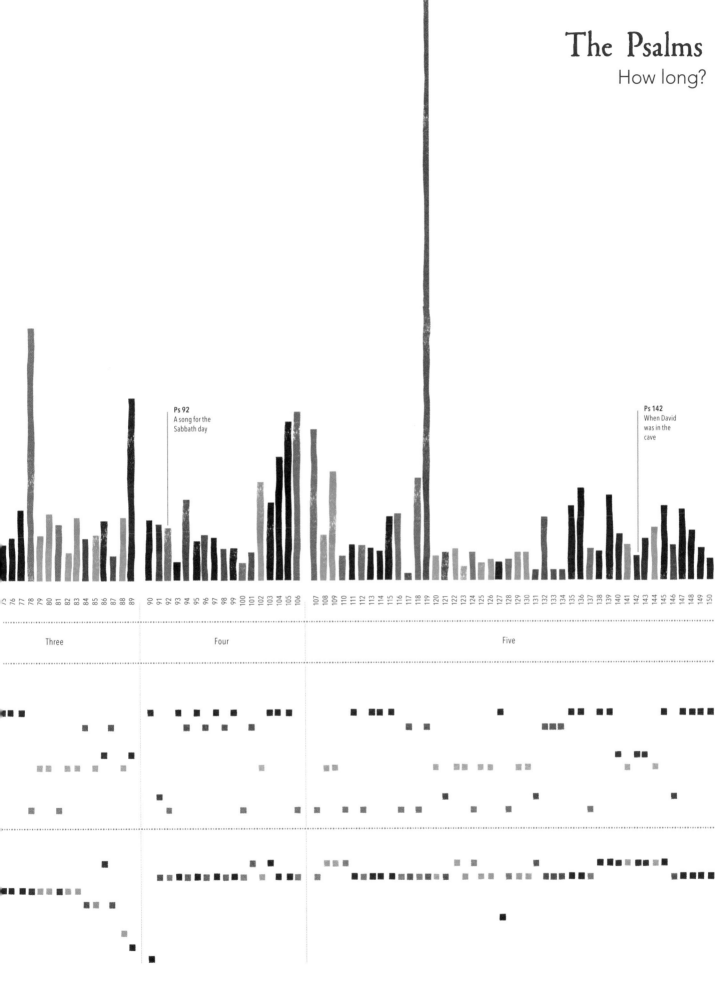

Ps 92
A song for the
Sabbath day

Ps 142
When David
was in the
cave

Three

Four

Five

source: Professor James Crossley. Psalms. Hebrew Masoretic Text
note: The number of Psalms varies according to different traditions. The 150 Psalms here are based on the Hebrew version and the major English translations of the Bible.

Praise & Worship Stances
Meaning in the moves

HALAL

To celebrate.
To rave about God.

PS 150:1

YADAH

To praise with thankfulness
and outstretched hands.

2 CHR 20:21

TOWDAH

To raise hands in adoration as well as
thankfulness for things not yet received.

PS 50:14

SHABACH

To shout, to address God in a loud tone
and to triumph.

PS 47:1

BARAK

To kneel down to bless God
as an act of adoration.

PS 95:6

ZAMAR

To make music in praise.
To celebrate with singing and playing.

PS 21:13

TEHILLAH

To be led by the Holy Spirit in spontaneous moments of overflow praise to God.

PS 22:3

see pp112-113

source: WORSHIPCENTRAL www.worshipcentral.org. 2 Chr, Ps.
note: The data contributor and author have drawn on their own opinions when selecting this data and these Scripture examples. This is not an exhaustive list.

Solomon's Temple
A response in worship

1 cubit = 0.45 metres

120 cubits
54m

20 cubits
9m

30 cubits
13.5m

15 cubits
6.75m

7 cubits
3.15m

60 cubits
27m

10 cubits
4.5m

Solomon's Temple
A response in worship

1 cubit ≈ 0.45 metres

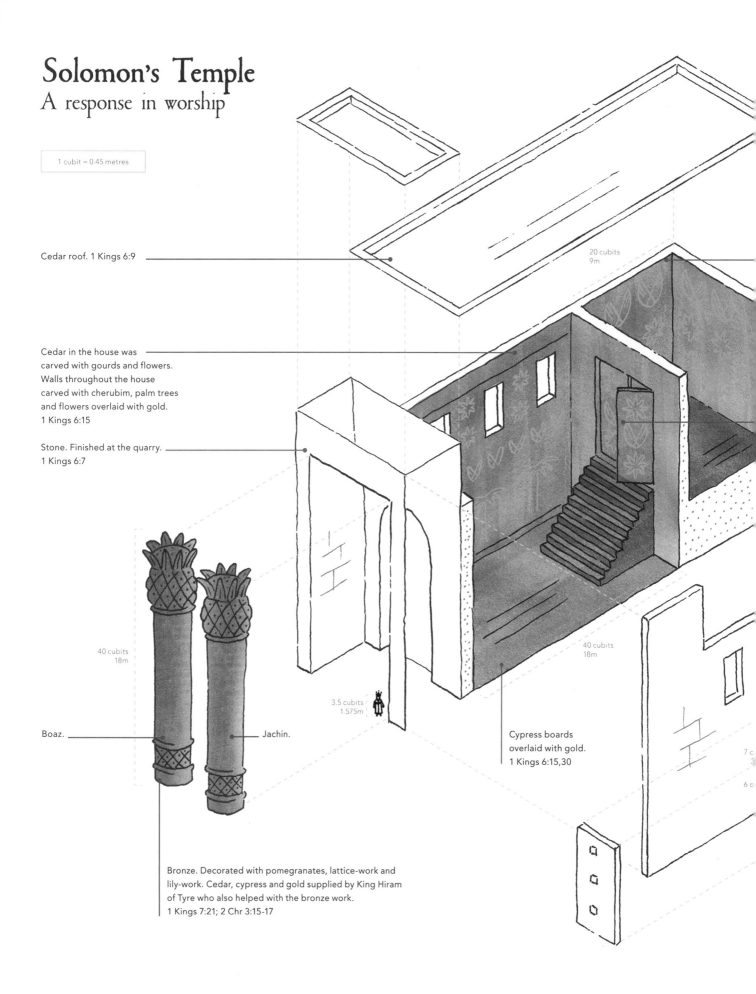

Cedar roof. 1 Kings 6:9

Cedar in the house was
carved with gourds and flowers.
Walls throughout the house
carved with cherubim, palm trees
and flowers overlaid with gold.
1 Kings 6:15

Stone. Finished at the quarry.
1 Kings 6:7

20 cubits
9m

40 cubits
18m

40 cubits
18m

3.5 cubits
1.575m

Boaz.

Jachin.

Cypress boards
overlaid with gold.
1 Kings 6:15,30

7 c
3

6 c

Bronze. Decorated with pomegranates, lattice-work and
lily-work. Cedar, cypress and gold supplied by King Hiram
of Tyre who also helped with the bronze work.
1 Kings 7:21; 2 Chr 3:15-17

see pp68-69, 70-71

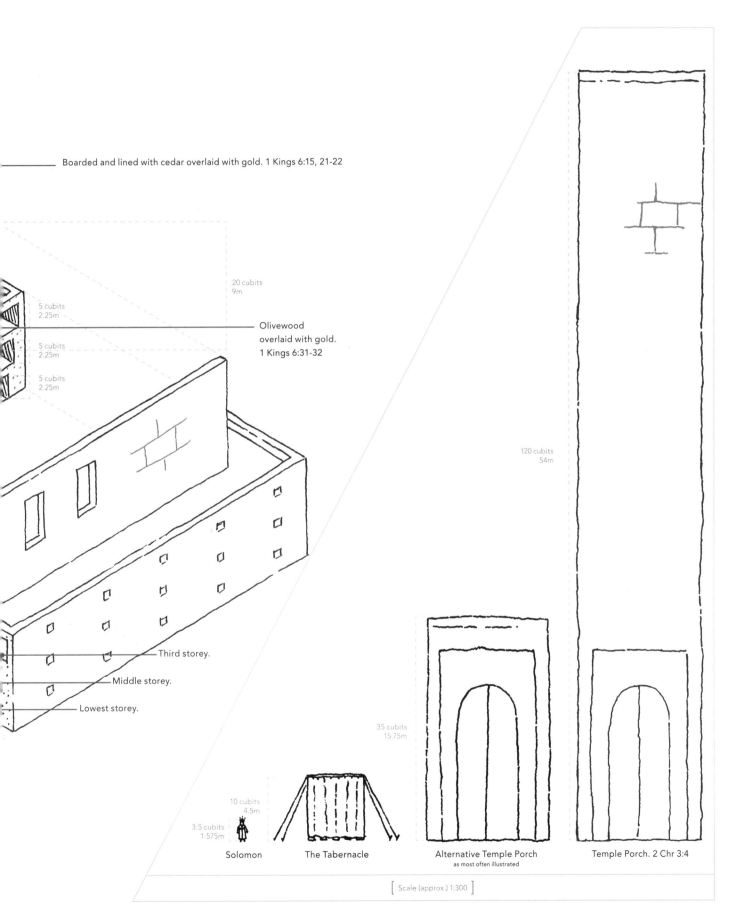

Boarded and lined with cedar overlaid with gold. 1 Kings 6:15, 21-22

20 cubits
9m

5 cubits
2.25m

5 cubits
2.25m

5 cubits
2.25m

Olivewood
overlaid with gold.
1 Kings 6:31-32

120 cubits
54m

Third storey.

Middle storey.

Lowest storey.

35 cubits
15.75m

10 cubits
4.5m

3.5 cubits
1.575m

Solomon

The Tabernacle

Alternative Temple Porch
as most often illustrated

Temple Porch. 2 Chr 3:4

[Scale (approx.) 1:300]

source: Professor James Crossley. 1 Kings 6-9; 2 Chr 3-8 (Hebrew Masoretic Text), Wikipedia Note: 2 Chr 3:4 appears to mention an especially high vestibule/porch.
This is a difficult text to interpret but our visualisation assumes that this reading of the text is correct. The alternative porch height is based on 'Solomon's Temple', https://en.wikipedia.org/wiki/Solomon%27s_Temple

Solomon's Wealth
Living the dream

ITEMS ATTRIBUTED TO WEALTH
Symbol : amount it represents = total wealth

BUILDINGS & CONTENTS:

 1 = 1 Temple

1 = 1 Great ivory throne overlaid with gold

1 = 2 Palaces

 : 100 = 40000 Stalls of horses for chariots

: 100 = 200 Large shields of beaten gold

: 100 = 300 Shields of beaten gold

TRANSPORT:

: 60 ships (1 Fleet) = 120 ships (2 Fleets)

: 100 = 1400 Chariots

: 100 = 12000 Horses

PEOPLE:

 : 100 = 300 Concubines

: 100 = 550 Chief officers

 : 100 = 700 Wives

: 100 = 3600 Supervisors

: 100 = 12000 Horsemen

: 200 = 70000 Labourers

: 200 = 80000 Stone cutters

WISDOM:

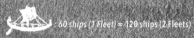 *: 100 = 3000 Proverbs*

: 100 = 1005 Songs

MONEY:

● *: 100 = over 26640 gold coins*

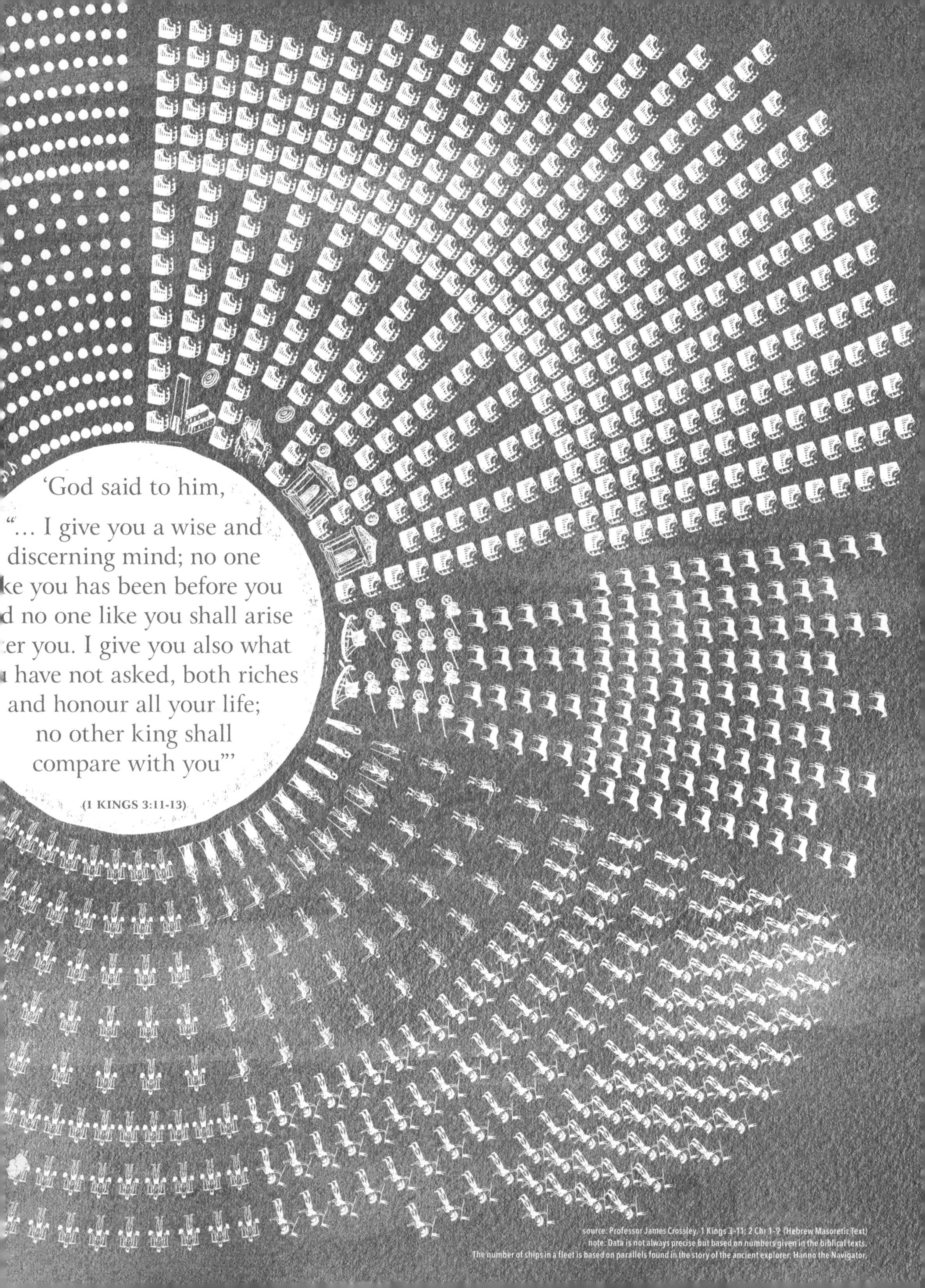

'God said to him,
"… I give you a wise and
discerning mind; no one
like you has been before you
and no one like you shall arise
after you. I give you also what
you have not asked, both riches
and honour all your life;
no other king shall
compare with you"'

(1 KINGS 3:11-13)

source: Professor James Crossley, 1 Kings 3-11; 2 Chr 1-9 (Hebrew Masoretic Text)
note: Data is not always precise but based on numbers given in the biblical texts.
The number of ships in a fleet is based on parallels found in the story of the ancient explorer, Hanno the Navigator.

LILIES 8

DEER / STAGS 8

GARDEN 9

WINE 8

MYRRH 8

DOVES / COOING 8

FRUIT 7

MOUNTAINS 5

ARMY 4

SPICES 8

JERUSALEM 6

DOOR 5

POMEGRANATES 5

APPLE 4

VINES / VINEYARD 8

BRIDE 6

TREASURE 5

GAZELLES 7

TOWER 5

CEDAR 4

source: David Painting 'Song.

Song of Songs Speech
The his and hers language of love...

THEMES: WHO TALKED ABOUT WHAT?

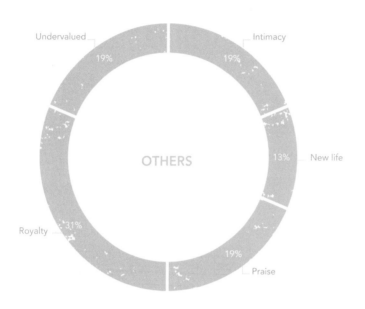

see pp164-165

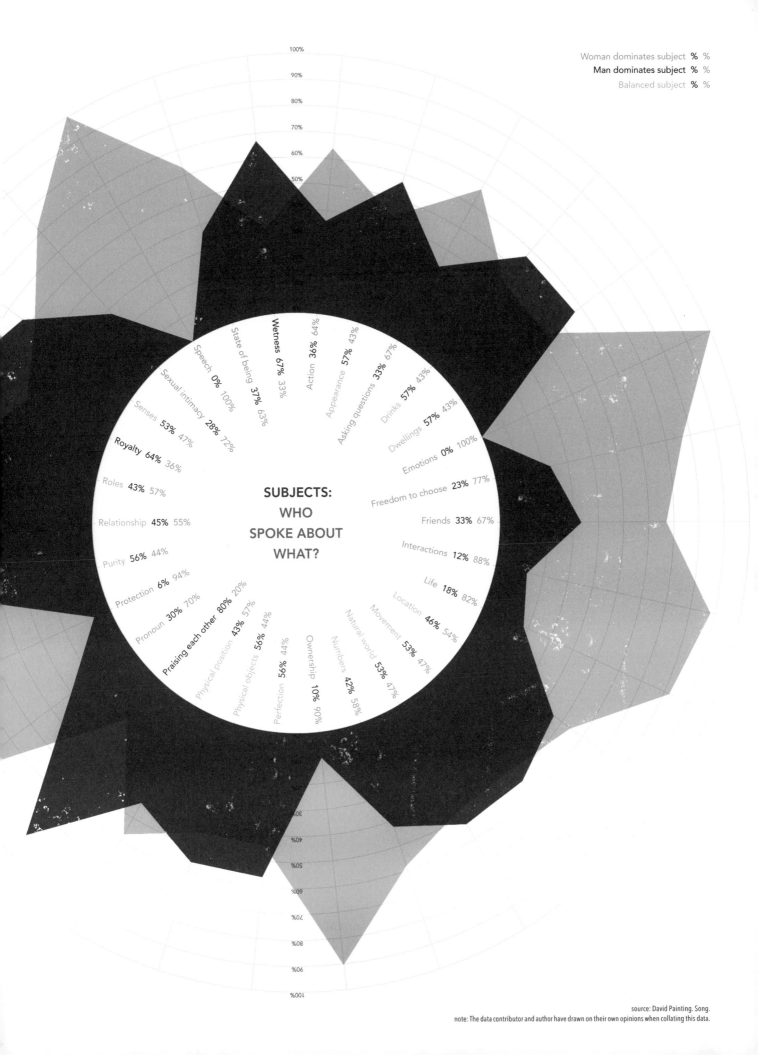

Wetness 67% 33%
State of being 37% 63%
Speech 0% 100%
Sexual intimacy 28% 72%
Senses 53% 47%
Royalty 64% 36%
Roles 43% 57%
Relationship 45% 55%
Purity 56% 44%
Protection 6% 94%
Pronoun 30% 70%
Praising each other 80% 20%
Physical position 43% 57%
Physical objects 56% 44%
Perfection 56% 44%
Ownership 10% 90%
Numbers 42% 58%
Natural world 53% 47%
Movement 53% 47%
Location 46% 54%
Life 18% 82%
Interactions 12% 88%
Friends 33% 67%
Freedom to choose 23% 77%
Emotions 0% 100%
Dwellings 57% 43%
Drinks 57% 43%
Asking questions 33% 67%
Appearance 57% 43%
Action 36% 64%

**SUBJECTS:
WHO
SPOKE ABOUT
WHAT?**

source: David Painting. Song.
note: The data contributor and author have drawn on their own opinions when collating this data.

Elijah the Prophet
Forerunner of Jesus as prophet

"Elijah was a human being like us, and he prayed fervently that it might not rain, and for three years and six months it did not rain on the earth."

(JAMES 5:17)

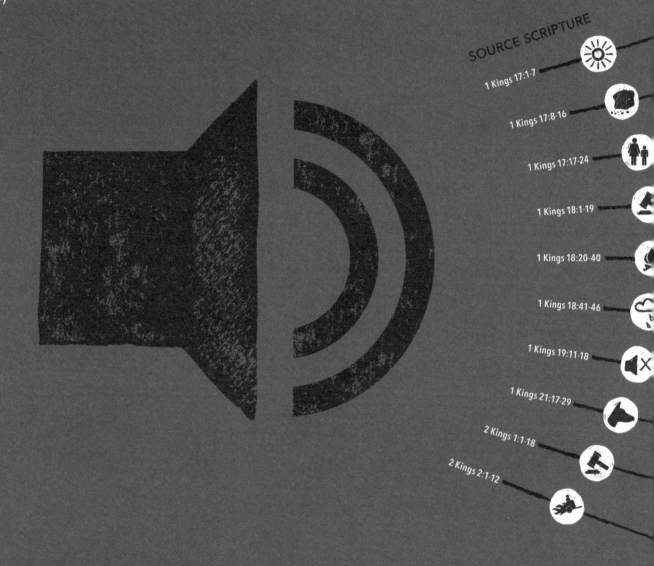

SOURCE SCRIPTURE

1 Kings 17:1-7

1 Kings 17:8-16

1 Kings 17:17-24

1 Kings 18:1-19

1 Kings 18:20-40

1 Kings 18:41-46

1 Kings 19:11-18

1 Kings 21:17-29

2 Kings 1:1-18

2 Kings 2:1-12

* Appears with Moses and Jesus at the Transfiguration Mt 17:3, Mk 9:4, Lk 9:30

see pp140-141, 164-165, 200-201

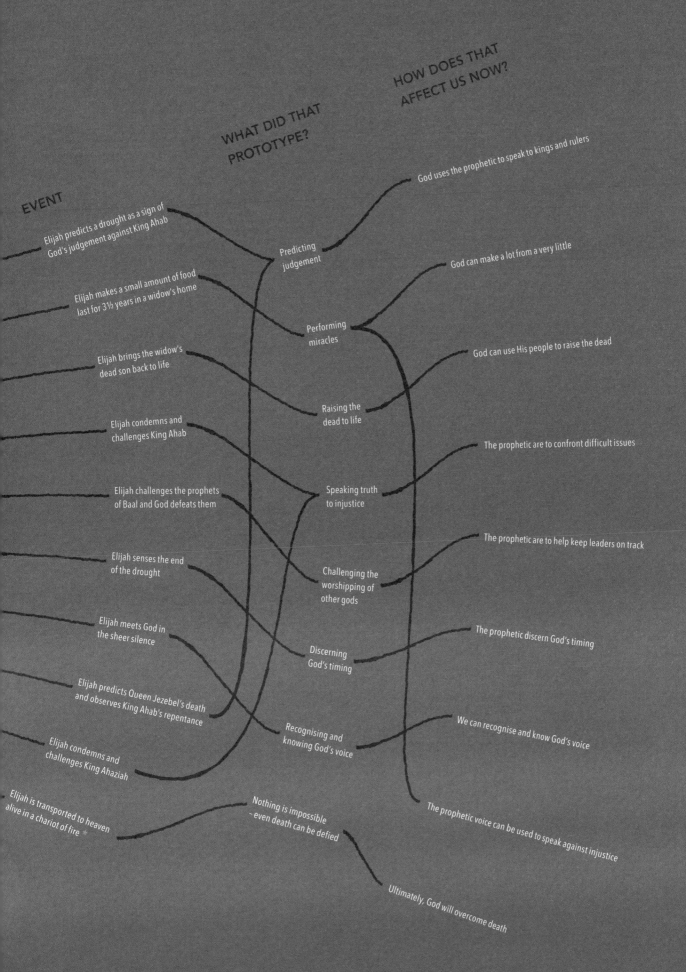

EVENT

WHAT DID THAT PROTOTYPE?

HOW DOES THAT AFFECT US NOW?

Elijah predicts a drought as a sign of God's judgement against King Ahab

Elijah makes a small amount of food last for 3½ years in a widow's home

Elijah brings the widow's dead son back to life

Elijah condemns and challenges King Ahab

Elijah challenges the prophets of Baal and God defeats them

Elijah senses the end of the drought

Elijah meets God in the sheer silence

Elijah predicts Queen Jezebel's death and observes King Ahab's repentance

Elijah condemns and challenges King Ahaziah

Elijah is transported to heaven alive in a chariot of fire

Predicting judgement

Performing miracles

Raising the dead to life

Speaking truth to injustice

Challenging the worshipping of other gods

Discerning God's timing

Recognising and knowing God's voice

Nothing is impossible – even death can be defied

God uses the prophetic to speak to kings and rulers

God can make a lot from a very little

God can use His people to raise the dead

The prophetic are to confront difficult issues

The prophetic are to help keep leaders on track

The prophetic discern God's timing

We can recognise and know God's voice

The prophetic voice can be used to speak against injustice

Ultimately, God will overcome death

source: Dr Stuart C. Weir, 1 Kings; 2 Kings; Mt.
note: The contributor and author have drawn on their own opinions when identifying prototypes within this data, and defining how those prototypes affect us now.

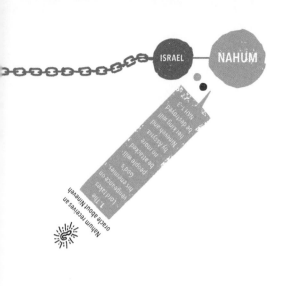

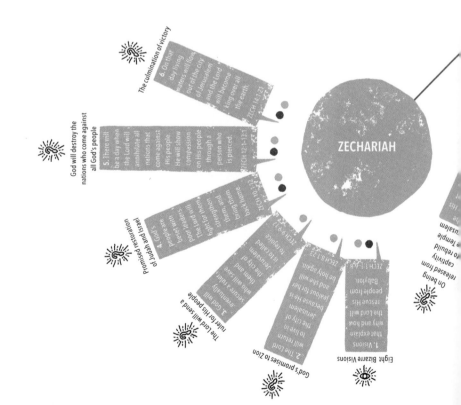

NAHUM — ISRAEL

Nahum receives an oracle about Nineveh

1. The Lord takes vengeance on his enemies. God's people will be attacked no more. Nineveh and her king will be destroyed by Assyria. Nah 1-3

ISAIAH

The Lord's servant and the restoration of all God's people
5. The Lord has followed His servant since conception in order that he may bring His people back to Him. All these enemies will reap the violence they have sown and know that the Lord is saviour. ISA 49:1-26

The Man of Sorrows
6. The Lord's servant will prosper, suffer, be despised, cover sin, and die for many. ISA 52:13-53:12

God's message to the wicked
7. The righteous among God's people perish as the wicked lust under every green tree and slaughter their children in the valleys. The Lord is looking for the humble hearted. ISA 56:9-57:21

The new heavens and new earth
8. The Lord will transform His creation so that God's people no longer remember the atrocities done to them and so that life's injustices are put to rights. ISA 65:17-25

The humiliation of Babylon
4. The Lord of hosts is the Holy One of all God's people. He will take vengeance on the idolatry of Babylon and bring their arrogance down to the dust. ISA 47:1-15

The Lord is greater than Babylon's gods
3. Bel and Nebo (Babylon's gods) are temporary but the Lord has no end. Trust in His coming deliverance from exile. ISA 46:1-13

Jacob is not forgotten
2. The Lord has swept her sins away and calls her to return to Him as her redeemer will use King Cyrus to accomplish the rebuilding of the city. ISA 44:1-45:25

Good news for God's people
1. The people have now paid their dues in exile and are promised a future return. ISA 40:1-11

The second deportation of Judah
2. The outcome of God's...

Fall of God's people and first deportation of Judah
1. The consequence of ignoring God's calls for repentance

ZECHARIAH

The culmination of victory
6. On that day living waters will flow out of the city of Jerusalem and the Lord will become king over all the earth. ZECH 14:1-21

God will destroy the nations who come against all God's people
5. There will be a day when the Lord will annihilate all nations that come against His people. He will show compassion on His people through a person who is pierced. ZECH 12:1-13:1

Promised restoration of Judah and Israel
4. God's people are blessed with the Lord's favour. The Lord will fight for them, strengthen them, and bring them back home. ZECH 9:1-11:17

The Lord will send a ruler for His people
3. God will secure a ruler who and will save the city of Jerusalem. ZECH 8:1-23

God's promises to Zion
2. The Lord will return to live in the city of Jerusalem and she will be holy again. ZECH 7:1-8:23

Eight Bizarre Visions
1. Visions that explain why and how the Lord will rescue His people from Babylon. ZECH 1:7-6:8

On being released from captivity to rebuild the temple ... Jerusalem ...

The Exiles
Messages of doom and hope

source: Dr Stuart C. Weir. 2 Kings, Isa, Jer, Ezek, Dan, Ob, Nah, Hag, Zech. <biblehub.org>; Frank E. Gaebelein, *The Expositor's Bible Commentary – Volume 6* (Isaiah – Ezekiel); A.C. Schultz, *'Exile' in Merrill* C. Tenney & Steven Barabas, *The Zondervan Pictorial Encyclopedia of the Bible – Volume 2 D-G*; Robert P. Carroll, *The Book of Jeremiah: A Commentary*; John N. Oswalt, *Isaiah – Chapters 40-66 (The New International Commentary on the Old Testament)*.
note: Scholars differ over the dates of some prophets' activities. One view in each case has been chosen for the purposes of this book.

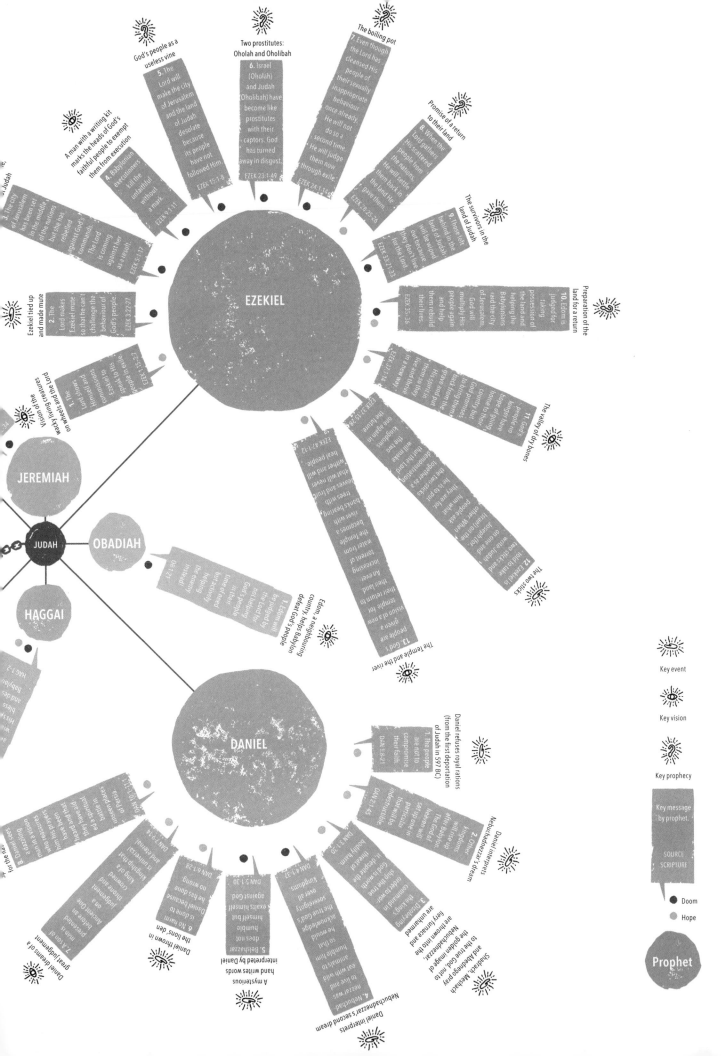

The Return from Exile
Rebuilding Jerusalem against the odds

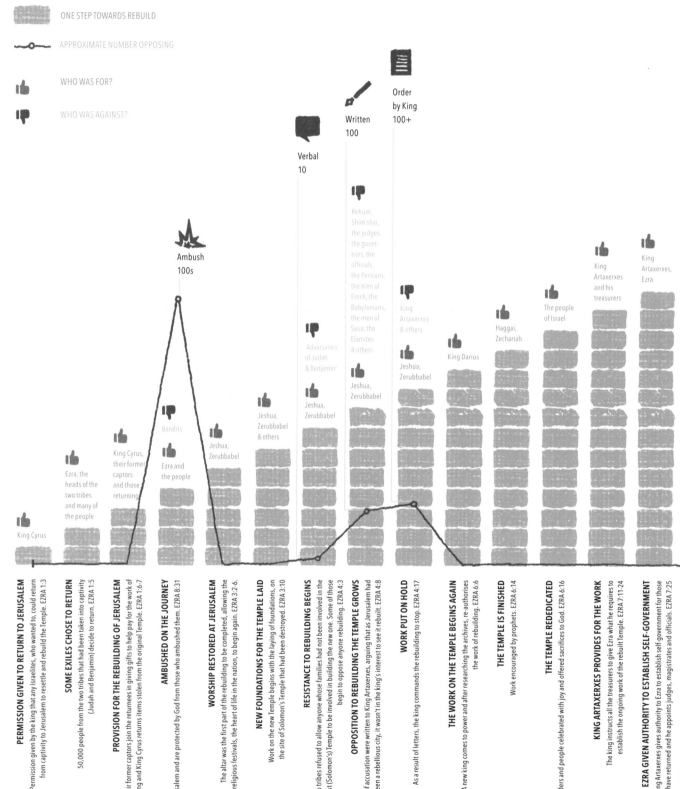

ONE STEP TOWARDS REBUILD

APPROXIMATE NUMBER OPPOSING

WHO WAS FOR?

WHO WAS AGAINST?

Order by King
100+

Written
100

Verbal
10

Ambush
100s

Rehum, Shim'shai, the judges, the governors, the officials, the Persians, the men of Erech, the Babylonians, the men of Susa, the Elamites & others

'Adversaries of Judah & Benjamin'

King Artaxerxes & others

King Artaxerxes, Ezra

King Artaxerxes and his treasurers

The people of Israel

Haggai, Zechariah

King Darius

Jeshua, Zerubbabel

Jeshua, Zerubbabel

Jeshua, Zerubbabel

Jeshua, Zerubbabel & others

Jeshua, Zerubbabel

Bandits

King Cyrus, their former captors and those returning

Ezra and the people

Ezra, the heads of the two tribes and many of the people

King Cyrus

PERMISSION GIVEN TO RETURN TO JERUSALEM
Permission given by the king that any Israelites, who wanted to, could return from captivity to Jerusalem to resettle and rebuild the Temple. EZRA 1:3

SOME EXILES CHOSE TO RETURN
50,000 people from the two tribes that had been taken into captivity (Judah and Benjamin) decide to return. EZRA 1:5

PROVISION FOR THE REBUILDING OF JERUSALEM
Their former captors join the returnees in giving gifts to help pay for the work of rebuilding and King Cyrus returns items stolen from the original Temple. EZRA 1:6-7

AMBUSHED ON THE JOURNEY
They journey to Jerusalem and are protected by God from those who ambushed them. EZRA 8:31

WORSHIP RESTORED AT JERUSALEM
The altar was the first part of the rebuilding to be completed, allowing the religious festivals, the heart of life in the nation, to begin again. EZRA 3:2-6.

NEW FOUNDATIONS FOR THE TEMPLE LAID
Work on the new Temple begins with the laying of foundations, on the site of Solomon's Temple that had been destroyed. EZRA 3:10

RESISTANCE TO REBUILDING BEGINS
The leaders of the two tribes refused to allow anyone whose families had not been involved in the building of the first (Solomon's) Temple to be involved in building the new one. Some of those begin to oppose anyone rebuilding. EZRA 4:3

OPPOSITION TO REBUILDING THE TEMPLE GROWS
Letters of accusation were written to King Artaxerxes, arguing that as Jerusalem had historically been a rebellious city, it wasn't in the king's interest to see it rebuilt. EZRA 4:8

WORK PUT ON HOLD
As a result of letters, the king commands the rebuilding to stop. EZRA 4:17

THE WORK ON THE TEMPLE BEGINS AGAIN
A new king comes to power and after researching the archives, re-authorises the work of rebuilding. EZRA 6:6

THE TEMPLE IS FINISHED
Work encouraged by prophets. EZRA 6:14

THE TEMPLE REDEDICATED
The priests, leaders and people celebrated with joy and offered sacrifices to God. EZRA 6:16

KING ARTAXERXES PROVIDES FOR THE WORK
The king instructs all the treasurers to give Ezra what he requires to establish the ongoing work of the rebuilt Temple. EZRA 7:11-24

EZRA GIVEN AUTHORITY TO ESTABLISH SELF-GOVERNMENT
King Artaxerxes gives authority to Ezra to establish self-government for those who have returned and he appoints judges, magistrates and officials. EZRA 7:25

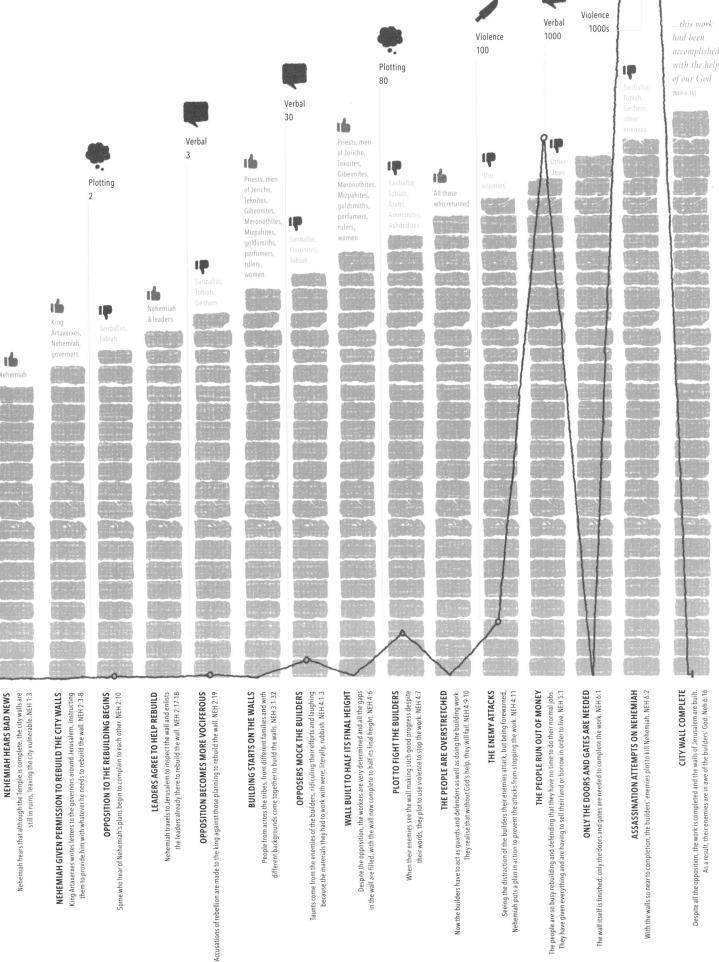

...this work had been accomplished with the help of our God
[NEH 6:16]

NEHEMIAH HEARS BAD NEWS
Nehemiah hears that although the Temple is complete, the city walls are still in ruins, leaving the city vulnerable. NEH 1:3

NEHEMIAH GIVEN PERMISSION TO REBUILD THE CITY WALLS
King Artaxerxes writes letters to the governors around Jerusalem, instructing them to provide him with whatever he needs to rebuild the wall. NEH 2:3-8

OPPOSITION TO THE REBUILDING BEGINS
Some who hear of Nehemiah's plans begin to complain to each other. NEH 2:10

LEADERS AGREE TO HELP REBUILD
Nehemiah travels to Jerusalem to inspect the wall and enlists the leaders already there to rebuild the wall. NEH 2:17-18

OPPOSITION BECOMES MORE VOCIFEROUS
Accusations of rebellion are made to the king against those planning to rebuild the wall. NEH 2:19

BUILDING STARTS ON THE WALLS
People from across the tribes, from different families and with different backgrounds come together to build the walls. NEH 3:1-32

OPPOSERS MOCK THE BUILDERS
Taunts come from the enemies of the builders, ridiculing their efforts and laughing because the materials they had to work with were, literally, rubbish. NEH 4:1-3

WALL BUILT TO HALF ITS FINAL HEIGHT
Despite the opposition, the workers are very determined and all the gaps in the wall are filled, with the wall now complete to half its final height. NEH 4:6

PLOT TO FIGHT THE BUILDERS
When their enemies see the wall making such good progress despite their words, they plot to use violence to stop the work. NEH 4:7

THE PEOPLE ARE OVERSTRETCHED
Now the builders have to act as guards and defenders as well as doing the building work. They realise that without God's help, they will fail. NEH 4:9-10

THE ENEMY ATTACKS
Seeing the distraction of the builders their enemies attack, but being forewarned, Nehemiah puts a plan in action to prevent the attacks from stopping the work. NEH 4:11

THE PEOPLE RUN OUT OF MONEY
The people are so busy rebuilding and defending that they have no time to do their normal jobs. They have given everything and are having to sell their land or borrow in order to live. NEH 5:1

ONLY THE DOORS AND GATES ARE NEEDED
The wall itself is finished; only the doors and gates are needed to complete the work. NEH 6:1

ASSASSINATION ATTEMPTS ON NEHEMIAH
With the walls so near to completion, the builders' enemies plot to kill Nehemiah. NEH 6:2

CITY WALL COMPLETE
Despite all the opposition, the work is completed and the walls of Jerusalem are built. As a result, their enemies are in awe of the builders' God. Neh 6:16

Plotting 2

Verbal 3

Verbal 30

Plotting 80

Violence 100

Verbal 1000

Violence 1000s

Nehemiah

King Artaxerxes, Nehemiah, governors

Sanballat, Tobiah

Nehemiah & leaders

Sanballat, Tobiah, Geshem

Priests, men of Jericho, Tekoites, Gibeonites, Meronothites, Mizpahites, goldsmiths, perfumers, rulers, women

Sanballat, Horonites, Tobiah

Priests, men of Jericho, Tekoites, Gibeonites, Meronothites, Mizpahites, goldsmiths, perfumers, rulers, women

Sanballat, Tobiah, Arabs, Ammonites, Ashdodites

All those who returned

'Our enemies'

Other Jews

Sanballat, Tobiah, Geshem, other enemies

source: David Painting. Ezra, Neh.
note: The division of the story into steps has been created by the contributor and author for the purposes of this graphic.

Suffering through the Eyes of Job
More questions than answers

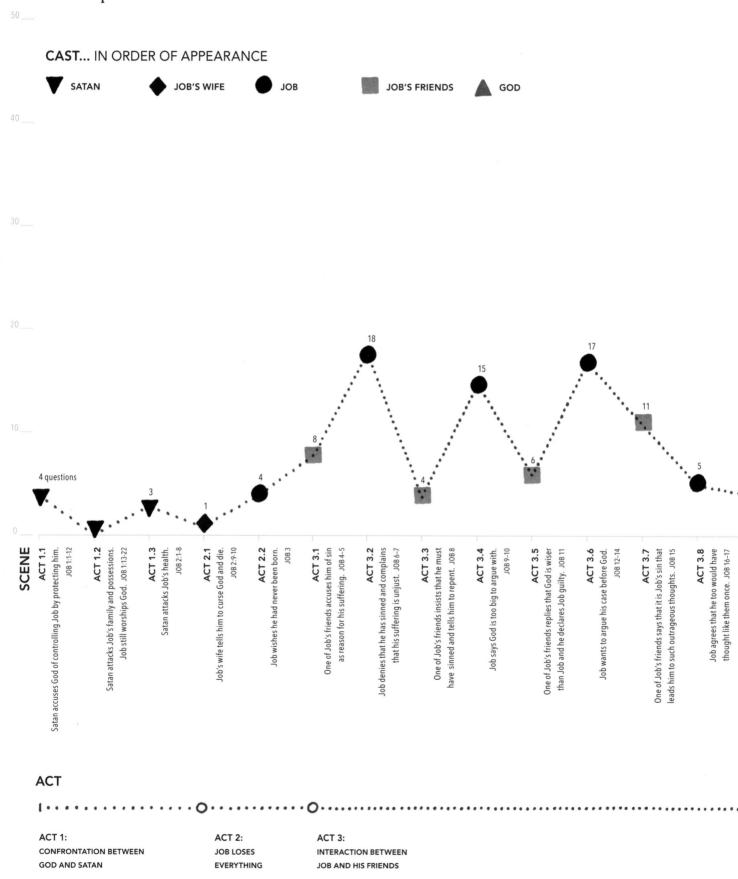

CAST... IN ORDER OF APPEARANCE

▼ SATAN   ◆ JOB'S WIFE   ● JOB   ◼ JOB'S FRIENDS   ▲ GOD

50

40

30

20

18

17

15

11

8

6

5

4 questions

4

3

1

SCENE

ACT 1.1 Satan accuses God of controlling Job by protecting him. JOB 1:1-12

ACT 1.2 Satan attacks Job's family and possessions. Job still worships God. JOB 1:13-22

ACT 1.3 Satan attacks Job's health. JOB 2:1-8

ACT 2.1 Job's wife tells him to curse God and die. JOB 2:9-10

ACT 2.2 Job wishes he had never been born. JOB 3

ACT 3.1 One of Job's friends accuses him of sin as reason for his suffering. JOB 4-5

ACT 3.2 Job denies that he has sinned and complains that his suffering is unjust. JOB 6-7

ACT 3.3 One of Job's friends insists that he must have sinned and tells him to repent. JOB 8

ACT 3.4 Job says God is too big to argue with. JOB 9-10

ACT 3.5 One of Job's friends replies that God is wiser than Job and he declares Job guilty. JOB 11

ACT 3.6 Job wants to argue his case before God. JOB 12-14

ACT 3.7 One of Job's friends says that it is Job's sin that leads him to such outrageous thoughts. JOB 15

ACT 3.8 Job agrees that he too would have thought like them once. JOB 16-17

ACT

● · · · · · · · · · · ○ · · · · · · ○ ·

ACT 1: CONFRONTATION BETWEEN GOD AND SATAN

ACT 2: JOB LOSES EVERYTHING

ACT 3: INTERACTION BETWEEN JOB AND HIS FRIENDS

see pp110-111, 204-205

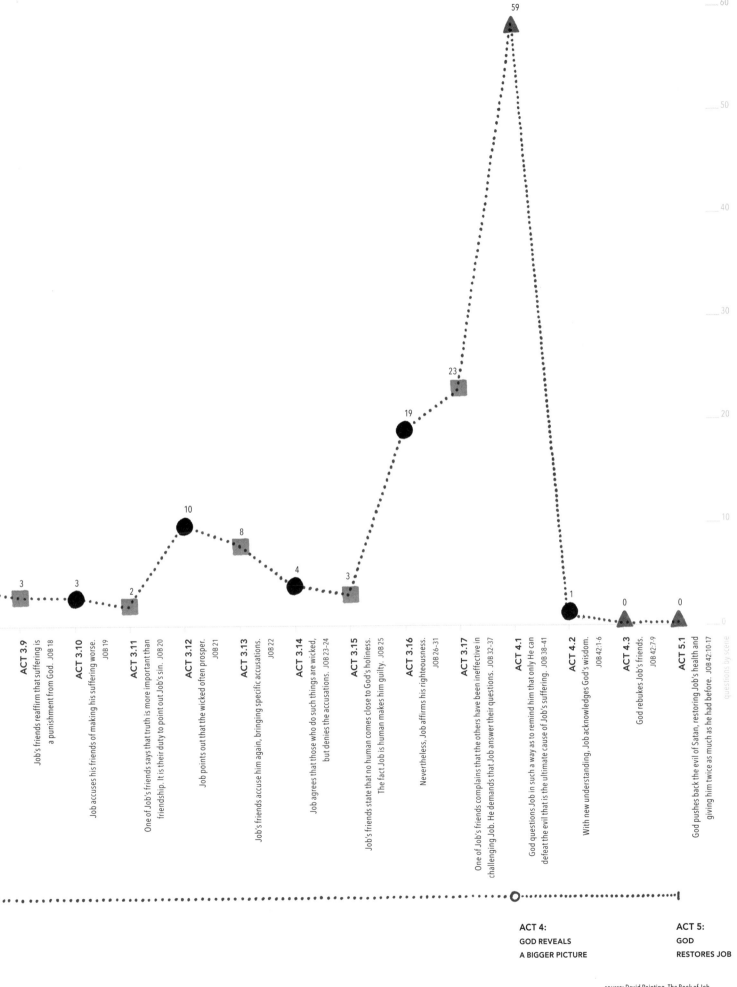

59

23

19

10

8

4

3   3   3

2

1

0   0

60

50

40

30

20

10

ACT 3.9
Job's friends reaffirm that suffering is
a punishment from God. JOB 18

ACT 3.10
Job accuses his friends of making his suffering worse.
JOB 19

ACT 3.11
One of Job's friends says that truth is more important than
friendship. It is their duty to point out Job's sin. JOB 20

ACT 3.12
Job points out that the wicked often prosper.
JOB 21

ACT 3.13
Job's friends accuse him again, bringing specific accusations.
JOB 22

ACT 3.14
Job agrees that those who do such things are wicked,
but denies the accusations. JOB 23-24

ACT 3.15
Job's friends state that no human comes close to God's holiness.
The fact Job is human makes him guilty. JOB 25

ACT 3.16
Nevertheless, Job affirms his righteousness.
JOB 26-31

ACT 3.17
One of Job's friends complains that the others have been ineffective in
challenging Job. He demands that Job answer their questions. JOB 32-37

ACT 4.1
God questions Job in such a way as to remind him that only He can
defeat the evil that is the ultimate cause of Job's suffering. JOB 38-41

ACT 4.2
With new understanding, Job acknowledges God's wisdom.
JOB 42:1-6

ACT 4.3
God rebukes Job's friends.
JOB 42:7-9

ACT 5.1
God pushes back the evil of Satan, restoring Job's health and
giving him twice as much as he had before. JOB 42:10-17

question, by scene

ACT 4:
GOD REVEALS
A BIGGER PICTURE

ACT 5:
GOD
RESTORES JOB

source: David Painting. The Book of Job
note: The contributor and author have drawn on personal opinions when creating the stages of the events in Job for the purposes of this graphic.

ABOUT THE BIBLE:
TOPICS FOR TODAY

ACROSS THE TESTAMENTS

Wellbeing & Wholeness
Meditating on words that bring us peace

MEDITATION:

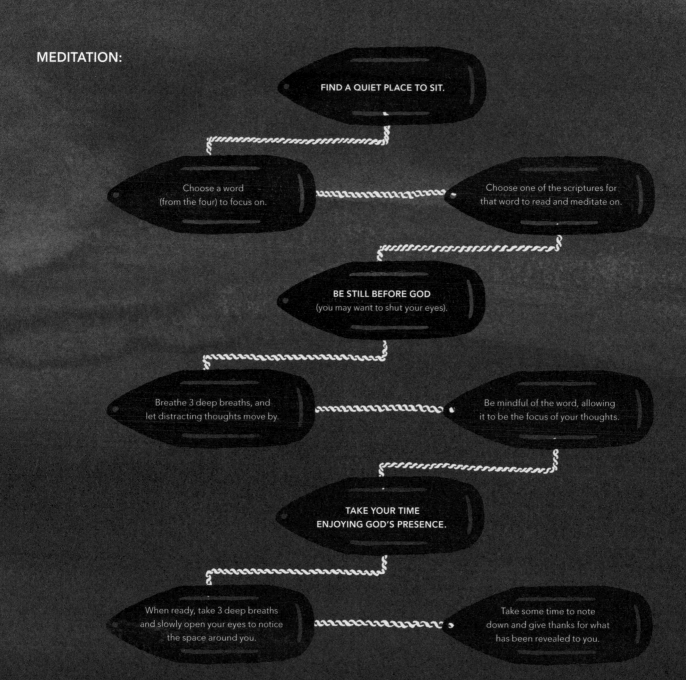

FIND A QUIET PLACE TO SIT.

Choose a word
(from the four) to focus on.

Choose one of the scriptures for
that word to read and meditate on.

BE STILL BEFORE GOD
(you may want to shut your eyes).

Breathe 3 deep breaths, and
let distracting thoughts move by.

Be mindful of the word, allowing
it to be the focus of your thoughts.

TAKE YOUR TIME
ENJOYING GOD'S PRESENCE.

When ready, take 3 deep breaths
and slowly open your eyes to notice
the space around you.

Take some time to note
down and give thanks for what
has been revealed to you.

see pp156-157, 204-205

19% HEALING

spoken of 131 times. (Words searched: heal, healed & healing)

PSALM 147:3 | 1 PETER 2:24

spoken of 232 times in the Bible. (Words searched: save, saved & salvation)

34% SALVATION

ISAIAH 12:2 | EPHESIANS 2:8

May the God of hope
fill you with all joy and peace
in believing, so that you may
abound in hope by the power
of the Holy Spirit.

[ROM 15:13]

EXODUS 33:14 | MATTHEW 11:28-29

spoken of 145 times. (Words searched: rest & restoration)

21% REST

ISAIAH 32:18 | JOHN 14:27

spoken of 179 times

26% PEACE

source: Contributor David Painting. Gen, Ex, Lev, Num, Deut, Josh, Judg, 1 Sam, 2 Sam, 1 Kings, 2 Kings, 1 Chr, 2 Chr, Ezra, Neh, Esth, Job, Ps, Prov, Eccl, Song, Isa, Jer, Lam, Ezek, Dan, Hos, Joel, Am, Ob, Mic, Nah, Hab, Zech, Mal, Mt, Mk, Lk, Jn, Acts, Rom, 1 Cor, 2 Cor, Gal, Eph, Phil, Col, 1 Thess, 2 Thess, 1 Tim, 2 Tim, Titus, Philem, Heb, Jas, 1 Pet, 2 Pet, 2 Jn, 3 Jn, Jude, Rev. Source for meditation words: Soni Cox (www.sonicox.com)
note: A number of words are used in the Bible to describe God's desire to see us whole. The contributor and author have drawn on personal opinion when collating this data and writing the meditation.

Why Worship Is Central

Encounter + Equip + Empower = Transformation

Worship sparks worship – whatever type we're talking about.

Whether we are singing or living, face down in silence at the foot of the Cross, or determined to sacrifice that which we value in pursuit of a deeper connection with God, when we live our whole lives as acts of worship we cannot help but be changed, made whole and inspired to want more.

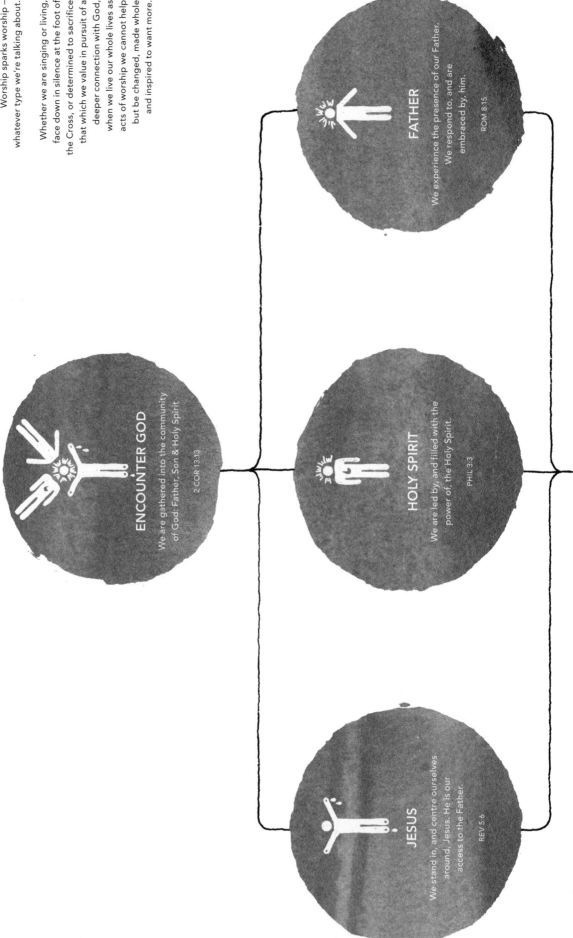

FATHER

We experience the presence of our Father. We respond to, and are embraced by, him.

ROM 8:15

ENCOUNTER GOD

We are gathered into the community of God: Father, Son & Holy Spirit

2 COR 13:13

HOLY SPIRIT

We are led by, and filled with the power of, the Holy Spirit.

PHIL 3:3

JESUS

We stand in, and centre ourselves around, Jesus. He is our access to the Father.

REV 5:6

TRANSFORMATION

We worship in response to the desires of our hearts being fulfilled. LK 2:21-38

We worship in response to His promises being fulfilled. LK 1:39-56

We respond with lives of gratitude as worship. EPH 5:18-20

We live out our purpose: that is, to worship. EPH 1:4-6

We can now encounter God through worship anywhere, anytime. JN 4:1-26

We are able to worship in times of suffering. JOB 1:18-22

Through worship we receive our true identities from the Father. ROM 8:15-17

Through worship we know we are loved. ROM 5:5

Through worship we grow in faith. JUDG 7:15-18

Through worship we gain intimacy and friendship with God. HOS 11

Through worship we gain freedom. 2 COR 3:17

Through worship we gain courage to speak about Him. ACTS 4:1-14

Through worship we experience joy. ISA 35:10

Through worship we encounter the Truth. JN 4:23-24

Through worship we are refreshed and made well. 1 SAM 16:23

Through worship we are equipped. 2 COR 9:8

Through worship we are encouraged. ISA 61:3

Through worship blessing is released. 2 CHR 20:1-26

The whole of our lives are acts of worship through serving. ROM 12:1

Like Jesus, we lead in worship from a place of humility. PHIL 2:5-8

In worship we experience the glory of God. 2 CHR 5:12-14

In worship we draw near to God and He to us. JAS 4:8

Creativity is released through worship. EX 31:1-5

As we worship we see miracles. ACTS 16:25-26

As we worship we bring glory to Him. REV 4:11

As we worship we bring life to others. LK 4:18

As we worship we are restored. PS 147:3

As we worship we are renewed. ISA 40:31

As we worship others can see Jesus. ACTS 16:25-34

As we worship awe and wonder are experienced. MT 2:1-12

All of our lives are an act of worship through total surrender. GEN 22

source: WORSHIP CENTRAL www.worshipcentral.org. Gen, Ex, Judg, 1 Sam, 1 Chr, 2 Chr, Job, Ps, Isa, Hos, Mt, Lk, Jn, Acts, Rom, 2 Cor, Eph, Phil, Jas, Rev. note: The data contributor and author have drawn on personal choices when collating and selecting this data and these Scripture examples.

SPOKEN TO WHOM

Fear
Hagar and her young son Ishmael thrown out of home into the desert.
'What is the matter? Do not be afraid.'
God cares and miraculously provides water.
Hagar and Ishmael saved. Ishmael fathers a great nation.

HAGAR
Gen 21:17

Fear
Elisha surrounded by enemies.
'Don't be afraid.'
Blinds the enemy
Elisha and his servant continue God's work. Israel less oppressed.

ELISHA'S SERVANT
2 Kings 6:15

Fear
Gideon, at home while Israel at war, called 'mighty warrior' by visiting angel.
'Peace. Do not be afraid; you are not going to die.'
Helped to understand that rejecting God's way of living made Israel vulnerable to attack.
Attacks stop when land cleansed of evil.

GIDEON
Judg 6:22

Terror
Shepherds fear for their lives when angels announce Jesus' birth to them.
'Do not be afraid.'
Reveal Jesus' birth, and where to find him.
Shepherds greet Jesus

SHEPHERDS
Lk 2:10

Fear
The two Marys, knocked to the ground by an earthquake, see angels at Jesus' tomb.
'Do not be afraid. He is not here: He is risen!'
Encouragement
Belief grows in the two Marys that Jesus is risen.

MARY (JESUS' MOTHER) & MARY MAGDALENE
Mt 28:4

Fear
Zechariah fears the implications of Gabriel's announcement of Elizabeth's longed-for pregnancy as God speaks for the first time in 400 years.
'Do not be afraid, Zechariah.'
Zechariah struck dumb: unable to speak God's word to the people because of his unbelief.
Despite Zechariah's unbelief, Elizabeth conceives John (the Baptist).

ZECHARIAH
Lk 1:13

Faith
Mary is not afraid of Gabriel. Although troubled by his announcement that she will give birth to God's son, she agrees to co-operate in God's plan.
'Greetings, highly favoured one!'
Mary conceives
Jesus, the Saviour of the World, is born.

MARY
Lk 1:28

Anxiety
Joseph, fearing blame for Mary's pregnancy, decides to part from Mary quietly.
'Joseph, son of David, do not be afraid to take Mary to be your wife.'
NA
Marries Mary

JOSEPH
Mt 1:20

SPEAKER

ANGEL

GABRIEL

Do Not Be Afraid
When was heavenly courage needed?

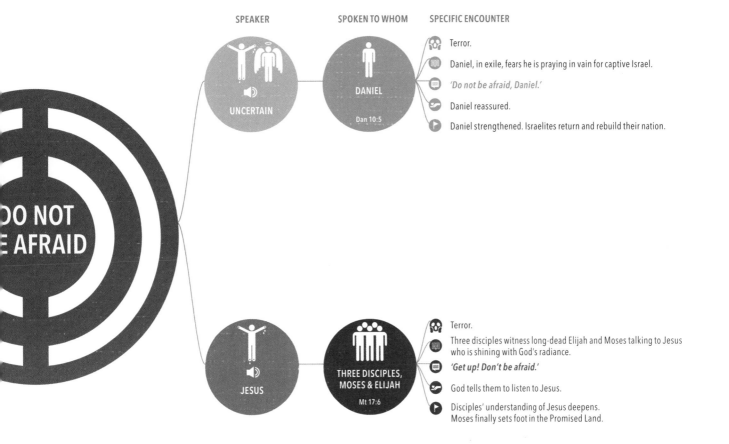

SPEAKER | SPOKEN TO WHOM | SPECIFIC ENCOUNTER

UNCERTAIN

DANIEL
Dan 10:5

Terror.

Daniel, in exile, fears he is praying in vain for captive Israel.

'Do not be afraid, Daniel.'

Daniel reassured.

Daniel strengthened. Israelites return and rebuild their nation.

JESUS

THREE DISCIPLES, MOSES & ELIJAH
Mt 17:6

Terror.

Three disciples witness long-dead Elijah and Moses talking to Jesus who is shining with God's radiance.

'Get up! Don't be afraid.'

God tells them to listen to Jesus.

Disciples' understanding of Jesus deepens. Moses finally sets foot in the Promised Land.

DO NOT BE AFRAID

WHERE IN THE BIBLE WAS THE COURAGE GIVEN?

- LAW
- OLD TESTAMENT NARRATIVE
- MAJOR PROPHETS
- NEW TESTAMENT NARRATIVE

THE ENCOUNTER

- Person's response to encounter
- Why courage was needed?
- First phrase spoken
- Angelic / God response
- Outcome

source: David Painting. Gen, Judg, 2 Kings, Dan, Mt, Lk.

Promised Children
Infertility and God's intervention

Joseph = 'He adds' (1915 BC)
God enabled her to conceive
Rachel gave her maid to Jacob
Rachel was barren

Jacob
Rachel

Samuel = 'He who is from God' (1105 BC)
God heard Hannah's prayer
Elkanah took second wife named Peninnah
Unknown but 'So it went on year after year'
Hannah was barren

Elkanah
Hannah

Jacob = 'He takes by the heel' (2006 BC)
Esau = 'Hairy' (2006 BC)
God enabled her to conceive
Isaac prayed
Rebekah was barren

Isaac
Rebekah

Isaac = 'Laughter, play' (2066 BC)
God repeated the promise then answered the promise
25 years between first promise and birth
Sarah gave Hagar to Abraham as surrogate
Sarah was barren. Both parents elderly.

Sarah (Sarai)
Abraham (Abram)

Hagar

Sarah and Abraham drove the pregnant Hagar away
Promise came after conception but prior to birth
God saw Hagar alone in desert, met with her and blessed her
Ishmael = 'God hears' (2080 BC)

God healed
Abraham prayed to God
God stopped all women in Abimelech's house conceiving
All women of Abimelech's house
Abimelech

Samuel 1 Sam 1:2, 7, 8, 15-21

Joseph Gen 29:31; 30:22-24; 35:16-18

Jacob Gen 25:21; 26, 28

Isaac Gen 12:2-3; 18-21

Ishmael Gen 16:9-12

Gen 20:17-18

A Symphony of Science & Scripture

All creation praises God

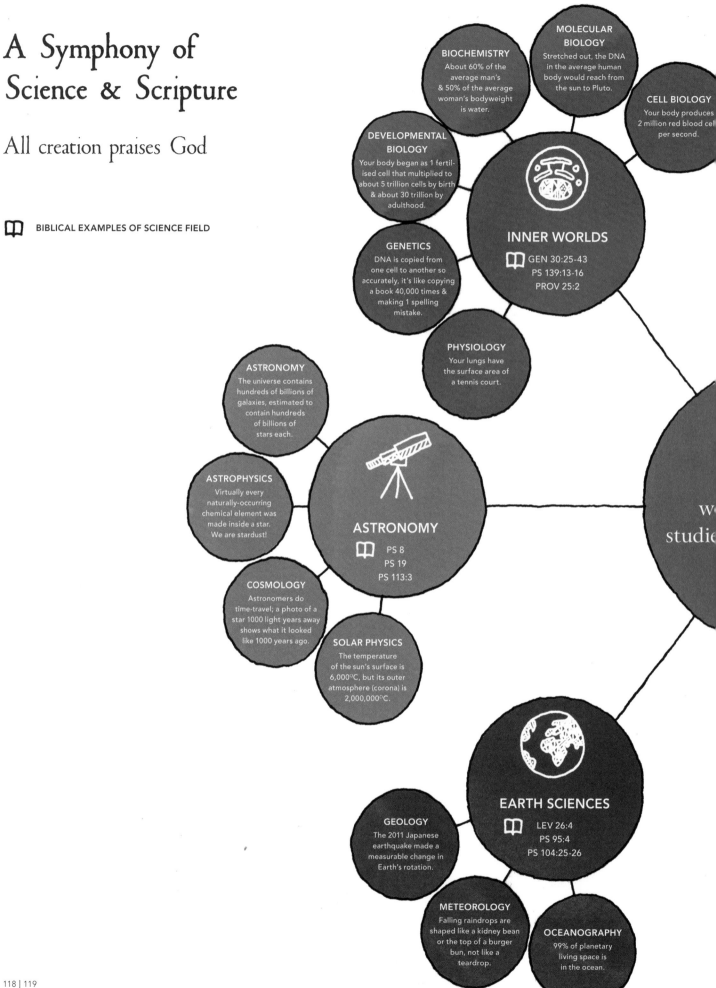

📖 BIBLICAL EXAMPLES OF SCIENCE FIELD

BIOCHEMISTRY
About 60% of the average man's & 50% of the average woman's bodyweight is water.

MOLECULAR BIOLOGY
Stretched out, the DNA in the average human body would reach from the sun to Pluto.

CELL BIOLOGY
Your body produces 2 million red blood cells per second.

DEVELOPMENTAL BIOLOGY
Your body began as 1 fertilised cell that multiplied to about 5 trillion cells by birth & about 30 trillion by adulthood.

INNER WORLDS
📖 GEN 30:25-43
PS 139:13-16
PROV 25:2

GENETICS
DNA is copied from one cell to another so accurately, it's like copying a book 40,000 times & making 1 spelling mistake.

PHYSIOLOGY
Your lungs have the surface area of a tennis court.

ASTRONOMY
The universe contains hundreds of billions of galaxies, estimated to contain hundreds of billions of stars each.

ASTROPHYSICS
Virtually every naturally-occurring chemical element was made inside a star. We are stardust!

ASTRONOMY
📖 PS 8
PS 19
PS 113:3

COSMOLOGY
Astronomers do time-travel; a photo of a star 1000 light years away shows what it looked like 1000 years ago.

SOLAR PHYSICS
The temperature of the sun's surface is 6,000°C, but its outer atmosphere (corona) is 2,000,000°C.

w...
studie...

EARTH SCIENCES
📖 LEV 26:4
PS 95:4
PS 104:25-26

GEOLOGY
The 2011 Japanese earthquake made a measurable change in Earth's rotation.

METEOROLOGY
Falling raindrops are shaped like a kidney bean or the top of a burger bun, not like a teardrop.

OCEANOGRAPHY
99% of planetary living space is in the ocean.

see pp26-27, 32-33

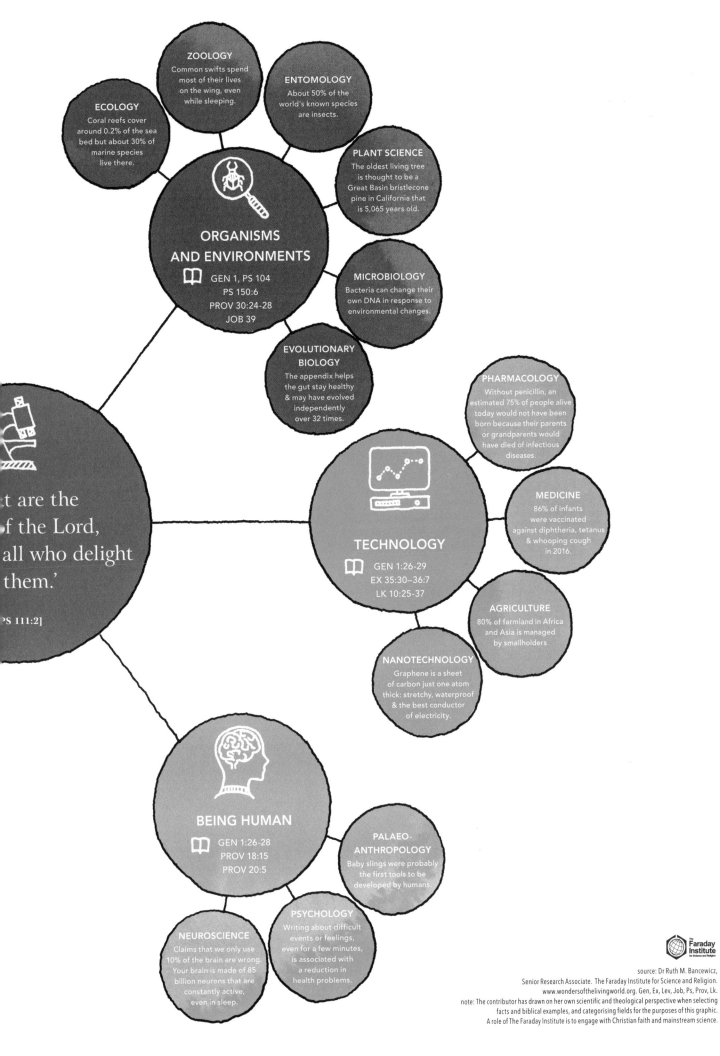

ZOOLOGY
Common swifts spend most of their lives on the wing, even while sleeping.

ENTOMOLOGY
About 50% of the world's known species are insects.

ECOLOGY
Coral reefs cover around 0.2% of the sea bed but about 30% of marine species live there.

PLANT SCIENCE
The oldest living tree is thought to be a Great Basin bristlecone pine in California that is 5,065 years old.

ORGANISMS AND ENVIRONMENTS
GEN 1, PS 104
PS 150:6
PROV 30:24-28
JOB 39

MICROBIOLOGY
Bacteria can change their own DNA in response to environmental changes.

EVOLUTIONARY BIOLOGY
The appendix helps the gut stay healthy & may have evolved independently over 32 times.

PHARMACOLOGY
Without penicillin, an estimated 75% of people alive today would not have been born because their parents or grandparents would have died of infectious diseases.

t are the
f the Lord,
all who delight
them.'

PS 111:2]

TECHNOLOGY
GEN 1:26-29
EX 35:30–36:7
LK 10:25-37

MEDICINE
86% of infants were vaccinated against diphtheria, tetanus & whooping cough in 2016.

AGRICULTURE
80% of farmland in Africa and Asia is managed by smallholders

NANOTECHNOLOGY
Graphene is a sheet of carbon just one atom thick: stretchy, waterproof & the best conductor of electricity.

BEING HUMAN
GEN 1:26-28
PROV 18:15
PROV 20:5

PALAEO-ANTHROPOLOGY
Baby slings were probably the first tools to be developed by humans.

NEUROSCIENCE
Claims that we only use 10% of the brain are wrong. Your brain is made of 85 billion neurons that are constantly active, even in sleep.

PSYCHOLOGY
Writing about difficult events or feelings, even for a few minutes, is associated with a reduction in health problems.

The Faraday Institute for Science and Religion

source: Dr Ruth M. Bancewicz,
Senior Research Associate. The Faraday Institute for Science and Religion.
www.wondersofthelivingworld.org. Gen, Ex, Lev, Job, Ps, Prov, Lk.
note: The contributor has drawn on her own scientific and theological perspective when selecting facts and biblical examples, and categorising fields for the purposes of this graphic.
A role of The Faraday Institute is to engage with Christian faith and mainstream science.

Parallel Passages: the Voice of the Old in the New

Threading the Testaments together

GENRE OF VOICE:

- ■ LAW
- ■ OLD TESTAMENT NARRATIVE
- ■ WISDOM LITERATURE
- ■ MAJOR PROPHETS
- ■ MINOR PROPHETS

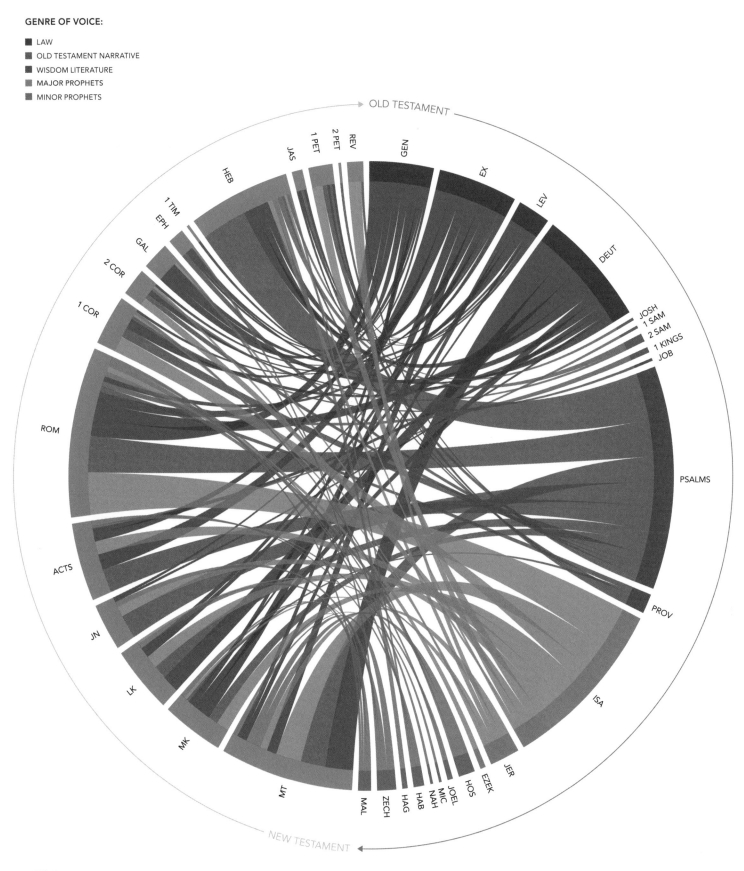

OLD TESTAMENT

NEW TESTAMENT

source: NT quoted from OT parallel passages, using direct citations only. Retrieved from https://www.blueletterbible.org/study/misc/quotes.cfmr.
note: The Blue Letter Bible ministry and the BLB Institute hold to the historical, conservative Christian faith, which includes a firm belief in the inerrancy of scripture. Since the text
content provided by BLB represent a range of evangelical traditions, all of the ideas and principles conveyed in the resource materials are not necessarily affirmed, in total, by this ministry.

How God Has Spoken

Before and after the silence

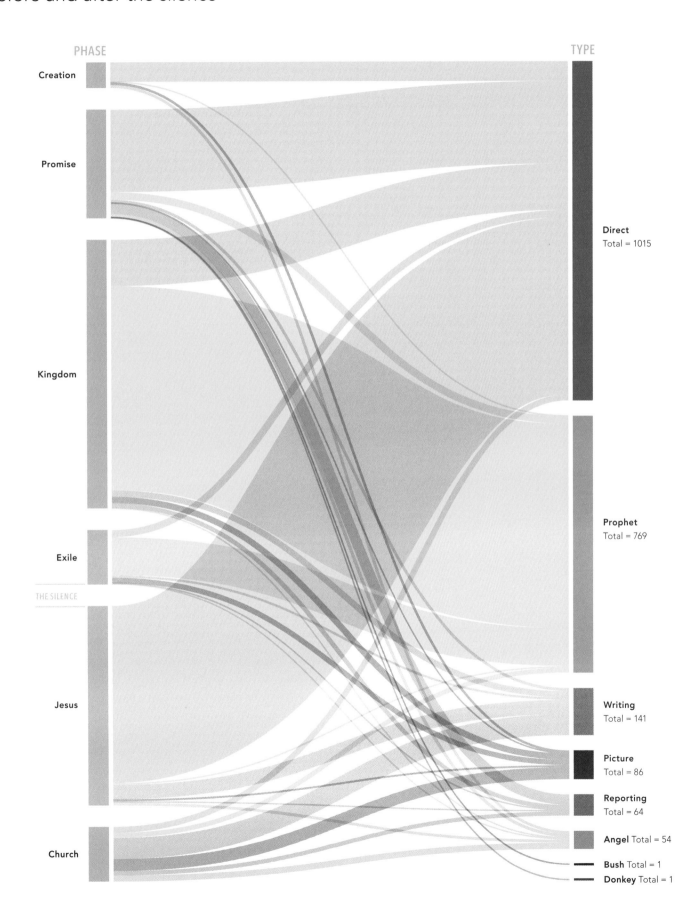

How God Has Spoken
Before and after the silence

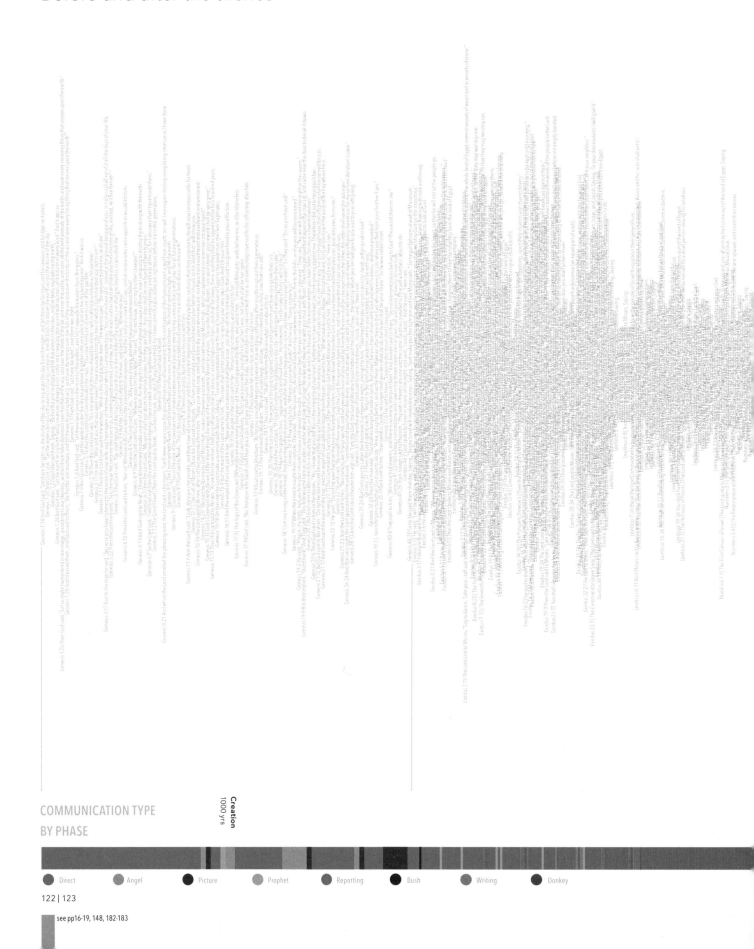

Direct ●   Angel ●   Picture ●   Prophet ●   Reporting ●   Bush ●   Writing ●   Donkey ●

see pp16-19, 148, 182-183

Promise
2000 yrs

Kingdom
400 yrs

Exile
70 yrs

Silence
400 yrs

Church
70 yrs

Jesus
33 yrs

How God Has Spoken

Before and after the silence

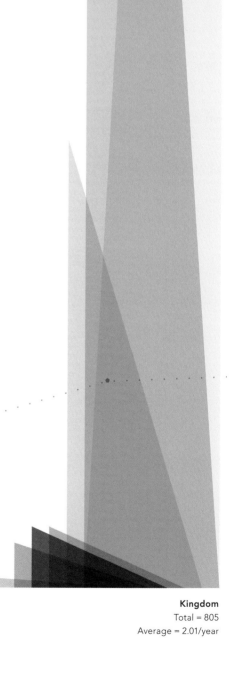

Creation
Total = 77
Average = 0.08/year

Promise
Total = 324
Average = 0.16/year

Kingdom
Total = 805
Average = 2.01/year

see p16-19, 148, 182-183

TYPE

Direct
Angel
Picture
Prophet
Eye-ening
Writing
Rain
Donkey
Total communications

● Average communication per year

Exile
Total = 164
Average = 2.34/year

Jesus
Total = 597
Average = 18.09/year

Church
Total = 164
Average = 2.34/year

source: David Painting. The Bible.
note: Data is a representative sample of God speaking in Scripture. Timescales are indicative and used for illustrative purposes.

Jesus Prophecies in the Gospels

The events and words where those were fulfilled

see pp200-201

THEME OF PROPHECY

- What the Messiah will be like
- The lineage of the Messiah
- His character
- How He will come
- What He will say
- How He will be received
- What He will do
- How others will respond
- How He will redeem
- How it will end

HOW THE PROPHECY WAS FULFILLED

Affirmation by others in canon order for first instance

Claim of Jesus in canon order for first instance

FULFILMENT BY JESUS IN GOSPELS

The angel stated that Jesus would be 'God with us': Immanuel (Mt 1:18-23)
The angel declared that Jesus would fulfil this (Mt 1:21; Lk 1:32-33)
The angel instructed that He was to be called Jesus: the one who saves (Mt 1:21)
NT author stated that prophecy had been fulfilled (Mt 12:18-21)
NT author stated that prophecy had been fulfilled by Jesus (Mt 16:18; Lk 23:34; Jn 12:40-41)
The people declared Jesus to be good, making Him one with God (Mt 19:16-17)
Quoting this scripture, Jesus was declared Lord and David's son (Mt 22:44-45)
The authorities quoted this verse to Jesus, unwittingly acknowledging that He was the Messiah (Mt 27:43)
John the Baptist foretold of the Messiah who was coming, using the same words to 'prepare the way' (Mk 1:1-8)
John the Baptist would bring Elijah's spirit of reconciliation in preparation for the coming of the Messiah (Lk 1:16-17)
Gabriel affirmed Jesus as the child who came from God to share our humanity (Lk 1:31)
Gabriel confirmed Jesus to be that child (Lk 1:31)
Jesus would reign over a kingdom which will have no end (Lk 1:31-33)
God said that Jesus would have David's throne (Lk 1:32)
The angel's declaration confirmed Jesus to be the son (Lk 1:32; Jn 1:14)
Gabriel declared to Mary that her son would establish that eternal kingdom (Lk 1:32-33)
Jesus declared to be the king whose kingdom would never end (Lk 1:32-33)
The angel declared that this referred to Jesus (Lk 1:32-33)
Jesus would rule over the house of Jacob (Israel) (Lk 1:33)
Mary, mother of Jesus, declared she was a virgin (Lk 1:34-35)
The angel said that Jesus will be holy and powerful (Lk 1:35)
These same words of prophecy were applied to Jesus (Lk 1:69-71)
Simeon declared Jesus to be the saviour of all (Lk 2:29-32)
Simeon declared Jesus to be the child of promise (Lk 2:32)
Anna stated that the prophecy was being fulfilled (Lk 2:38)
Jesus declared Himself to Moses as 'I AM' (Lk 3:34)
Satan quoted this scripture to Jesus, tacitly acknowledging who He was (Lk 4:10-11)
Grace came to us through Jesus (Lk 4:22; Jn 1:17)
Jesus declared to have been with God before the world was created (Jn 1:1)
John the Baptist declared Jesus to be 'the Lamb of God' (Jn 1:29)
Angels confirmed that Jesus will ascend as Jacob dreamed it (Jn 1:51)
Nicodemus declared that Jesus is a teacher (Jn 3:2)
The woman stated that Jesus fulfilled this prophecy in talking to her (Jn 4:25)
John declared Jesus to be the prophet foretold to Moses (Jn 6:14)
Pharisees confirmed the whole world had run after Him (Jn 12:18-21)
Jesus declared Himself as having been living before Abraham (Jn 8:58)
Jesus stated that the prophecy was being fulfilled by the people He was speaking to (Mt 13:13-15; Jn 12:40)
Jesus prophesied that He would be killed (Mt 16:21)
Jesus stated that this prophecy was being fulfilled in Him (Mt 20:28)
Jesus claimed to be the stone which would break other kingdoms (Mt 21:44)
Jesus declared Himself a safe place (Mt 23:37)
Jesus declared that His blood was a sign of the new covenant (Mt 26:28)
Jesus described Himself being mocked, quoting the same words (Mt 27:39-44)
Jesus applied these words to Himself as He was crucified (Mt 27:46)
Jesus was given all authority as a result of His suffering (Mt 28:18)
Jesus claimed to be with us always (Mt 28:20)
Jesus declared He is the light of the world (Lk 2:29-32; Jn 8:12)
Jesus used these words of commitment as He died (Lk 23:46)
Jesus declared that He is the first and the last (Jn 1:30)
Jesus took the name God had revealed, saying, 'I AM' her' when describing who He is (Jn 4:26; 8:58)
Jesus declared that His aim was to carry out the will of God (Jn 4:34)
Jesus claimed to be entrusted with settling all things (Jn 5:22)
Jesus claimed to be just in all His ways (Jn 5:30)
Jesus invoked this prophecy as referring to Him (Jn 5:45-47)
Jesus stated that He was fulfilling that prophecy (Jn 6:40)
Jesus claimed that His teaching fulfilled this prophecy (Jn 8:28-29)
Jesus revealed that He is the everlasting God (Jn 8:31-58)
Jesus declared Himself to have been living before Abraham (Jn 8:58)
Jesus said He was the good shepherd (Jn 10:10-18)
Jesus declared He was the good shepherd (Jn 10:11)
Jesus said peace can be found in Him (Jn 16:33)
Jesus was a direct descendant of David (Mt 1:1; Lk 1:31-33; 3:23-31)
Jesus was a son of David (Mt 1:1)
Mary became pregnant by the Holy Spirit (Mt 1:18)
The wise men came to Jesus (Mt 2:1-11)
Jesus was born in Bethlehem (Mt 2:1-6)
Jesus lived as a refugee in Egypt before returning to Israel (Mt 2:15)
The wise men sought the one born to be king (Mt 2:2)
Jesus was filled with the Spirit (Mt 3:16)
Jesus was baptised, and the Spirit fell on Him (Mt 3:16-17)

OLD TESTAMENT PROPHECY ABOUT THE MESSIAH

(Ex 15:11) God was revealed as holy and powerful
(Ps 2:6) The Messiah would be king
(Ps 18:2-3) God promised one who would be the saviour
(Ps 22:8; 31:14-15) The Messiah would trust God for His deliverance
(Ps 23:1) God was the 'Lord Shepherd'
(Ps 90:2) God was the creator of everything
(Ps 100:5) God was proclaimed to be the source of good
(Isa 9:6) His name would be wonderful counsellor
(Isa 9:6) His name would be Everlasting Father
(Isa 11:3) He would know their thoughts
(Isa 28:16) He would be the Sure Foundation
(Isa 40:11) A shepherd who was a compassionate life-giver
(Isa 42:2) He would be gentle and humble
(Isa 42:1-4) He would be the Servant: a faithful, patient redeemer
(Mic 5:2c) A ruler would come from before time
(Gen 28:14) Jacob's offspring would be the redeemer
(2 Sam 7:12; 1 Chr 17:11) God told David that one of His descendants would establish God's kingdom
(Ps 89:35-37) The Messiah would come from the line of David
(Ps 110:1) David's offspring would one day be called 'Lord'
(Ps 132:11) The Lord told one of his sons would be on the throne
(Isa 11:1) He would be from the family tree of Jesse
(Jer 33:14-15) A descendant of David's would bring righteousness and justice
(Ezek 34:23-24) The line of David would shepherd God's people
(Ezek 37:24-25) David's line would reign for ever
(Ex 3:13-15) God described Himself to Moses as 'I AM'
(Ps 31:5) The Messiah would commit His spirit to God
(Isa 48:12) He was the only God, the first and the last
(Dan 10:5-6) The Messiah was described in all His glory
(Zech 11:7) The shepherd would look after the vulnerable sheep
(Deut 18:15) Moses told that God would one day raise up a prophet like Him
(1 Chr 17:13) God promised that the one to come would be His son
(Ps 45:7) The Messiah would be anointed by the Spirit
(Isa 6:8) He would be sent by God
(Isa 7:14) He would be called Immanuel – God with us
(Isa 8:8) God would live with His people
(Isa 9:6) He was to be born a child, sharing our humanity
(Isa 9:6) A son was to be given who will become the Messiah
(Isa 11:2) The Spirit of God would rest upon Jesus
(Isa 40:9) God would come in person
(Isa 49:1) The Messiah would be born to a mother
(Isa 49:5) He was a servant born to a mother
(Isa 61:1a) The Spirit of God would be upon Him
(Hos 11:1) God's son would be called out of Egypt
(Mic 5:2a) A ruler would come from Bethlehem
(Mal 3:1a) God would send a messenger to prepare the way
(Mal 4:6) Elijah would bring a spirit of reconciliation
(Deut 18:15-16) Moses warned that the people would not listen to the prophet who was to come
(Ps 69:8) The psalmist acknowledged that He was a stranger to His own brethren
(Ps 72:10-11) Great people would come to visit the Messiah
(Deut 18:18) The prophet that God would send would speak God's words
(Ps 78:1-2) The Messiah would teach in parables
(Isa 2:3) He would teach us the way He works
(Isa 52:7) The Messiah would bring good news
(Isa 61:1b) The Messiah would preach the good news
(Isa 61:1c) The Messiah would announce freedom to all captives
(Ps 40:6-8) The psalmist wrote of His delight in doing the will of the Father
(Ps 69:9) The Messiah would be zealous for God's house
(Ps 91:11-12) The Messiah would be defended by angels
(Ps 147:3-6) The Messiah would bind up the broken-hearted
(Isa 9:1-2) His ministry would begin in Galilee
(Isa 9:7) There would be no limits to the wholeness He brings
(Isa 9:7) The Messiah would establish fair dealing and right living
(Isa 29:13) He would reveal people's double standards
(Isa 32:2) He would be a refuge
(Isa 35:4) He was coming to rescue you
(Isa 35:5-6) The Messiah would perform miracles

Record
of an event
in canon order for
first instance

Events (top labels):

- (Mt 3:16-17) The Spirit of God rested upon Jesus
- (Mt 3:17) God declared Jesus His son at His baptism
- (Mt 4:12-17) Jesus' ministry began in Galilee
- (Mt 9:27) Jesus was called 'Son of David'
- (Mt 9:35-36) Jesus had compassion on the crowds because they were like sheep without a shepherd
- (Mt 10:32) Jesus interceded for us
- (Mt 11:2-6) Jesus performed miracles
- (Mt 7:29; 11:28-29) Jesus amazed with His wise teaching
- (Mt 11:5; Mk 1:14; Lk 4:18) Jesus brought good news
- (Mt 12:40) Jesus said that He would be in the heart of the earth' for three days and nights, fulfilling what had happened to Jonah
- (Mt 13:34-35) Jesus taught in parables
- (Mt 13:54) The people recognised His wisdom and miracles
- (Mt 15:7-9; Mk 7:7) Jesus revealed the religious leaders' double standards
- (Mt 16:4) Jesus declared that what happened to Jonah was about to happen to Him
- (Mt 17:2) Jesus was seen in all His glory
- (Mt 21:38-39) Jesus told a parable prophesying His death
- (Mt 21:6-9) Jesus entered Jerusalem, riding on a donkey
- (Mt 21:8-10) As Jesus entered Jerusalem the crowds rejoiced
- (Mt 21:9) The crowd welcomed Jesus as the Messiah by echoing this prophecy on Palm Sunday
- (Mt 26:14-15) Jesus, the good shepherd, was betrayed for 30 pieces of silver
- (Mt 26:28) Jesus' blood was poured out for the forgiveness of sin
- (Mt 26:31-56; Mk 14:27) Jesus prophesied that people would fall away as He, the shepherd, was struck
- (Mt 26:36-45) Jesus was in anguish as He faced the suffering of the Cross
- (Mt 26:37-38; Lk 19:41) His soul was overwhelmed with sorrow
- (Mt 26:39) Jesus did His Father's will
- (Mt 26:47-27:31) Jesus imprisoned
- (Mt 26:67) Jesus was struck
- (Mt 27:1) The priests and elders plotted to kill Jesus
- (Mt 27:12-14) He didn't answer their accusations
- (Mt 27:21-23) The crowd chose His crucifixion
- (Mt 27:24-31) Jesus was ripped apart by being flogged, beaten and then crucified
- (Mt 27:26) Jesus was 'scourged' (whipped) and beaten before being crucified
- (Mt 27:27-31) Jesus tortured
- (Mt 27:30) Jesus was spat on
- (Mt 27:34; Jn 19:28) Jesus said that He was thirsty whilst on the Cross
- (Mt 27:35) Jesus crucified
- (Mt 27:39) Jesus was ridiculed in exactly the way foretold
- (Mt 27:50-51) Jesus was killed before the Temple was destroyed (in AD70)
- (Mt 27:50-54) The earth shook when Jesus' resurrected body touched it
- (Mt 27:57) Rich man, Joseph from Arimathea buried Him
- (Mt 28:19-20) Jesus commissioned His followers to go all nations
- (Mk 8:31) Jesus was rejected and suffered
- (Mk 10:45) Jesus gave His life, not as a symbol, but as a ransom for many
- (Mk 14:50) The crowds and His friends left Jesus
- (Mk 14:50-52) Jesus was deserted by His friends
- (Mk 15:27-28) Jesus was crucified with criminals
- (Mk 16:19) Jesus 'seated at the right hand of God' fulfilling the prophecy
- (Lk 1:32-33) Jesus was born in the line of David
- (Lk 3:23-32) Jesus' family tree confirmed this
- (Lk 4:16-21) Jesus preached the good news of the kingdom
- (Lk 4:18) Throughout Jesus' ministry, He fulfilled this prophecy and the writer quoted this by way of confirmation
- (Lk 4:28-29) The people drove Jesus out of town, wanting to throw Him off a cliff
- (Lk 6:8; Jn 2:25) Jesus knew what they were thinking
- (Lk 23:34-35; Jn 19:23-24) When Jesus was crucified, He was stripped and the soldiers gambled for His clothes
- (Lk 23:41; Jn 18:38) A criminal declared Him innocent
- (Lk 23:46) Jesus died on the Cross
- (Lk 23:49) Jesus' friends kept their distance when He was accused
- (Lk 23:49) The people deserted Jesus
- (Lk 24:51) Jesus ascended into heaven, fulfilling this prophecy
- (Lk 24:6) Angels announced the Resurrection
- (Jn 1:11; 8:48-49; 19:14-15) Jesus was despised by those He came to rescue
- (Jn 1:11) Jesus was rejected by His own people
- (Jn 1:36; 19:14) Jesus came in person
- (Jn 2:17) Jesus demonstrated His zeal for God's house by throwing out illegal traders
- (Jn 8:31-36) Jesus taught about true freedom
- (Jn 9:25-38) Jesus healed a blind man
- (Jn 11:44) As an example of this being fulfilled, Jesus brought freedom to Lazarus
- (Jn 11:53) The Pharisees plotted to kill Jesus
- (Jn 12:27) Jesus questioned the suffering but was satisfied that it would accomplish what was needed
- (Jn 12:37-38) Quoting the Old Testament scriptures, the author described how people did not believe Jesus
- (Jn 13:19) Judas, a close friend of Jesus, betrayed Him
- (Jn 16:7-13) Jesus declared that the Holy Spirit would come
- (Jn 17:1-5) Jesus asked to be brought into glory
- (Jn 18:11) Jesus was obedient to God's plan, even when it required His death
- (Jn 18:13-22) Jesus put on trial
- (Jn 18:37) Jesus told Pilate that He came into the world to be a witness to the truth about God
- (Jn 19:31-36) Jesus, representing that lamb, had no bones broken
- (Jn 19:34-37) Jesus' body was pierced with a spear

Prophecies (bottom labels):

- (Isa 42:6) The giving of the child would be a sign that God had kept His promise
- (Isa 42:7) He would open the eyes of the blind
- (Isa 42:7) He would bring freedom to those held captive
- (Isa 44:3) He would send the Spirit of God
- (Isa 48:16-17) He came as a teacher
- (Isa 49:6) He would be salvation to all
- (Isa 50:5) He would be willing to do His Father's will
- (Isa 53:10d) He would prosper
- (Isa 55:4a) The Messiah would be a witness to the people about God
- (Isa 59:16a) He would come to Zion as their Redeemer
- (Isa 59:20) He would step in to save/rescue them
- (Zech 9:9f) The Messiah would come, riding on a donkey
- (Dan 9:26c) The one who was to come would be cut off before the Temple is destroyed
- (Ps 22:1) The Messiah would feel forsaken
- (Ps 22:7) The Messiah would be mocked
- (Ps 22:17-18) People would gamble for the Messiah's clothes
- (Ps 31:11) The people would distance themselves from Him
- (Ps 35:19; 69:4) The Messiah would be hated without cause
- (Ps 38:11) Those nearest the Messiah would stand apart from Him
- (Ps 41:9; 55:12-14) The Messiah would be betrayed by a friend
- (Ps 88:8) God's enemies would cause the people to desert Him
- (Ps 109:25) The Messiah would be ridiculed
- (Ps 118:26a) The Messiah, coming in the name of the Lord, would be blessed
- (Isa 6:9-10) People heard but didn't understand
- (Isa 49:7) He would be despised by the nations
- (Isa 50:6a) They would strike Him with their fists
- (Isa 50:6c) They would spit on Him
- (Isa 53:1) People would not believe Him
- (Isa 53:3a) He would be despised
- (Isa 53:3b) He would be rejected
- (Isa 53:3d) Men would hide from being associated with Him
- (Isa 53:4b) The Messiah would be rejected and suffer
- (Zech 9:9a) A king would be greeted with rejoicing in Jerusalem
- (Zech 11:12-13a) 30 pieces of silver would be given as the wage for a false shepherd
- (Ex 12:46; Num 9:12; Ps 34:20) No bones of the sacrificial lamb were to be broken
- (Lev 17:11) An animal's blood on the altar symbolised people being made right with God
- (Ps 22:15; 69:21) The Messiah would thirst as part of His suffering
- (Ps 69:14-20) The Messiah would be in anguish over the suffering He would face
- (Ps 89:27) The Messiah would be the highest king
- (Ps 129:3) The Messiah would be whipped and beaten
- (Isa 25:8) The Resurrection was predicted
- (Isa 26:19) His power of resurrection was predicted
- (Isa 52:14) He would be disfigured beyond human recognition
- (Isa 53:10a) God's plan was that He die for mankind
- (Isa 53:10b) He would be an offering for sin
- (Isa 53:11a) God would be fully satisfied that His suffering had accomplished what was needed
- (Isa 53:12a) God would give His stamp of approval because of His Messiah's suffering
- (Isa 53:12b) He would give up His life to save mankind
- (Isa 53:12c) He would be counted among the rebels
- (Isa 53:12e) The Messiah would take the place of mankind
- (Isa 53:3c) He would know great sorrow and grief
- (Isa 53:7a) He would be oppressed and treated harshly
- (Isa 53:7b) He would be silent before His accusers
- (Isa 53:7c) The Messiah would be led like a lamb to the slaughter
- (Isa 53:8a) He would be imprisoned and persecuted
- (Isa 53:8b) He would be tried and condemned
- (Isa 53:8c) He would be killed
- (Isa 53:9a) The Messiah would be buried in a rich man's grave
- (Isa 53:9b) He would be innocent and do no violence
- (Jer 31:31) Jeremiah told of God's plan to make a new covenant with His people
- (Dan 9:26a) Daniel prophesied that one anointed by God would be cut off
- (Jon 1:17) Jonah was in a large sea creature for three days and three nights
- (Zech 12:10a) God said people would look at Him who they had pierced
- (Zech 13:7b) The shepherd would be struck and the sheep would fall away
- (Gen 28:12) Jacob dreamed of those who ascend to heaven
- (1 Chr 17:12-13) The King who was to come would establish an eternal kingdom
- (Ps 45:2) God poured grace onto the son of man
- (Ps 68:18) The Messiah would ascend into heaven
- (Ps 110:1) The Messiah would take His place at the right hand of God
- (Isa 2:4) He would settle things between nations
- (Isa 6:1) His glory/beauty would be seen
- (Isa 11:10) The nations would come to Him
- (Isa 12:2) The Messiah would save (yeshua) His people
- (Isa 42:6) He would be a light to the nations
- (Isa 49:6) He would be a light to the nations
- (Dan 2:44-45) Daniel talked of an everlasting kingdom which would break other kingdoms
- (Dan 7:13-14c) A son of man would be given a kingdom which would not be destroyed

source: David Painting. Gen, Ex, Lev, Num, Deut, 2 Sam, 1 Chr, Ps, Isa, Jer, Ezek, Dan, Hos, Jon, Mic, Zech, Mal, Mt, Mk, Lk, Jn.
note: The data contributor and author have drawn on personal choices when selecting the prophecies and creating the themes and categories.

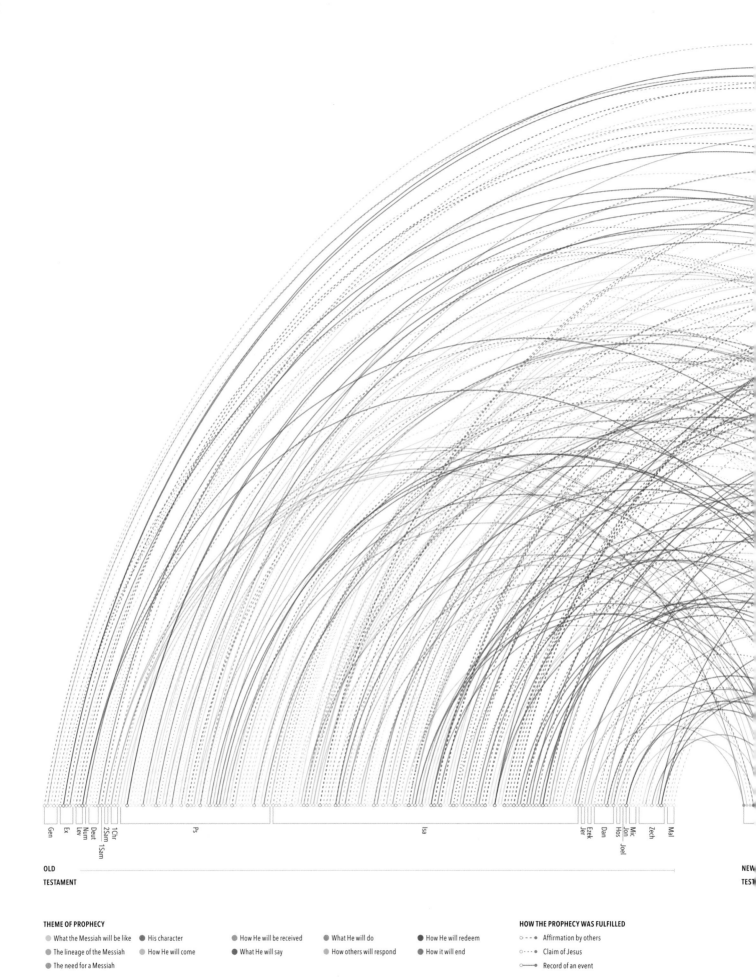

OLD
TESTAMENT

NEW
TEST

THEME OF PROPHECY

- What the Messiah will be like
- His character
- How He will be received
- What He will do
- How He will redeem
- The lineage of the Messiah
- How He will come
- What He will say
- How others will respond
- How it will end
- The need for a Messiah

HOW THE PROPHECY WAS FULFILLED

○ - - - ● Affirmation by others

○ - - - ● Claim of Jesus

○———● Record of an event

Gen
Ex
Num
Lev
Deut
2Sam
1Sam
1Chr
Ps
Isa
Jer
Ezek
Dan
Hos
Jon
Mic
Joel
Zech
Mal

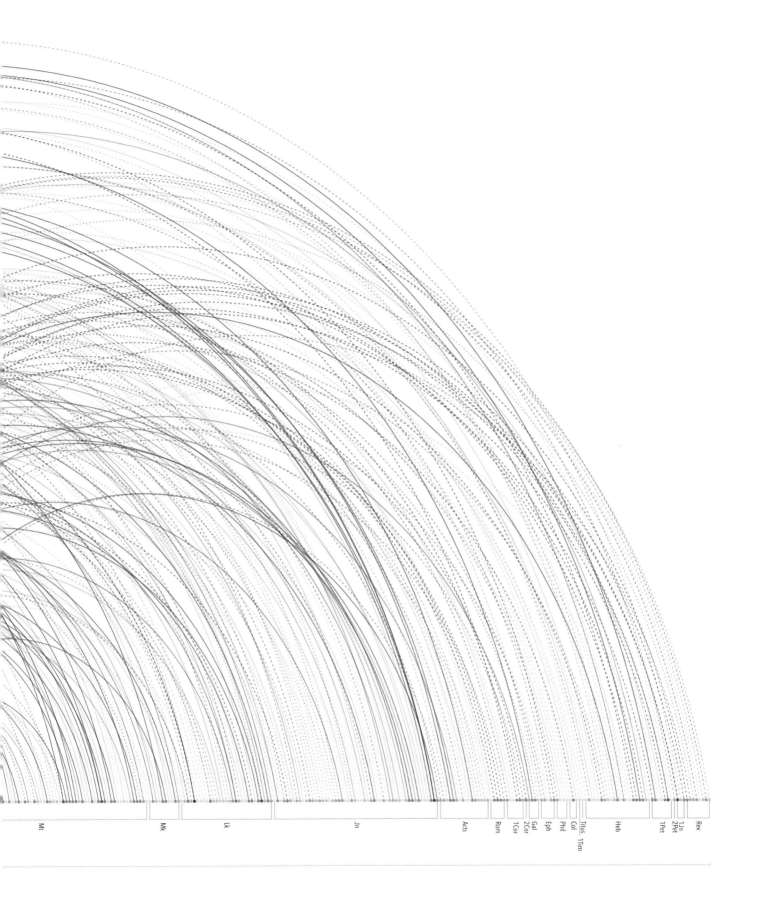

All Prophecies about Jesus

A big picture view of those promised in the Old & fulfilled in the New

source: David Painting. Gen, Ex, Lev, Num, Deut, 1 Sam, 2 Sam, 1 Chr, Ps, Isa, Jer, Ezek, Dan, Hos, Joel, Jon, Mic, Zech, Mal, Mt, Mk, Lk, Jn, Acts, Rom, 1 Cor, 2 Cor, Gal, Eph, Phil, Col, 1 Tim, Titus, Heb, 1 Pet, 2 Pet, 1 Jn, Rev.
note: The data contributor and author have drawn on personal choices when selecting the prophecies and creating the themes and categories.

THE OLD TESTAMENT

JESUS COMES

God is King

JN 1:10-14

THE NEW TESTAMENT

NEW TESTAMENT

- With us: 2
- Creative: 2
- Holy: 2
- Spirit: 2
- Like a gardener: 2
- Unique: 2
- Greater than Jesus: 1
- King: 3
- Perfect: 1
- Compassionate: 5
- Praiseworthy: 1
- One with Jesus: 12
- Righteous: 1
- Glorious: 15
- Trustworthy: 1

OLD TESTAMENT

- He is the Father of individuals: 5
- He is the Father of Israel: 12
- He acts as a Father would: 13

THE FATHER IS

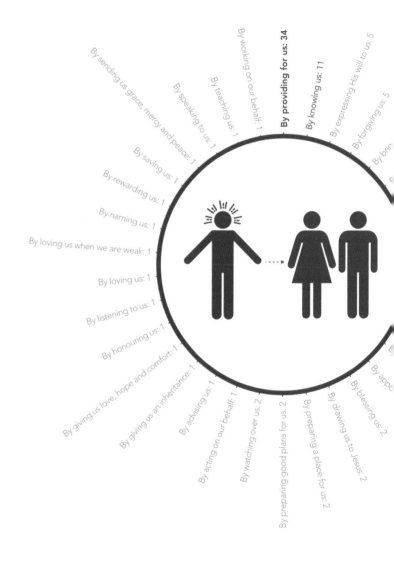

- By sending us grace, mercy and peace: 1
- By speaking to us: 1
- By teaching us: 1
- By working on our behalf: 1
- **By providing for us: 34**
- By knowing us: 11
- By expressing His will to us: 5
- By saving us: 1
- By forgiving us: 5
- By rewarding us: 1
- By brin...
- By naming us: 1
- By loving us when we are weak: 1
- By loving us: 1
- By listening to us: 1
- By appo...
- By honouring us: 1
- By blessing us: 2
- By giving us love, hope and comfort: 1
- By drawing us to Jesus: 2
- By giving us an inheritance: 1
- By preparing a place for us: 2
- By advising us: 1
- By preparing good plans for us: 2
- By acting on our behalf: 1
- By watching over us: 2

HOW FATHER GOD RELATES TO US
NEW TESTAMENT

see pp26-27, 142, 182-183

God the Father

How He relates to us: how we relate to Him

TIMES MENTIONED: 1-10 11-20 **21+**

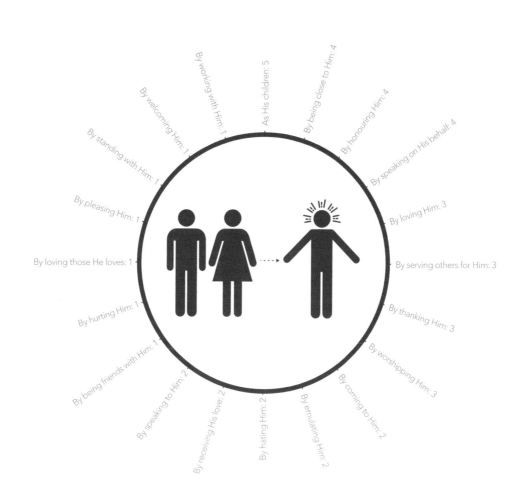

By working with Him: 1
As His children: 5
By being close to Him: 4
By welcoming Him: 1
By honouring Him: 4
By standing with Him: 1
By speaking on His behalf: 4
By pleasing Him: 1
By loving Him: 3
By loving those He loves: 1
By serving others for Him: 3
By hurting Him: 1
By thanking Him: 3
By being friends with Him: 1
By worshipping Him: 3
By speaking to Him: 2
By coming to Him: 2
By receiving His love: 2
By hating Him: 2
By emulating Him: 2

...4
...us: 4
...g what is right: 4
Father: 3
...feating our enemies: 3
...eping His promises: 3
...iving our worship: 3
...ding to our prayers: 3
...self to the humble: 3

HOW WE RELATE TO FATHER GOD
NEW TESTAMENT

source: David Painting. Ex, Deut, 2 Sam, 1 Chr, Prov, Ps, Isa, Jer, Hos, Mal, Mt, Mk, Lk Jn, Acts, Rom, 1 & 2 Cor, Gal, Eph, Col, Phil, 1 & 2 Tim, 1 & 2 Thess, Philem, Titus, Heb, 1 & 2 Pet, 1 & 2 Jn, Jas, Jude, Rev.
OT reference document http://www.etsjets.org/files/JETS-PDFs/31/31-4/31-4-pp385-398_JETS.pdf . note: The data contributor and author have drawn on personal opinions when categorising the data.

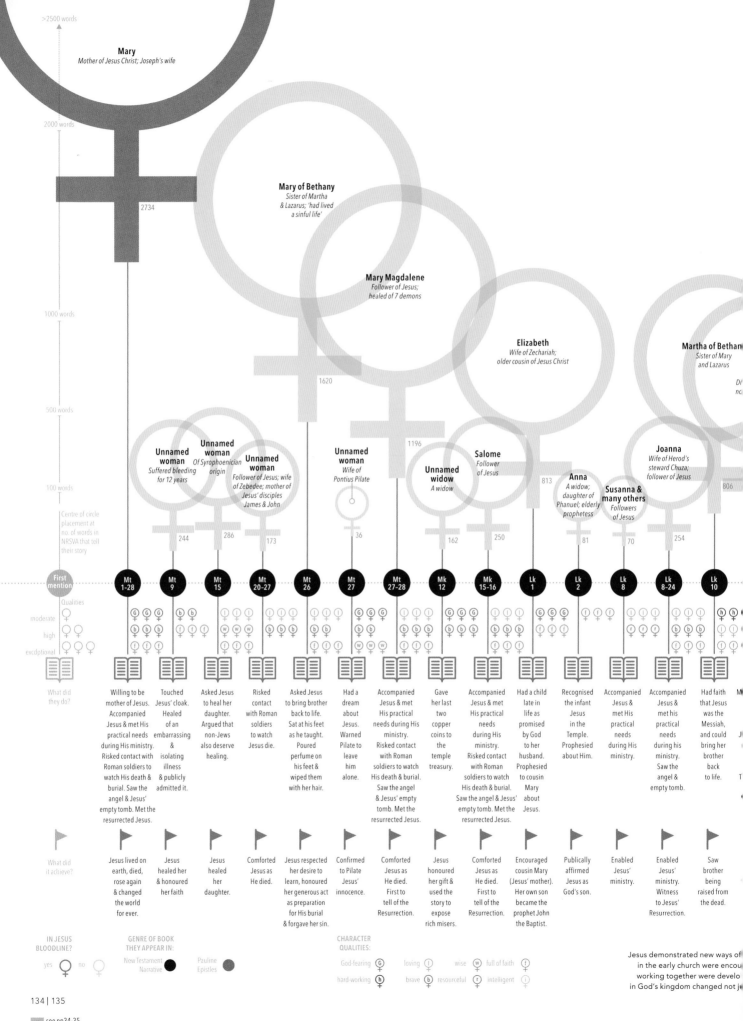

Mary
Mother of Jesus Christ; Joseph's wife

Mary of Bethany
Sister of Martha & Lazarus; 'had lived a sinful life'

Mary Magdalene
Follower of Jesus; healed of 7 demons

Elizabeth
Wife of Zechariah; older cousin of Jesus Christ

Martha of Bethan...
Sister of Mary and Lazarus

Unnamed woman
Suffered bleeding for 12 years

Unnamed woman
Of Syrophoenician origin

Unnamed woman
Follower of Jesus; wife of Zebedee; mother of Jesus' disciples James & John

Unnamed woman
Wife of Pontius Pilate

Unnamed widow
A widow

Salome
Follower of Jesus

Anna
A widow; daughter of Phanuel; elderly prophetess

Susanna & many others
Followers of Jesus

Joanna
Wife of Herod's steward Chuza; follower of Jesus

>2500 words

2000 words

2734

1000 words

1620

500 words

1196

813

100 words

806

Centre of circle placement at no. of words in NRSVA that tell their story

244 286 173 36 162 250 81 70 254

First mention

Qualities
moderate
high
exceptional

Mt 1–28 | Mt 9 | Mt 15 | Mt 20–27 | Mt 26 | Mt 27 | Mt 27–28 | Mk 12 | Mk 15–16 | Lk 1 | Lk 2 | Lk 8 | Lk 8–24 | Lk 10

What did they do?

Willing to be mother of Jesus. Accompanied Jesus & met His practical needs during His ministry. Risked contact with Roman soldiers to watch His death & burial. Saw the angel & Jesus' empty tomb. Met the resurrected Jesus.	Touched Jesus' cloak. Healed of an embarrassing & isolating illness & publicly admitted it.

Asked Jesus to heal her daughter. Argued that non-Jews also deserve healing.

Risked contact with Roman soldiers to watch Jesus die.

Asked Jesus to bring brother back to life. Sat at his feet as he taught. Poured perfume on his feet & wiped them with her hair.

Had a dream about Jesus. Warned Pilate to leave him alone.

Accompanied Jesus & met His practical needs during His ministry. Risked contact with Roman soldiers to watch His death & burial. Saw the angel & Jesus' empty tomb. Met the resurrected Jesus.

Gave her last two copper coins to the temple treasury.

Accompanied Jesus & met His practical needs during His ministry. Risked contact with Roman soldiers to watch His death & burial. Saw the angel & Jesus' empty tomb. Met the resurrected Jesus.

Had a child late in life as promised by God to her husband. Prophesied to cousin Mary about Jesus.

Recognised the infant Jesus in the Temple. Prophesied about Him.

Accompanied Jesus & met His practical needs during His ministry.

Accompanied Jesus & met his practical needs during his ministry. Saw the angel & empty tomb.

Had faith that Jesus was the Messiah, and could bring her brother back to life.

What did it achieve?

Jesus lived on earth, died, rose again & changed the world for ever.

Jesus healed her & honoured her faith

Jesus healed her daughter.

Comforted Jesus as He died.

Jesus respected her desire to learn, honoured her generous act as preparation for His burial & forgave her sin.

Confirmed to Pilate Jesus' innocence.

Comforted Jesus as He died. First to tell of the Resurrection.

Jesus honoured her gift & used the story to expose rich misers.

Comforted Jesus as He died. First to tell of the Resurrection.

Encouraged cousin Mary (Jesus' mother). Her own son became the prophet John the Baptist.

Publically affirmed Jesus as God's son.

Enabled Jesus' ministry.

Enabled Jesus' ministry. Witness to Jesus' Resurrection.

Saw brother being raised from the dead.

IN JESUS BLOODLINE?
yes ♀ no ♀

GENRE OF BOOK THEY APPEAR IN:
● New Testament Narrative   ● Pauline Epistles

CHARACTER QUALITIES:
ⓖ God-fearing   ⓘ loving   ⓦ wise   Ⓕ full of faith
ⓗ hard-working   ⓑ brave   ⓡ resourceful   ⓘ intelligent

Jesus demonstrated new ways of ...
in the early church were encou...
working together were develo...
in God's kingdom changed not ju...

see pp34-35

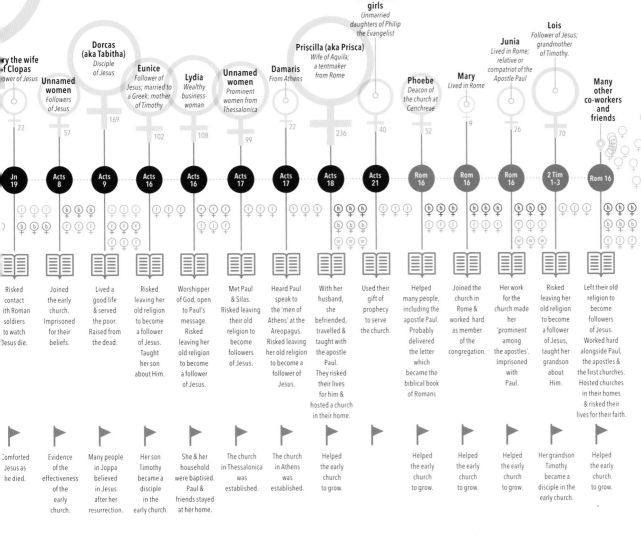

Women of Influence in the New Testament

Courage, faith and calling

...ry the wife ...f Clopas
...ower of Jesus

Unnamed women
Followers of Jesus

Dorcas (aka Tabitha)
Disciple of Jesus

Eunice
Follower of Jesus; married to a Greek; mother of Timothy

Lydia
Wealthy business-woman

Unnamed women
Prominent women from Thessalonica

Damaris
From Athens

Priscilla (aka Prisca)
Wife of Aquila; a tentmaker from Rome

4 unknown girls
Unmarried daughters of Philip the Evangelist

Phoebe
Deacon of the church at Cenchreae

Mary
Lived in Rome

Junia
Lived in Rome; relative or compatriot of the Apostle Paul

Lois
Follower of Jesus; grandmother of Timothy.

Many other co-workers and friends

22 | 57 | 169 | 102 | 108 | 99 | 22 | 236 | 40 | 52 | 9 | 26 | 70

Jn 19 | Acts 8 | Acts 9 | Acts 16 | Acts 16 | Acts 17 | Acts 17 | Acts 18 | Acts 21 | Rom 16 | Rom 16 | Rom 16 | 2 Tim 1–3 | Rom 16

Risked contact ...ith Roman soldiers to watch Jesus die.

Joined the early church. Imprisoned for their beliefs.

Lived a good life & served the poor. Raised from the dead.

Risked leaving her old religion to become a follower of Jesus. Taught her son about Him.

Worshipper of God, open to Paul's message. Risked leaving her old religion to become followers of Jesus.

Met Paul & Silas. Risked leaving their old religion to become followers of Jesus.

Heard Paul speak to the 'men of Athens' at the Areopagus. Risked leaving her old religion to become a follower of Jesus.

With her husband, she befriended, travelled & taught with the apostle Paul. They risked their lives for him & hosted a church in their home.

Used their gift of prophecy to serve the church.

Helped many people, including the apostle Paul. Probably delivered the letter which became the biblical book of Romans

Joined the church in Rome & worked hard as member of the congregation.

Her work for the church made her 'prominent among the apostles'. Imprisoned with Paul.

Risked leaving her old religion to become a follower of Jesus, taught her grandson about Him.

Left their old religion to become followers of Jesus. Worked hard alongside Paul, the apostles & the first churches. Hosted churches in their homes & risked their lives for their faith.

...Comforted Jesus as ...he died.

Evidence of the effectiveness of the early church.

Many people in Joppa believed in Jesus after her resurrection.

Her son Timothy became a disciple in the early church.

She & her household were baptised. Paul & friends stayed at her home.

The church in Thessalonica was established.

The church in Athens was established.

Helped the early church.

Helped the early church to grow.

Helped the early church to grow.

Helped the early church to grow.

Her grandson Timothy became a disciple in the early church.

Helped the early church to grow.

...h women. Following his lead, women ...ctive roles, as new ways of living and ...ngness to accept new responsibilities ...ut also the world in which they lived.

source: Ruth M. Bancewicz, with thanks to Dr Hilary Marlow, Faraday Institute for Science and Religion, Mt, Mk, Lk, Jn, Acts, Rom, 1 Cor, Phil, Col, 2 Tim, Titus, Philem, 3 Jn.
All About Jesus: The Single Story from Matthew, Mark, Luke and John, compiled by Roger Quy (Authentic, 2007).
note: The data contributor and author have drawn on personal interpretation and choices when collating this data.

HEROD AGRIPPA I
Eaten by worms
5

JOSEPH OF ARIMATHEA
Secret follower who
buried Jesus
7

STEPHEN
Martyr who
was stoned
8

CORNELIUS
Roman centurion:
first non-Jewish
follower of Jesus
8

CAIAPHAS
High priest
9

HEROD I
'The Great':
the baby killer
9

THOMAS
The doubter
11

KING AGRIPPA II
Last in Herodian
dynasty
11

BARABBAS
Set free instead
of Jesus
11

LAZARUS
Jesus' friend:
raised from the dead
12

FESTUS
Procurator of Judea
13

MARTHA
Lazarus' sister
& Jesus' friend
13

ANDREW
Peter's brother
13

MARY MAGDALENE
Restored woman
14

JOSEPH
Jesus' dad
14

SILAS
Fellow prisoner of Paul
16

CAESAR
The Roman emperor
20

TIMOTHY
Paul's blood brother
24

BARNABAS
The encourager
24

HEROD II
'That fox':
beheaded John the Baptist
25

JOHN, SON OF ZEBEDEE
'Son of thunder'
26

MARY
Jesus' mum
31

PHILIP
The evangelist
32

JUDAS ISCARIOT
The betrayer
33

JAMES, SON OF ZEBEDEE
'Son of thunder'
40

PONTIUS PILATE
Jesus' judge
58

SATAN
'Father of lies'
81

JOHN THE BAPTIST
Jesus' forerunner & cousin
107

PAUL
Messenger to non-Jews
156

PETER
'The rock'
160

JESUS   JESUS' FAMILY   12 DISCIPLES   FOLLOWER OF JESUS   SPIRITUAL BEING

ROMAN AUTHORITIES   RELIGIOUS RULERS   JEWISH ROYALTY   JEWISH PRISONER

see pp36-37

Most-mentioned Characters in the New Testament
Each playing their part

source: Dr Stuart C. Weir. New Testament

The Birth of Jesus
A tale of two Gospels

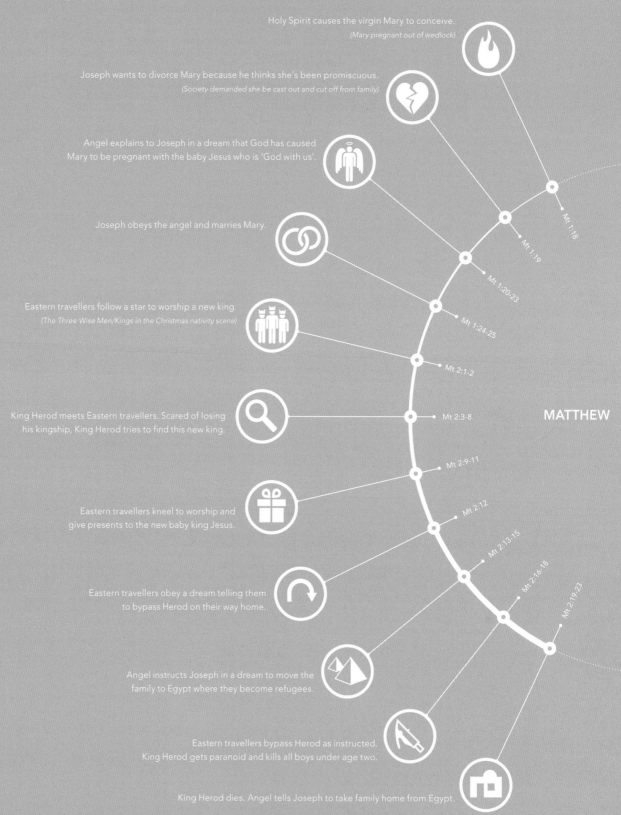

Holy Spirit causes the virgin Mary to conceive.
(Mary pregnant out of wedlock)

Joseph wants to divorce Mary because he thinks she's been promiscuous.
(Society demanded she be cast out and cut off from family)

Angel explains to Joseph in a dream that God has caused
Mary to be pregnant with the baby Jesus who is 'God with us'.

Joseph obeys the angel and marries Mary.

Eastern travellers follow a star to worship a new king.
(The Three Wise Men/Kings in the Christmas nativity scene)

King Herod meets Eastern travellers. Scared of losing
his kingship, King Herod tries to find this new king.

Eastern travellers kneel to worship and
give presents to the new baby king Jesus.

Eastern travellers obey a dream telling them
to bypass Herod on their way home.

Angel instructs Joseph in a dream to move the
family to Egypt where they become refugees.

Eastern travellers bypass Herod as instructed.
King Herod gets paranoid and kills all boys under age two.

King Herod dies. Angel tells Joseph to take family home from Egypt.

Mt 1:18
Mt 1:19
Mt 1:20-23
Mt 1:24-25
Mt 2:1-2
Mt 2:3-8
Mt 2:9-11
Mt 2:12
Mt 2:13-15
Mt 2:16-18
Mt 2:19-23

MATTHEW

see pp32-33, 116-117,

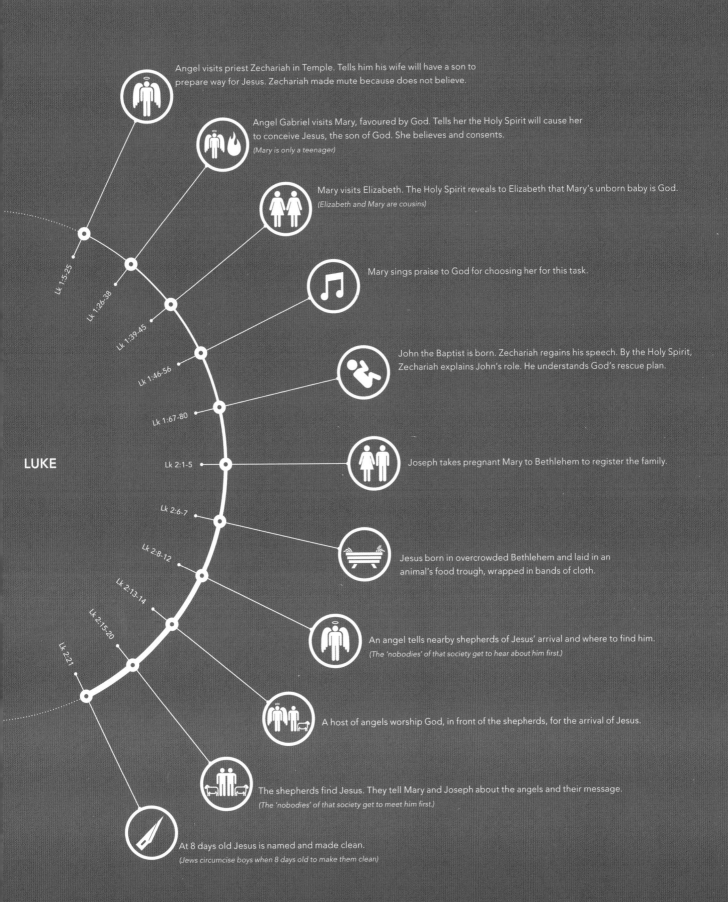

Angel visits priest Zechariah in Temple. Tells him his wife will have a son to prepare way for Jesus. Zechariah made mute because does not believe.

Angel Gabriel visits Mary, favoured by God. Tells her the Holy Spirit will cause her to conceive Jesus, the son of God. She believes and consents.
(Mary is only a teenager)

Mary visits Elizabeth. The Holy Spirit reveals to Elizabeth that Mary's unborn baby is God.
(Elizabeth and Mary are cousins)

Mary sings praise to God for choosing her for this task.

John the Baptist is born. Zechariah regains his speech. By the Holy Spirit, Zechariah explains John's role. He understands God's rescue plan.

Joseph takes pregnant Mary to Bethlehem to register the family.

Jesus born in overcrowded Bethlehem and laid in an animal's food trough, wrapped in bands of cloth.

An angel tells nearby shepherds of Jesus' arrival and where to find him.
(The 'nobodies' of that society get to hear about him first.)

A host of angels worship God, in front of the shepherds, for the arrival of Jesus.

The shepherds find Jesus. They tell Mary and Joseph about the angels and their message.
(The 'nobodies' of that society get to meet him first.)

At 8 days old Jesus is named and made clean.
(Jews circumcise boys when 8 days old to make them clean)

LUKE

Lk 1:5-25
Lk 1:26-38
Lk 1:39-45
Lk 1:46-56
Lk 1:67-80
Lk 2:1-5
Lk 2:6-7
Lk 2:8-12
Lk 2:13-14
Lk 2:15-20
Lk 2:21

source: Dr Stuart C. Weir. Gospel of Matthew 1-2, Gospel of Luke 1-2.
note: The contributor and author have divided the story into steps for the purposes of this graphic.

Key Events in the Life of Jesus

Alpha and Omega: the beginning and the end

'Now, there are many other things that Jesus
did. If they were all written down one by one,
I suppose that the whole world could not hold
the books that would be written.'

JOHN, 'SON OF THUNDER' GNT

Jesus comes back
Ascension of Jesus
Beach BBQ & Peter restored
Great Commission
Jesus meets with the apostles
Emmaus road
Mary hugs Jesus
Resurrection
Empty tomb
Women at the tomb
Crucifixion
Carrying the cross
The crowds curse themselves
Trial
Arrest of Jesus
Kiss of Judas
Praying in the Garden of Gethsemane
The Last Supper
Jesus anointed with perfume
Prophecies of Jesus' return
The Great Banquet
Clearing the Temple
Palm Sunday
Raising Lazarus from the dead
The Good Shepherd
The blind man
Predicting His death
Woman in adultery
The Unforgiving Servant

see pp126-127

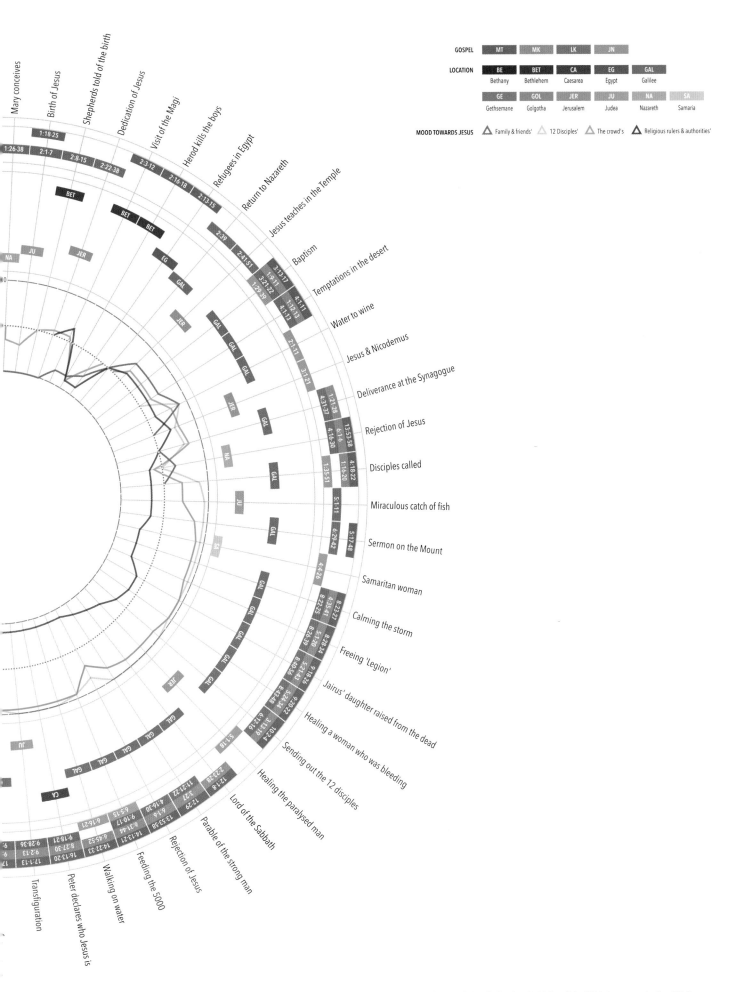

GOSPEL   MT   MK   LK   JN

LOCATION   BE   BET   CA   EG   GAL
            Bethany Bethlehem Caesarea Egypt Galilee

            GE   GOL   JER   JU   NA   SA
            Gethsemane Golgotha Jerusalem Judea Nazareth Samaria

MOOD TOWARDS JESUS   △ Family & friends'   △ 12 Disciples'   △ The crowd's   △ Religious rulers & authorities'

Mary conceives
Birth of Jesus
Shepherds told of the birth
Dedication of Jesus
Visit of the Magi
Herod kills the boys
Refugees in Egypt
Return to Nazareth
Jesus teaches in the Temple
Baptism
Temptations in the desert
Water to wine
Jesus & Nicodemus
Deliverance at the Synagogue
Rejection of Jesus
Disciples called
Miraculous catch of fish
Sermon on the Mount
Samaritan woman
Calming the storm
Freeing 'Legion'
Jairus' daughter raised from the dead
Healing a woman who was bleeding
Sending out the 12 disciples
Healing the paralysed man
Lord of the Sabbath
Parable of the strong man
Rejection of Jesus
Feeding the 5000
Walking on water
Peter declares who Jesus is
Transfiguration

1:18-25
1:26-38   2:1-7   2:8-15   2:22-38   2:3-12   2:16-18   2:13-15
BET
BET   BET
JU   JER   BET   EG
NA   GAL   2:39
        JER   2:41-51
        GAL   3:13-17
        GAL   1:9-11   4:1-11
        GAL   3:21-22   1:12-13
        JER   1:29-39   4:1-13
                2:1-11
                3:1-21
                1:21-28   4:31-37
        GAL   13:53-58   6:1-6
                4:16-30
        NA   1:16-20   4:18-22
                1:35-51
        GAL   5:1-11
                6:29-42
        SA   5:17-48
                4:4-26
        GAL   4:35-41   8:23-27
        GAL   8:22-25   5:1-20   8:28-34
                8:26-39
        GAL   5:21-43   8:40-56
                8:48-68   9:24-34
        JER   4:43-19   9:20-22
                10:24   5:1-18
        GAL   11:21-22   2:23-28
        GAL   12:1-8
        GAL   3:27
                12:29
        GAL   13:53-58   9:10-17
                14:13-21   6:45-52
        CA   6:16-21
                16:13-20   8:27-30
                17:1-13   9:2-13   9:28-36
                17

source: David Painting. The Gospels of Matthew, Mark, Luke and John. GNT. Scriptures researched from BibleGateway.
note: The data contributor and author have drawn on personal choices when collating this data. The 'mood towards Jesus' is the assessment of the author and contributor and based on the effect on those involved, and/or the consequences, of the key event.

King

Gentle & humble in heart

One with the Father   Way, Truth & Life

Messiah   Lord   Master

Son of God

Gate   Cornerstone   Light

Son of Man

Bread   Sent by the Father   Vine

Teacher   Servant   I AM   Shepherd

Prophet   Resurrection & Life

Bridegroom

Christ

Jesus: in His Own Words

I AM

see pp28-29

As promised I dedicate this one, my very first idea in 2013, to you Sara Hogg. Without you the book would not be possible.

said: 1-9. 10-49. **50-99.**

Jesus: in the Words of Other People

Who is this?

Jesus: ?

The Lord
King of the Jews
The Son of God
The Messiah of God
The chosen one
A Prophet

Jesus: if you are…

Life

Not dem[o]

One with God Spi[r]

Blasphemer Sign fr[om]

Come from God

A

King of Israel

Giver

Emmanuel

Miracle wo[rker]

Innoce[nt]

A drunkard

Blessed Holy One of God

Denied

Just

(Ancient) Prophet

L[o]

Sincere Creator Incarnate

Redeemer Saviour

Insurgent Son of God K

Truth A good man The Word Ex[

Auth[

King of the Jews

Knows al[l

Son of Mary & Jospeh Dem[

God's Chosen One Carpente[r

Beloved of God Cr[

God's Servant A frien[d

The

Jesus: in the Words of Other People

Jesus: you are… A

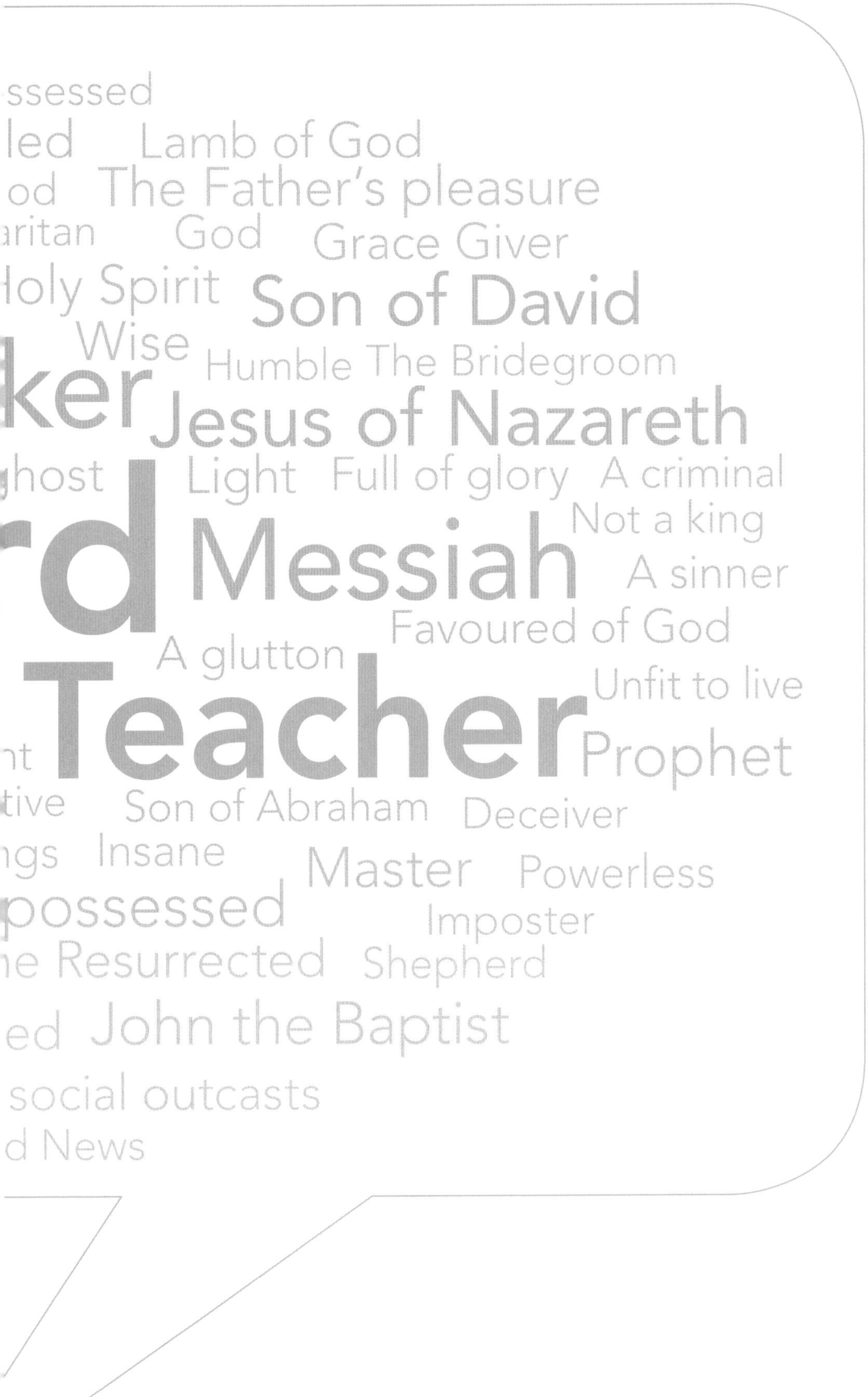

ssessed

led   Lamb of God

od   The Father's pleasure

aritan   God   Grace Giver

Holy Spirit   Son of David

Wise   Humble The Bridegroom

ker   Jesus of Nazareth

ghost   Light   Full of glory   A criminal

Not a king

rd   Messiah   A sinner

Favoured of God

A glutton   Unfit to live

nt   Teacher   Prophet

tive   Son of Abraham   Deceiver

ngs   Insane   Master   Powerless

possessed   Imposter

he Resurrected   Shepherd

ed   John the Baptist

social outcasts

d News

said: 1-9. 10-49. **50-99.**

source: Yolanda Oosthuizen and Miriam Lowe. The Gospels of Matthew, Mark, Luke and John.
note: The data contributor and author have drawn on personal interpretation when collating this data.

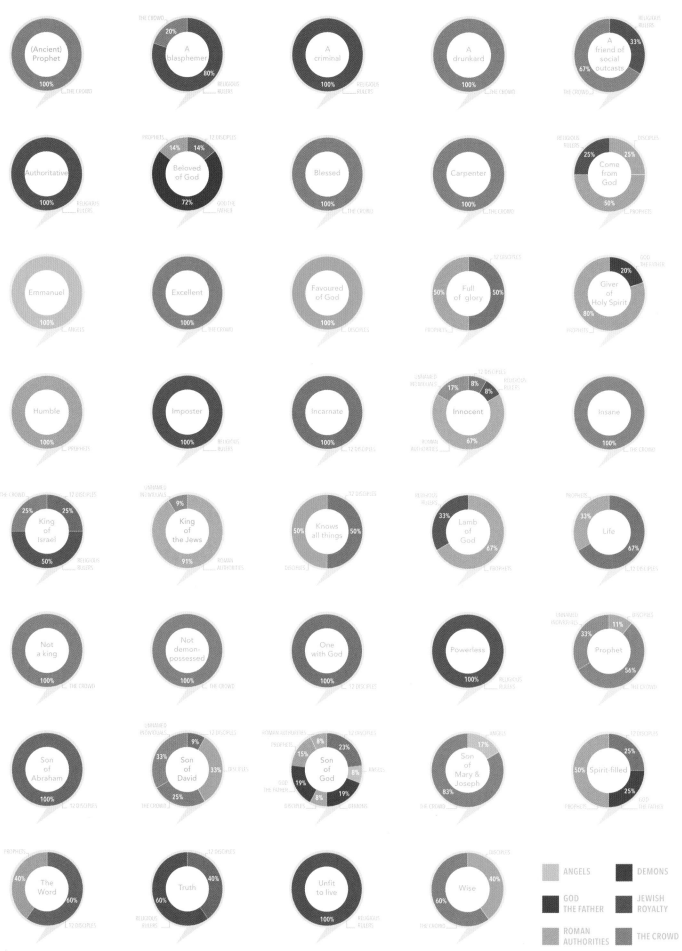

(Ancient) Prophet 100% THE CROWD

A blasphemer THE CROWD 20% / RELIGIOUS RULERS 80%

A criminal 100% RELIGIOUS RULERS

A drunkard 100% THE CROWD

A friend of social outcasts RELIGIOUS RULERS 33% / THE CROWD 67%

Authoritative 100% RELIGIOUS RULERS

Beloved of God PROPHETS 14% / 12 DISCIPLES 14% / GOD THE FATHER 72%

Blessed 100% THE CROWD

Carpenter 100% THE CROWD

Come from God RELIGIOUS RULERS 25% / DISCIPLES 25% / PROPHETS 50%

Emmanuel 100% ANGELS

Excellent 100% THE CROWD

Favoured of God 100% DISCIPLES

Full of glory 12 DISCIPLES 50% / PROPHETS 50%

Giver of Holy Spirit GOD THE FATHER 20% / PROPHETS 80%

Humble 100% PROPHETS

Imposter 100% RELIGIOUS RULERS

Incarnate 100% 12 DISCIPLES

Innocent UNNAMED INDIVIDUALS 17% / 12 DISCIPLES 8% / RELIGIOUS RULERS 8% / ROMAN AUTHORITIES 67%

Insane 100% THE CROWD

King of Israel THE CROWD 25% / 12 DISCIPLES 25% / RELIGIOUS RULERS 50%

King of the Jews UNNAMED INDIVIDUALS 9% / ROMAN AUTHORITIES 91%

Knows all things 50% / 50% DISCIPLES

Lamb of God RELIGIOUS RULERS 33% / 67% PROPHETS

Life PROPHETS 33% / 67% 12 DISCIPLES

Not a king 100% THE CROWD

Not demon-possessed 100% THE CROWD

One with God 100% 12 DISCIPLES

Powerless 100% RELIGIOUS RULERS

Prophet UNNAMED INDIVIDUALS 33% / DISCIPLES 11% / 56% THE CROWD

Son of Abraham 100% 12 DISCIPLES

Son of David UNNAMED INDIVIDUALS 9% / 12 DISCIPLES 33% / DISCIPLES 33% / 25% THE CROWD

Son of God ROMAN AUTHORITIES / PROPHETS 15% / 12 DISCIPLES 23% / 8% ANGELS / 8% / GOD THE FATHER 19% / DISCIPLES 8% / 19% DEMONS

Son of Mary & Joseph ANGELS 17% / 83% THE CROWD

Spirit-filled 12 DISCIPLES 25% / 50% / PROPHETS 25% GOD THE FATHER

The Word PROPHETS 40% / 60% / 12 DISCIPLES

Truth 12 DISCIPLES 40% / RELIGIOUS RULERS 60%

Unfit to live 100% RELIGIOUS RULERS

Wise DISCIPLES 40% / 60% THE CROWD

ANGELS
DEMONS
GOD THE FATHER
JEWISH ROYALTY
ROMAN AUTHORITIES
THE CROWD

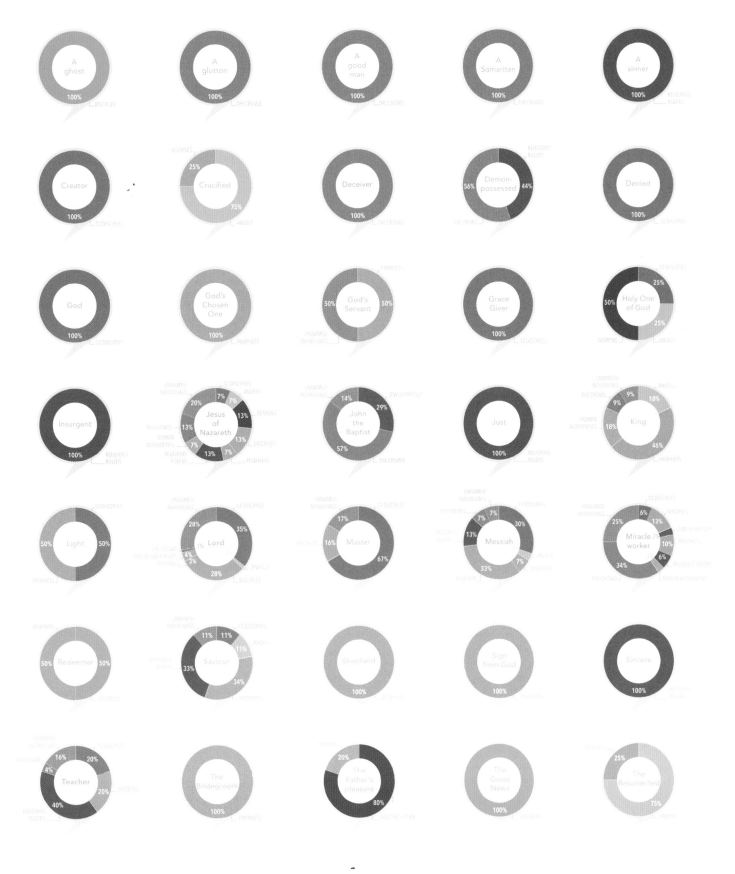

Accusation & Adoration
Who said what about Jesus?

12 DISCIPLES DISCIPLES
PROPHETS RELIGIOUS RULERS
UNNAMED INDIVIDUALS

said: 1-9. 10-49. **50-99.**

source: Yolanda Oosthuizen and Miriam Lowe. The Gospels of Matthew, Mark, Luke and John.
note: The data contributors and author have drawn on personal interpretation when collating this data.

The Top 50 Subjects Jesus Taught On

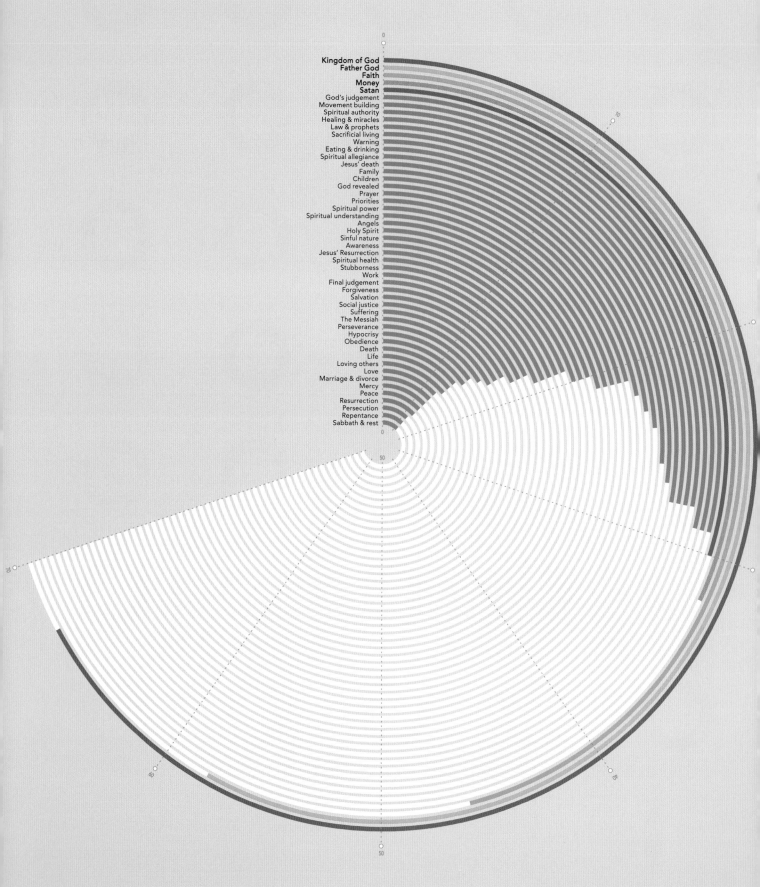

Kingdom of God
Father God
Faith
Money
Satan
God's judgement
Movement building
Spiritual authority
Healing & miracles
Law & prophets
Sacrificial living
Warning
Eating & drinking
Spiritual allegiance
Jesus' death
Family
Children
God revealed
Prayer
Priorities
Spiritual power
Spiritual understanding
Angels
Holy Spirit
Sinful nature
Awareness
Jesus' Resurrection
Spiritual health
Stubborness
Work
Final judgement
Forgiveness
Salvation
Social justice
Suffering
The Messiah
Perseverance
Hypocrisy
Obedience
Death
Life
Loving others
Love
Marriage & divorce
Mercy
Peace
Resurrection
Persecution
Repentance
Sabbath & rest

see pp154-155

source: Dr Stuart C.Weir. The Gospels of Matthew, Mark, Luke and John
note: The data contributor and author have drawn on personal opinions when creating the wider subject categories.
Although debated by some authorities, and omitted from some translations, John 5:4 and Mark 16:9-20 are included in this count.

The Top 5 Subjects Jesus Taught On
Shedding some more light

Each teaching can be complex, appearing in just one or multiple Gospels covering multiple subjects, using different teaching types which can change depending on the audience.

TEACHINGS THAT INCLUDE THE TOP 5 SUBJECTS:

- Kingdom of God
- Father God
- Faith
- Money
- Satan

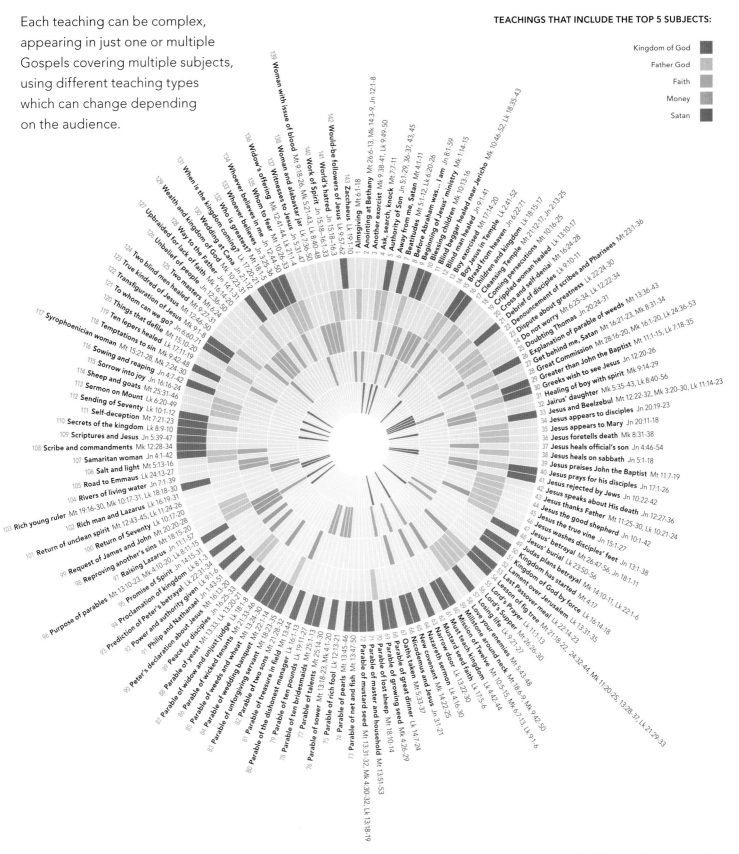

1 Almsgiving Mt 6:1-18
2 Anointing at Bethany Mt 26:6-13, Mk 14:3-9, Jn 12:1-8
3 Another exorcist Mk 9:38-41, Lk 9:49-50
4 Ask, search, knock Mt 7:7-11
5 Authority of Son Jn 5:1-29, 36-37, 43, 45
6 Away from me, Satan Mt 4:1-11
7 Beatitudes Mt 5:1-12, Lk 6:20-26
8 Before Abraham was... I am Jn 8:1-59
9 Beginning of Jesus' ministry Mk 1:14-15
10 Blessing children Mk 10:13-16
11 Blind beggar healed near Jericho Mk 10:46-52, Lk 18:35-43
12 Blind man healed Jn 9:1-41
13 Boy exorcised Mt 17:14-20
14 Boy Jesus in Temple Lk 2:41-52
15 Bread from heaven Jn 6:22-71
16 Children and kingdom Mt 21:12-17, Jn 2:13-25
17 Cleansing Temple Mt 21:12-17, Jn 2:13-25
18 Coming persecutions Mt 10:16-25
19 Crippled woman healed Lk 13:10-17
20 Cross and self-denial Mt 16:24-28
21 Debrief of disciples Lk 9:10-11
22 Denouncement of scribes and Pharisees Mt 23:1-36
23 Dispute about greatness Mt 6:25-34, Lk 12:22-34
24 Do not worry Lk 20:24-31
25 Doubting Thomas Jn 20:24-31
26 Explanation of parable of weeds Mt 13:36-43
27 Get behind me, Satan Mt 16:21-23, Mk 8:31-34
28 Great Commission Mt 28:16-20, Mk 16:1-20, Lk 24:36-53
29 Greater than John the Baptist Mt 11:1-15, Lk 7:18-35
30 Greeks wish to see Jesus Jn 12:20-26
31 Healing of boy with spirit Mk 9:14-29
32 Jairus' daughter Mk 5:35-43, Lk 8:40-56
33 Jesus and Beelzebul Mt 12:22-32, Mk 3:20-30, Lk 11:14-23
34 Jesus appears to disciples Jn 20:19-23
35 Jesus appears to Mary Jn 20:11-18
36 Jesus foretells death Mk 8:31-38
37 Jesus heals official's son Jn 4:46-54
38 Jesus heals on sabbath Jn 5:1-18
39 Jesus praises John the Baptist Mt 11:7-19
40 Jesus prays for his disciples Jn 17:1-26
41 Jesus rejected by Jews Jn 10:22-42
42 Jesus speaks about His death Jn 12:27-36
43 Jesus thanks Father Mt 11:25-30, Lk 10:21-24
44 Jesus the good shepherd Jn 10:1-42
45 Jesus the true vine Jn 15:1-27
46 Jesus washes disciples' feet Jn 13:1-38
47 Jesus' betrayal Lk 22:47-56, Jn 18:1-38
48 Jesus' burial Lk 23:50-56
49 Judas plans betrayal Mk 14:10-11, Lk 22:1-6
50 Kingdom has started Lk 4:17
51 Kingdom of God by force Lk 4:17
52 Lament over Jerusalem Lk 13:31-35
53 Last Passover meal Lk 16:14-18
54 Lesson of fig tree Mk 21:18-22, 24:32-44, Mk 11:20-25, 13:28-37, Lk 21:29-33
55 Lord's Prayer Lk 11:1-13
56 Lord's Supper Mt 26:26-30
57 Losing life Lk 22:14-23
58 Love your enemies Mt 5:43-48
59 Millstone around neck Mt 18:6-9, Mk 9:42-50
60 Mission of twelve Mt 10:5-15, Mk 6:7-13, Lk 9:1-6
61 Must teach kingdom Lk 4:42-44
62 Mustard seed faith Lk 17:5-6
63 Narrow door Lk 13:22-30
64 Nazareth sermon Lk 4:16-30
65 New covenant Mk 14:22-25
66 Nicodemus and Jesus Jn 3:1-21
67 Oaths taken Mt 5:33-37
68 Parable of great dinner Lk 14:7-24
69 Parable of growing seed Mk 4:26-29
70 Parable of lost sheep Mt 18:10-14
71 Parable of master and household Mt 13:51-53
72 Parable of mustard seed Mt 13:31-32, Mk 4:30-32, Lk 13:18-19
73 Parable of net and fish Mt 13:47-50
74 Parable of pearls Mt 13:45-46
75 Parable of rich fool Lk 12:13-21
76 Parable of sower Mt 13:18-23, Mk 4:1-20
77 Parable of talents Mt 25:14-30
78 Parable of ten bridesmaids Mt 25:1-13
79 Parable of ten pounds Lk 19:11-27
80 Parable of the dishonest manager Mt 13:44
81 Parable of treasure in field Mt 13:44
82 Parable of two sons Mt 21:28-32
83 Parable of unforgiving servant Mt 18:23-35
84 Parable of wedding banquet Mt 22:1-14
85 Parable of weeds and wheat Mt 13:24-30
86 Parable of widow and unjust judge Mt 21:33-46
87 Parable of wicked tenants Mt 13:45-46
88 Parable of yeast Mt 13:33, Lk 13:20-21
89 Peace for disciples Jn 16:25-33
90 Peter's declaration about Jesus Mt 16:13-20
91 Philip and Nathanael Jn 1:43-51
92 Power and authority given Jn 14:15-31
93 Prediction of Peter's betrayal Lk 22:31-34
94 Proclamation of kingdom Lk 9:1-6
95 Promise of Spirit Jn 14:15-31
96 Purpose of parables Mt 13:10-23, Mk 4:10-20, Lk 8:11-15
97 Raising Lazarus Jn 11:1-57
98 Reproving another's sins Mt 18:15-20
99 Request of James and John Mt 20:20-28
100 Return of Seventy Lk 10:17-20
101 Return of unclean spirit Mt 12:43-45, Lk 11:24-26
102 Rich man and Lazarus Lk 16:19-31
103 Rich young ruler Mt 19:16-30, Mk 10:17-31, Lk 18:18-30
104 Rivers of living water Jn 7:1-39
105 Road to Emmaus Lk 24:13-27
106 Salt and light Mt 5:13-16
107 Samaritan woman Jn 4:1-42
108 Scribe and commandments Mk 12:28-34
109 Scriptures and Jesus Jn 5:39-47
110 Secrets of the kingdom Lk 8:9-10
111 Self-deception Mt 7:21-23
112 Sending of Seventy Lk 10:1-12
113 Sermon on Mount Lk 6:20-49
114 Sheep and goats Mt 25:31-46
115 Sorrow into joy Jn 16:16-24
116 Sowing and reaping Jn 4:7-42
117 Syrophoenician woman Mt 15:21-28, Mk 7:24-30
118 Temptations to sin Mk 9:42-48
119 Ten lepers healed Lk 17:11-20
120 Things that defile Mk 7:1-23
121 To whom can we go? Jn 6:60-71
122 Transfiguration of Jesus Mt 12:46-50
123 True kindred of Jesus Mt 9:27-31
124 Two blind men healed Mt 6:16-34
125 Two masters Lk 12:36-50
126 Unbelief of people Jn 12:36-50
127 Upbraided for lack of faith Mk 12:41-44
128 Way to the Father Jn 14:1-31
129 Wealth and kingdom of God Lk 7:20-21
130 Wedding at Cana Jn 2:1-12
131 When is the kingdom coming? Jn 3:25-36
132 Whoever believes Jn 10:2-3.31
133 Whoever believes in me Mt 12:41-44
134 Widow's offering Mk 12:41-44, Mk 5:21-43, Lk 8:40-48
135 Whom to fear Mt 10:26-33
136 Who is greatest? Lk 7:36-50
137 Witnesses to Jesus Lk 5:31-47
138 Woman and alabaster jar Lk 7:36-50
139 Woman with issue of blood Mt 9:18-26, Mk 5:21-43, Lk 8:40-48
140 Work of Spirit Jn 15:18-16:1-33
141 World's hatred Jn 15:18-16:33
142 Would-be followers of Jesus Lk 9:57-62
143 Zacchaeus Lk 19:1-10

note: Calculation for top 5 totals = Each Gospel containing a teaching on the subject is 1 count. For clarity a teaching which appears in 2 Gospels would count as 2.

JESUS' TEACHINGS MEASURED & DIVIDED

How long is each teaching on the subject, what type is it and which Gospels does it appear in?

Position = number of verses within the

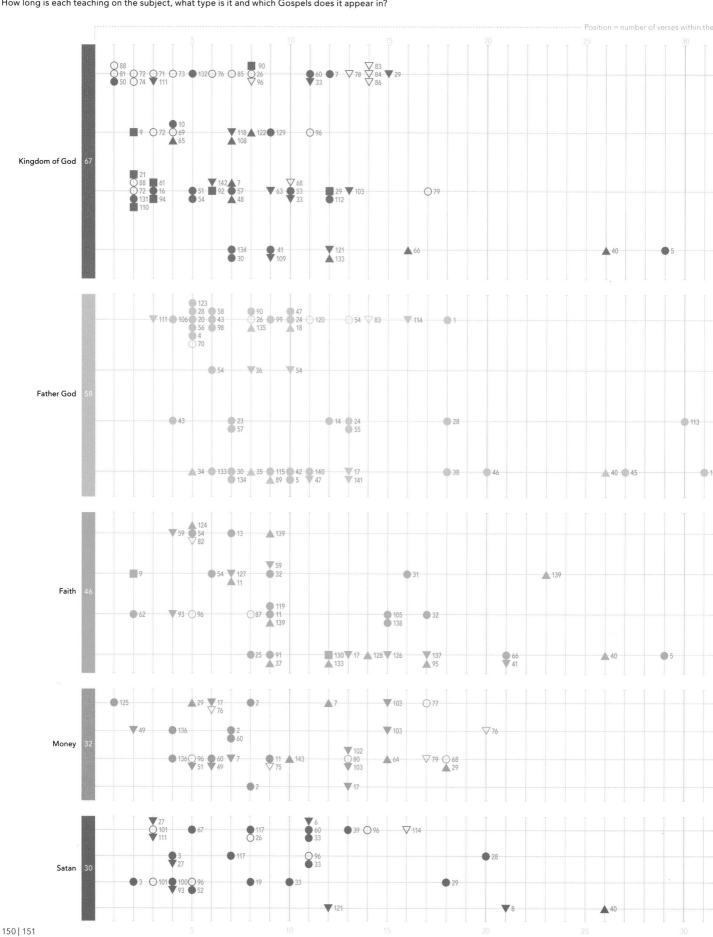

Kingdom of God 67

Father God 58

Faith 46

Money 32

Satan 30

see pp132-133, 187

ed to subject

Teachings per Gospel

35   40   45   50   55   60

● 116   ● 15
▲ 107

Matthew 22

Mark 10

Luke 23

John 12

▼ 22

● 44   ● 97   ● 8   ● 15
● 107

Matthew 24

Mark 3

Luke 8

John 23

● 46 ● 104 ▲ 12 ▲ 107 ▲ 140   ● 15   ● 97 ▼ 8

Matthew 6

Mark 8

Luke 10

John 22

Matthew 8

Mark 6

Luke 16

John 2

Matthew 12

Mark 6

Luke 9

John 3

35   40   45   50   55   60

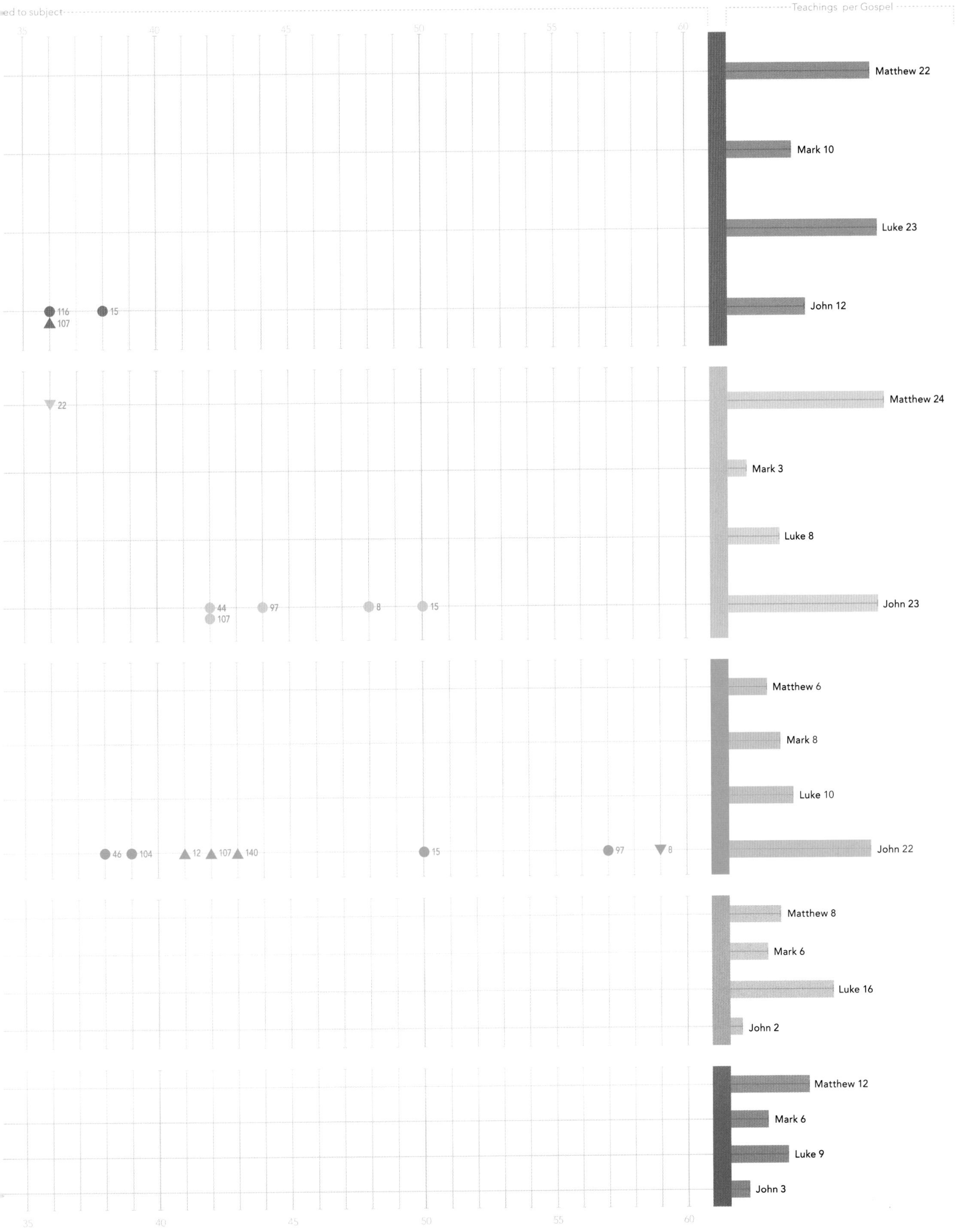

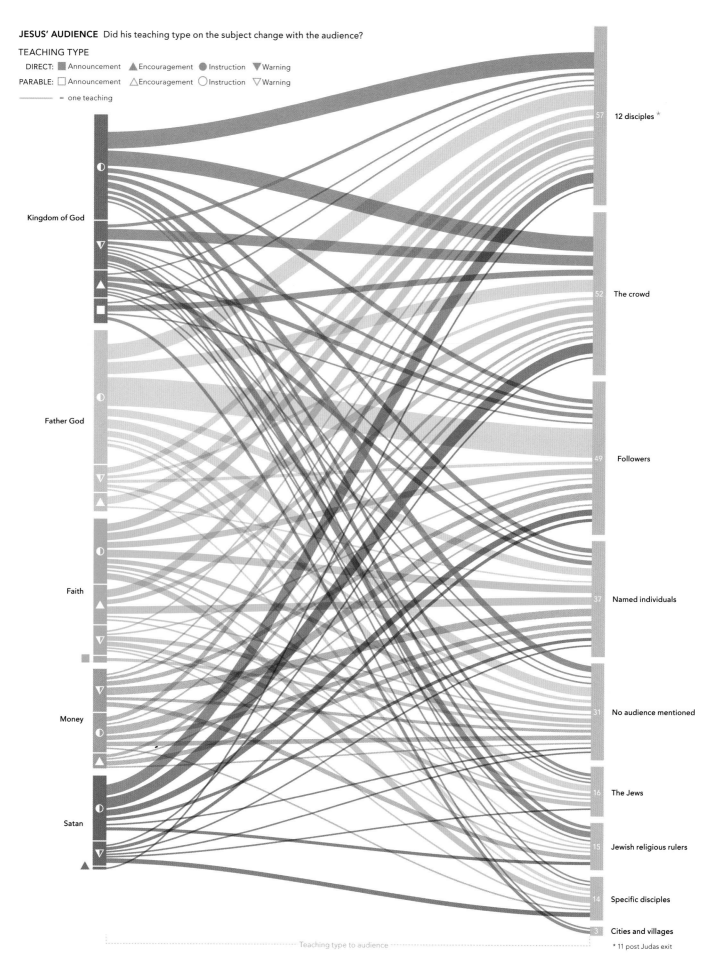

JESUS' AUDIENCE Did his teaching type on the subject change with the audience?

TEACHING TYPE

DIRECT: ■ Announcement ▲ Encouragement ● Instruction ▼ Warning

PARABLE: □ Announcement △ Encouragement ○ Instruction ▽ Warning

———— = one teaching

Kingdom of God

Father God

Faith

Money

Satan

57 12 disciples *

52 The crowd

49 Followers

37 Named individuals

31 No audience mentioned

16 The Jews

15 Jewish religious rulers

14 Specific disciples

3 Cities and villages

·········· Teaching type to audience ··········

* 11 post Judas exit

see p187
for 'Where Did Jesus Minister?' see pp156-157, 169, 198

source: Dr Stuart C. Weir. The Gospels of Matthew, Mark, Luke and John. Personal communication.
note: Types of teaching and categories allocated for graphic.

Where Did Jesus Minister?

On the road, by the sea, around the table …
and every place of encounter in between

IN THE COUNTRYSIDE
4%

ON THE ROAD
3%

IN GARDENS
2%

IN PEOPLE'S HOMES
22%

IN THE MOUNTAINS
11%

AT THE BEACH/LAKE
17%

'The Spirit of
the Lord is upon me,
because he has anointed me
to bring good news to the poor.
He has sent me to proclaim release
to the captives and recovery of sight
to the blind, to let the oppressed
go free, to proclaim the year
of the Lord's favour.'

[LUKE 4:18-19]

IN THE
SYNAGOGUE/TEMPLE
22%

IN THE CITIES, TOWNS & VILLAGES
19%

source: Revd Paul Sawrey. Gospels of Matthew, Mark, Luke and John
note: The data contributor and author have drawn on personal interpretation when selecting and categorising this data. Only ministry events where the Gospel description includes mention of the location have been shown.

Parables of Jesus

Visual storytelling

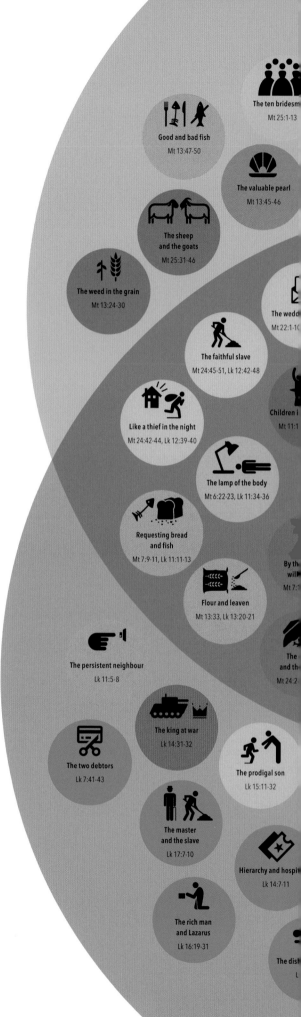

JOHN

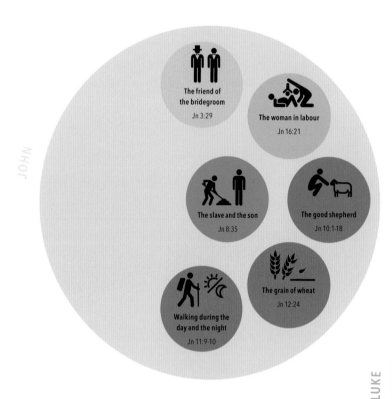

The friend of
the bridegroom
Jn 3:29

The woman in labour
Jn 16:21

The slave and the son
Jn 8:35

The good shepherd
Jn 10:1-18

Walking during the
day and the night
Jn 11:9-10

The grain of wheat
Jn 12:24

LUKE

Good and bad fish
Mt 13:47-50

The ten bridesm
Mt 25:1-13

The valuable pearl
Mt 13:45-46

The sheep
and the goats
Mt 25:31-46

The weed in the grain
Mt 13:24-30

The wedd
Mt 22:1-1

The faithful slave
Mt 24:45-51, Lk 12:42-48

Children i
Mt 11:1

Like a thief in the night
Mt 24:42-44, Lk 12:39-40

The lamp of the body
Mt 6:22-23, Lk 11:34-36

Requesting bread
and fish
Mt 7:9-11, Lk 11:11-13

By th
wil
Mt 7:1

Flour and leaven
Mt 13:33, Lk 13:20-21

The
and the
Mt 24:2

The persistent neighbour
Lk 11:5-8

The king at war
Lk 14:31-32

The two debtors
Lk 7:41-43

The prodigal son
Lk 15:11-32

The master
and the slave
Lk 17:7-10

Hierarchy and hospi
Lk 14:7-11

The rich man
and Lazarus
Lk 16:19-31

The dish

AGRICULTURE AND NATURE

ARCHITECTURE

BODY AND MEDICINE

FOOD AND DRINK

HOUSEHOLD AND FAMILY

KINGS AND KINDGOMS

MUSIC

RICHES

SOCIO-ECONOMIC STRUCTURE

see pp148, 187

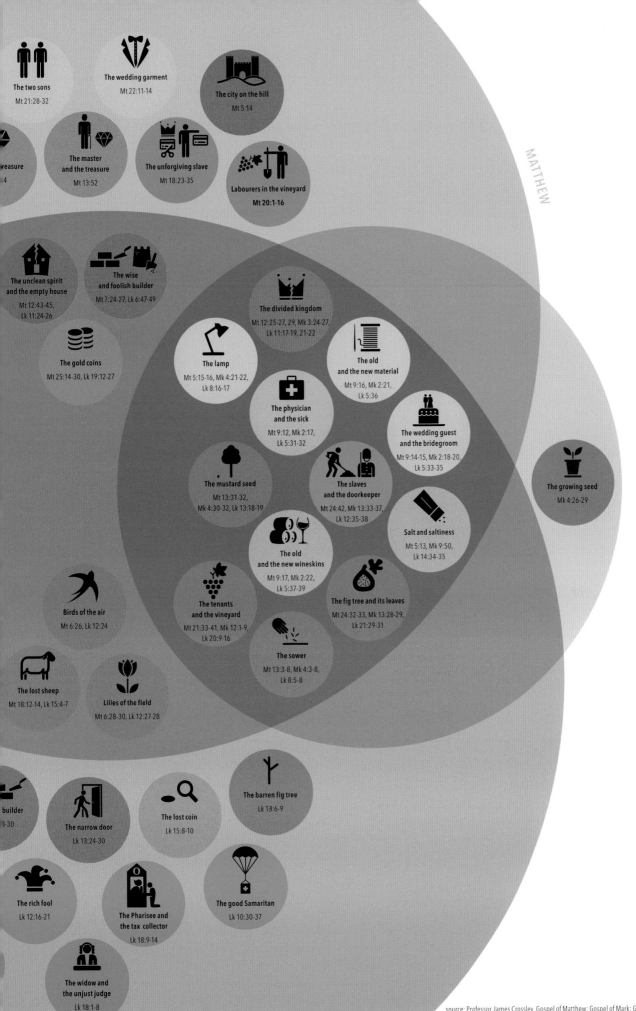

The two sons
Mt 21:28-32

The wedding garment
Mt 22:11-14

The city on the hill
Mt 5:14

...reasure
...4

The master
and the treasure
Mt 13:52

The unforgiving slave
Mt 18:23-35

Labourers in the vineyard
Mt 20:1-16

The unclean spirit
and the empty house
Mt 12:43-45,
Lk 11:24-26

The wise
and foolish builder
Mt 7:24-27, Lk 6:47-49

The divided kingdom
Mt 12:25-27, 29, Mk 3:24-27,
Lk 11:17-19, 21-22

The gold coins
Mt 25:14-30, Lk 19:12-27

The lamp
Mt 5:15-16, Mk 4:21-22,
Lk 8:16-17

The old
and the new material
Mt 9:16, Mk 2:21,
Lk 5:36

The physician
and the sick
Mt 9:12, Mk 2:17,
Lk 5:31-32

The wedding guest
and the bridegroom
Mt 9:14-15, Mk 2:18-20,
Lk 5:33-35

The growing seed
Mk 4:26-29

The mustard seed
Mt 13:31-32,
Mk 4:30-32, Lk 13:18-19

The slaves
and the doorkeeper
Mt 24:42, Mk 13:33-37,
Lk 12:35-38

Salt and saltiness
Mt 5:13, Mk 9:50,
Lk 14:34-35

The old
and the new wineskins
Mt 9:17, Mk 2:22,
Lk 5:37-39

Birds of the air
Mt 6:26, Lk 12:24

The tenants
and the vineyard
Mt 21:33-41, Mk 12:1-9,
Lk 20:9-16

The fig tree and its leaves
Mt 24:32-33, Mk 13:28-29,
Lk 21:29-31

The sower
Mt 13:3-8, Mk 4:3-8,
Lk 8:5-8

The lost sheep
Mt 18:12-14, Lk 15:4-7

Lilies of the field
Mt 6:28-30, Lk 12:27-28

...builder
...-30

The narrow door
Lk 13:24-30

The lost coin
Lk 15:8-10

The barren fig tree
Lk 13:6-9

The rich fool
Lk 12:16-21

The Pharisee and
the tax collector
Lk 18:9-14

The good Samaritan
Lk 10:30-37

The widow and
the unjust judge
Lk 18:1-8

MATTHEW

MARK

source: Professor James Crossley. Gospel of Matthew; Gospel of Mark; Gospel of Luke; Gospel of John
note: The classification of what constitutes a 'parable' is not always clear and the list used here is not necessarily exhaustive. The classification by type of imagery used here is for illustrative purposes.

Healings of Jesus
What did He do?

		ONE PERSON HEALED			PUBLIC			JESUS WAS PRESENT FOR HEALING

Legend:
- ONE PERSON HEALED
- MORE THAN ONE PERSON HEALED
- PUBLIC
- NON-PUBLIC
- JESUS WAS PRESENT FOR HEALING
- HEALING OCCURED REMOTELY
- % CATEGORY TOTAL ALL HEALINGS

SOURCE SCRIPTURES	WHAT DID JESUS DO OR SAY?	WHERE AND HOW DID JESUS HEAL?	WHO NEEDED HEALING?
MT 4:23-24; MK 3:9-12		The sick brought to Him as He was teaching and preaching across Galilee.	MANY SICK & DEMON-POSSESSED PEOPLE
MT 8:16; MK 1:32-34; LK 4:40	Laid hands on each one and drove out demons.	Many people brought to Him at Peter's home.	DEMON-POSSESSED & SICK PEOPLE
MT 8:28-34; MK 5:1-20; LK 8:26-39	Demons asked to be cast into pigs; He commanded that to happen.	Approached by the people as He got off the boat at the lakeside	DEMON-POSSESSED PEOPLE
MT 9:35		He was travelling through villages and cities, teaching and healing the sick.	MANY CURED OF THEIR DISEASES
MT 12:15-16; MK 3:7-12	He warned them not to reveal who He was.	Realising the Pharisees were conspiring, He left the synagogue, healing many people.	MANY SICK & DEMON-POSSESSED PEOPLE
MT 14:13-14	Jesus had compassion on them.	John the Baptist died. He left to be alone. The crowds followed Him.	PEOPLE IN THE CROWD
MT 14:34-36; MK 6:53-56		People brought those who were sick at Gennesaret.	PEOPLE IN THE CROWD
MT 15:29-31		Climbed a hill and sat down - a crowd of people was brought to Him	MANY PEOPLE
MT 19:2		Leaving Galilee and arriving at Judea, large crowds followed Him.	LARGE CROWDS
MT 20:29-33	He had compassion on them.	Leaving Jericho with the disciples, a large crowd followed Him.	ANOTHER TWO BLIND MEN
MT 21:12-15		People came to Him while at the Temple	BLIND & LAME PEOPLE
MK 1:39		While teaching in synagogues throughout Galilee	MANY PEOPLE
LK 5:15		Crowds were drawn to listen to Him, and received healing.	MANY PEOPLE
LK 6:5		He was in His home town and was only able to heal a few people	A FEW PEOPLE
LK 6:17-19		Coming down from the mountain on to a level place, people were healed as they touched Him	MANY SICK & DEMON-POSSESSED PEOPLE
LK 7:21-22		John the Baptist's disciples reported what He was doing.	MANY SICK & BLIND PEOPLE
LK 9:11		He withdrew with the disciples in Bethsaida. Crowds followed Him.	MANY SICK PEOPLE
LK 17:11-19	He said, 'Go and show yourselves to the priests.'	Walking along the roadside, the lepers approached Him.	TEN MEN WITH LEPROSY
MT 9:27-31	He said that because of their faith it would happen, but not to tell anyone about it.	Followed by the men as He left the girl's home	TWO BLIND MEN

81%

45%

19%

> I am telling you the truth: those who believe in me will do what I do—yes, they will do even greater things, because I am going to the Father.
>
> JOHN 14:12 (GNT)

see pp110-111, 204-205

WHO NEEDED HEALING?	WHERE AND HOW DID JESUS HEAL?	WHAT DID JESUS DO OR SAY?	SOURCE SCRIPTURES
81%			
MAN WITH LEPROSY	After He taught, a leper approached at the foot of the mountain.	He told him to tell no one except the priest what had happened to him.	MT 8:1-4; MK 1:40-45; LK 5:12-14
PARALYSED SERVANT	On His way to the centurion's home.	Told him to go	MT 8:5-13; LK 7:2-10
PARALYSED MAN	Arriving at His home town, people carried a man on a bed to Him	He told the man to stand up, pick up his mat and go home.	MT 9:2-8; MK 2:1-12; LK 5:17-26
WOMAN WITH BLEEDING ISSUE	En-route to heal dying girl, the woman approached Him and touched His cloak.	Calling her 'Daughter', He encouraged her, and said that her faith had made her well.	MT 9:19-22; MK 5:25-34; LK 8:42-48
MAN WITH DEFORMED HAND	He was questioned in the synagogue about healing on the Sabbath, then healed this man.		MT 12:9-14; MK 3: 1-6; LK 6:6-11
DEMON-POSSSESSED, BLIND & MUTE MAN	In among the crowds, a man was brought to Him.		MT 12:22-24; LK 11:14-15
DEMON-POSSESSED WOMAN	A Gentile woman approached in the region of Tyre & Sidon on behalf of her sick daughter	He said her faith was great and her request was granted.	MT 15:21-28; MK 7:24-29
DEMON-POSSESSED BOY	At the foot of the mountain after the Transfiguration, a man brought his son to Him.	He helped him up.	MT 17: 14-21; MK 9:14-29; LK 9:37-42
MAN WITH AN EVIL SPIRIT	While teaching in a synagogue, the man spoke out and He healed him.	He said, 'Be silent and come out of him.'	MK 1:23-28; LK 4:31-37
BARTIMAEUS THE BLIND MAN	Walking along with disciples, the man called out to Him.	He said, 'What do you want me to do for you?', healed him, then told him his faith had made him well.	MK 10:46-52; LK 18:35-43
YOUNG MAN WHO HAD DIED	Walking into the village of Nain, the dead man was being carried out of the gates.	He said, 'Young man, I say to you, rise!'	LK 7:11-16
DEMON-POSSESSED & SICK WOMAN	Teaching in a synagogue, He called her over.	He said, 'Woman, you are set free from your ailment!'	LK 13:11-13
HIGH PRIEST'S SLAVE WHOSE EAR HAD BEEN CUT OFF	As Jesus was being betrayed by Judas, a slave's ear was cut off.	He said, 'No more of this!' and touched his ear.	LK 22:49-51
MAN SICK FOR 38 YEARS	Arriving at Jerusalem, He came across the man.	He said, 'Stand up, take your mat and walk!'	JN 5:2-15
BLIND MAN	Walking along, He saw the man.	Spat on the ground, made mud with saliva and spread it over the man's eyes. Then said, 'Go, wash in the pool of Siloam'.	JN 9:1-12; 35-37
LAZARUS WHO HAD DIED	Visiting Lazarus in Bethany.	In front of the tomb He said, 'Lazarus, come out!'	JN 11:19-28; 39-44
19%			
PETER'S MOTHER-IN LAW SICK WITH FEVER	Entered Peter's home and found her unwell.	Rebuked the fever, and touched her hand.	MT 8:14:15; MK 1:29-31; LK 4:38-39
DYING GIRL	Interrupted while talking by a synagogue leader telling Him his daughter was dying	He said *Talitha cum* – little girl, get up!'	MT 9:18-19, 23-26; MK 5: 21-24, 35-43; LK 8:40-42; 49-56
MUTE & DEMON-POSSESSED MAN	The man was brought to Him at the house He was in.		MT 9:32-34
DEAF MAN WITH SPEECH IMPEDIMENT	On the way to Sidon a man was brought to Him	Put His fingers in the man's ears then spat and touched the man's tongue saying '*Ephphatha* – be opened.'	MK 7:31-37
BLIND MAN	Man brought to Him in Bethsaida. Takes man out of village.	He spat on the man's eyes and laid hands on him twice.	MK 8:22-26
MAN WITH SWOLLEN ARMS & LEGS (DROPSY)	At the home of the leader of the Pharisees to eat a meal, He came across the man.		LK 14:1-4
OFFICIAL'S DYING SON	Travelling through Galilee, He prayed for official's son without visiting him. The son was healed.	He told him to go back home saying, 'Your son will live!'	JN 4:46-54

source: Mark Marx www.healingonthestreets.com. The Gospels of Matthew, Mark, Luke and John.
note: The data contributor and author have drawn on personal choices when collating this data. It is not always clear from the Gospel
accounts of healing which descriptions occur only once and which are present in more than one Gospel. Opinions on this differ between scholars.

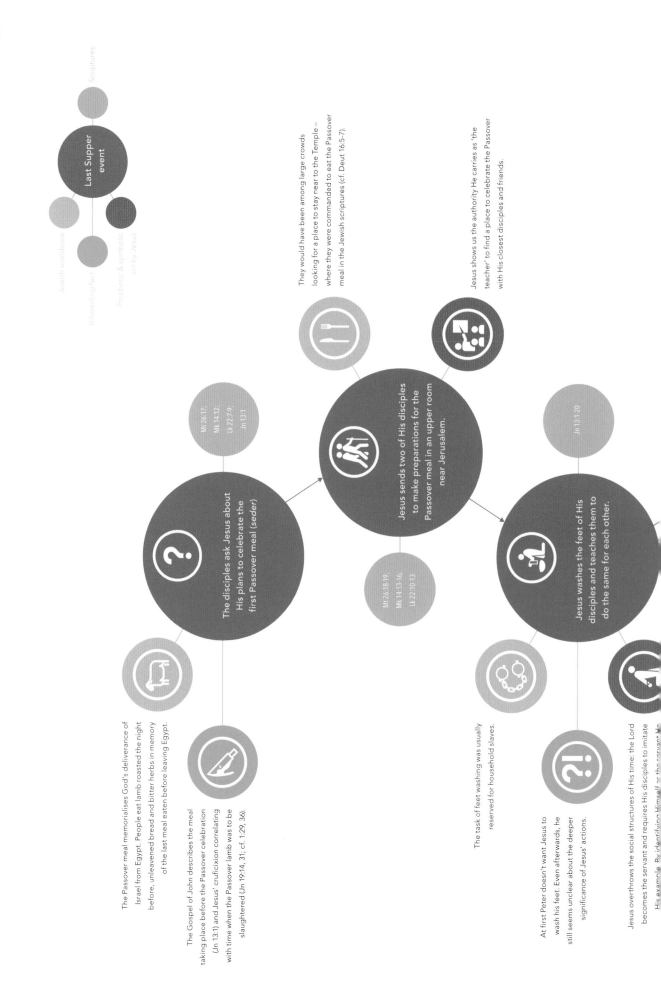

Scriptures

Last Supper event

Jewish worldview

Interesting fact

Prophetic & symbolic act by Jesus

The Passover meal memorialises God's deliverance of Israel from Egypt. People eat lamb roasted the night before, unleavened bread and bitter herbs in memory of the last meal eaten before leaving Egypt.

The Gospel of John describes the meal taking place before the Passover celebration (Jn 13:1) and Jesus' crucifixion correlating with time when the Passover lamb was to be slaughtered (Jn 19:14, 31; cf. 1:29, 36).

Mt 26:17; Mk 14:12; Lk 22:7-9; Jn 13:1

The disciples ask Jesus about His plans to celebrate the first Passover meal (seder)

They would have been among large crowds looking for a place to stay near to the Temple – where they were commanded to eat the Passover meal in the Jewish scriptures (cf. Deut 16:5-7).

Jesus shows us the authority He carries as 'the teacher' to find a place to celebrate the Passover with His closest disciples and friends.

Jesus sends two of His disciples to make preparations for the Passover meal in an upper room near Jerusalem.

Mt 26:18-19; Mk 14:13-16; Lk 22:10-13

The task of feet washing was usually reserved for household slaves.

Jn 13:1-20

Jesus washes the feet of His disciples and teaches them to do the same for each other.

At first Peter doesn't want Jesus to wash his feet. Even afterwards, he still seems unclear about the deeper significance of Jesus' actions.

Jesus overthrows the social structures of His time: the Lord becomes the servant and requires His disciples to imitate His example. By identifying Himself as the servant He

see p59

longing for restoration of the twelve tribes of Israel.

Jesus shows that His betrayal is as scripture said it would be. The expression 'the one who is eating with me' refers to Ps 41:9, a psalm that was part of the prayer life of His contemporaries.

An explanation of the symbolism of the wine is usual at this point in the Passover meal but, by saying 'this is my blood', Jesus offers an alternative and unprecedented explanation of the wine's significance.

No one is expecting the Messiah's death to be the event that brings about a new Passover and inaugurates the new covenant.

Jesus identifies the wine as 'my blood of the covenant which is poured out for many', thereby indicating that the giving of His life brings about a new covenant.

Jesus reveals that one of the twelve will betray Him.

Jesus blesses the bread and distributes it to His disciples saying 'this is my body'.

Jesus blesses the wine and distributes it to His disciples saying, 'this is my blood of the covenant'.

Jesus speaks of the coming kingdom of God.

Mt 26:26;
Mk 14:22;
Lk 22:19;
Jn 6:51-55

Mt 26:20-25;
Mk 14:17-21;
Lk 22:21-23;
Jn 13:21-30

Mt 26:26-28;
Mk 14:23-24;
Lk 22:17-18;
Jn 6:51-55

Mt 26:29;
Mk 14:25;
Lk 22:15-16

An explanation of the symbolism of the bread is usual at this point in the Passover meal but, by saying 'this is my body', Jesus gives the bread an alternative and unprecedented significance.

The earliest tradition of the Lord's Supper comes from Paul's first letter to the churches in Corinth (1 Cor 11:23-24). The practice continues today in a variety of forms, such as Eucharist, Communion, Mass, and the Lord's Supper.

The point is not about eating Jesus' body, but about reframing the significance of Passover – freedom from sin, Satan and death which is brought about by the Messiah giving His life.

Some Jews in the first century looked forward to a banquet in the last days.

Jesus says the Lord's Supper is to be celebrated in anticipation of His return.

source: Dr Max Botner, Ph.D. Goethe-Universität Frankfurt am Main; LOEWE-Projekt: Religiöse Positionierung. The Gospels of Matthew, Mark, Luke and John note: The data contributor and author have drawn on personal opinions when collating this data.

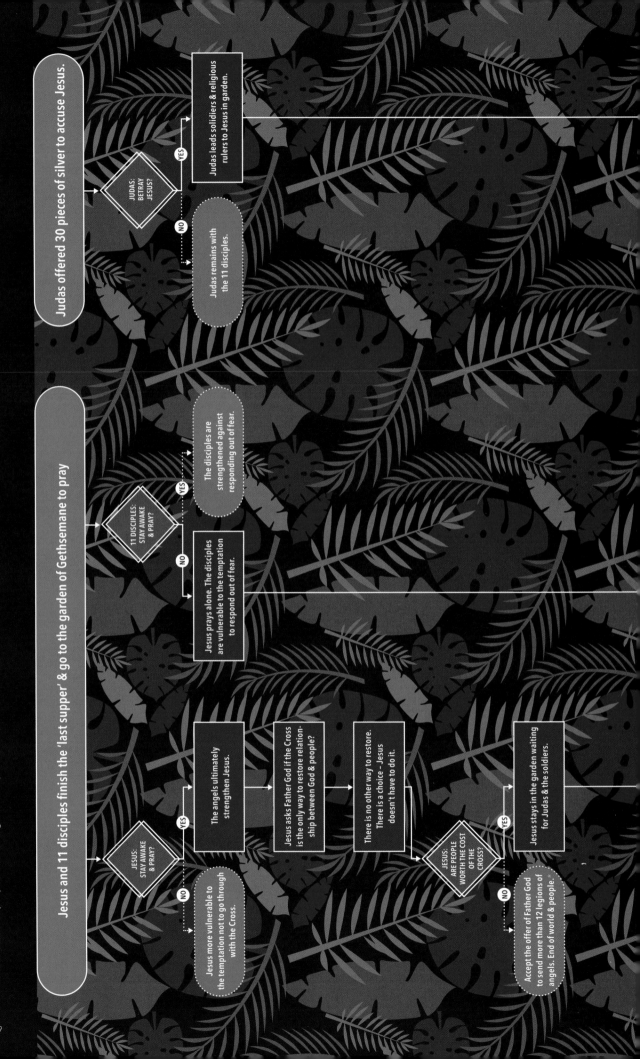

Garden of Gethsemane
A decision tree

see pp106-107, 196-199

* Passover reminded people that one angel had the power to wipe out the first-born in a whole nation.

ACTUAL OUTCOME •••••••• POTENTIAL SUGGESTED OUTCOME

START/END OF OUTCOME

EVENT/OUTCOME

CHOICE

Judas offered 30 pieces of 'silver' to accuse Jesus.

JUDAS: BETRAY JESUS?

YES → Judas leads soldiers & religious rulers to Jesus in garden.

NO ••• Judas remains with the 11 disciples.

Jesus and 11 disciples finish the 'last supper' & go to the garden of Gethsemane to pray

11 DISCIPLES: STAY AWAKE & PRAY?

YES ••• The disciples are strengthened against responding out of fear.

NO → Jesus prays alone. The disciples are vulnerable to the temptation to respond out of fear.

JESUS: STAY AWAKE & PRAY?

YES → The angels ultimately strengthen Jesus.

NO ••• Jesus more vulnerable to the temptation not to go through with the Cross.

Jesus asks Father God if the Cross is the only way to restore relationship between God & people?

There is no other way to restore. There is a choice – Jesus doesn't have to do it.

JESUS: ARE PEOPLE WORTH THE COST OF THE CROSS?

YES → Jesus stays in the garden waiting for Judas & the soldiers.

NO ••• Accept the offer of Father God to send more than 12 legions of angels. End of world & people. *

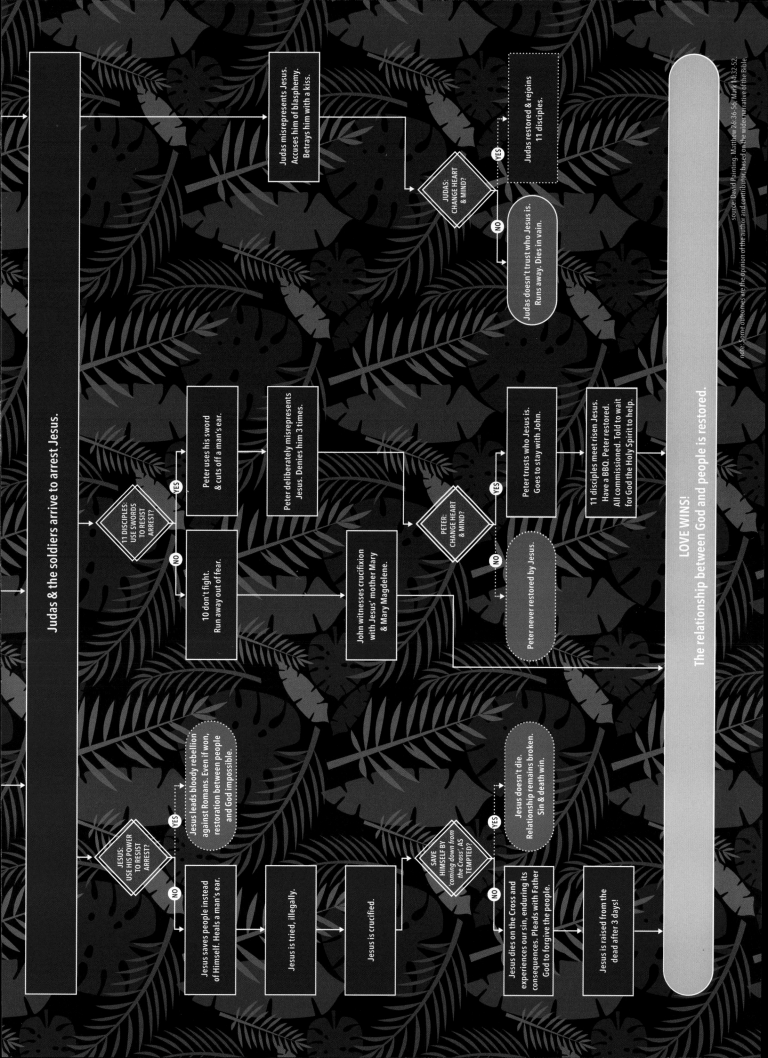

Judas & the soldiers arrive to arrest Jesus.

JESUS: USE HIS POWER TO RESIST ARREST?
- YES → Jesus leads bloody rebellion against Romans. Even if won, restoration between people and God impossible.
- NO → Jesus saves people instead of Himself. Heals a man's ear. → Jesus is tried, illegally. → Jesus is crucified.

SAVE HIMSELF BY coming down from the Cross, AS TEMPTED?
- YES → Jesus doesn't die. Relationship remains broken. Sin & death win.
- NO → Jesus dies on the Cross and experiences our sin, enduring its consequences. Pleads with Father God to forgive the people. → Jesus is raised from the dead after 3 days!

11 DISCIPLES: USE SWORDS TO RESIST ARREST?
- YES → Peter uses his sword & cuts off a man's ear. → Peter deliberately misrepresents Jesus. Denies him 3 times.
- NO → 10 don't fight. Run away out of fear. → John witnesses crucifixion with Jesus' mother Mary & Mary Magdelene.

PETER: CHANGE HEART & MIND?
- YES → Peter trusts who Jesus is. Goes to stay with John. → 11 disciples meet risen Jesus. Have a BBQ. Peter restored. All commissioned. Told to wait for God the Holy Spirit to help.
- NO → Peter never restored by Jesus.

Judas misrepresents Jesus. Accuses him of blasphemy. Betrays him with a kiss.

JUDAS: CHANGE HEART & MIND?
- YES → Judas restored & rejoins 11 disciples.
- NO → Judas doesn't trust who Jesus is. Runs away. Dies in vain.

LOVE WINS!
The relationship between God and people is restored.

source: David Painting. Matthew 26:36-56. Mark 14:32-52.
note: Some outcomes are the opinion of the author and contributor, based on the wider narrative of the Bible.

Stations of the Cross
From trial of Jesus to His death

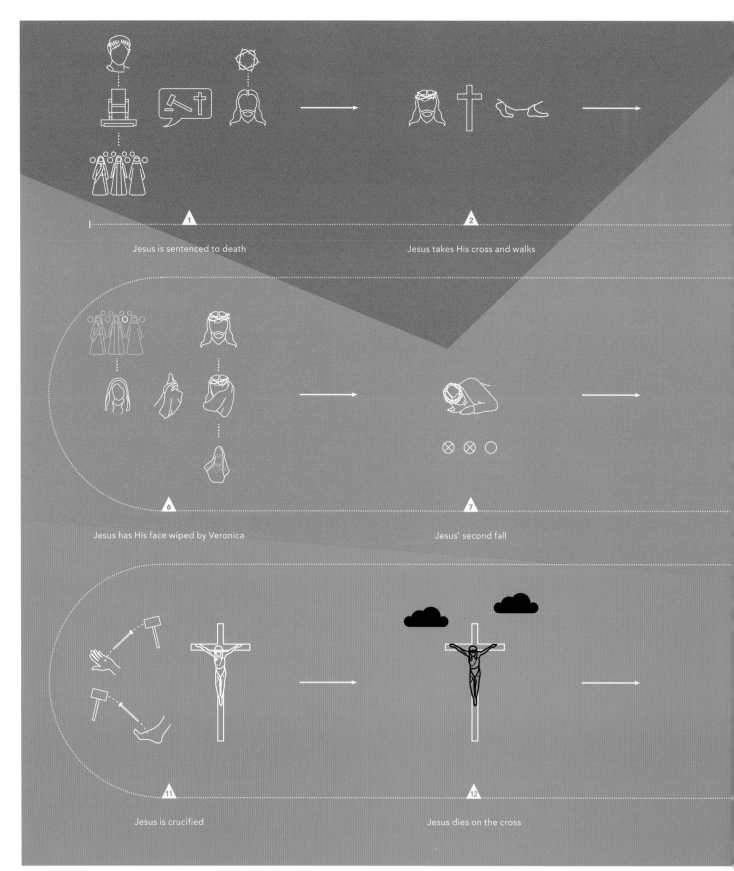

1 Jesus is sentenced to death

2 Jesus takes His cross and walks

6 Jesus has His face wiped by Veronica

7 Jesus' second fall

11 Jesus is crucified

12 Jesus dies on the cross

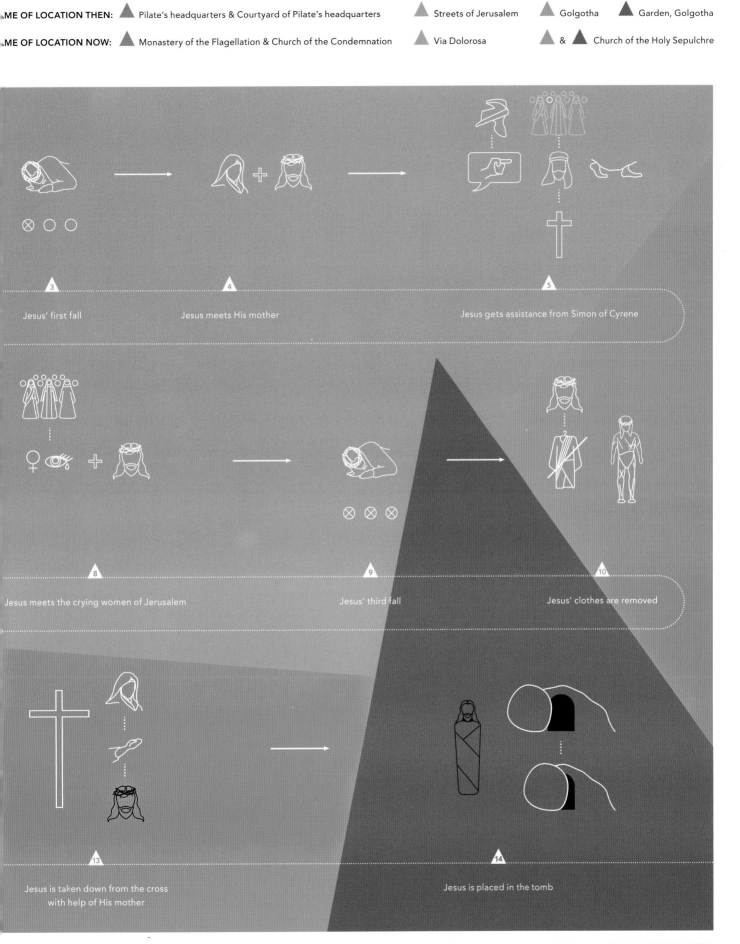

source: Professor James Crossley. Christian devotional traditions; Gospel of Matthew; Gospel of Mark; Gospel of Luke; Gospel of John
note: This traditional Easter devotion has been further supplemented by the Gospel accounts. The record of those present differs between Gospel accounts, but it may be that they are same people named differently by each Gospel writer. Here those named in each Gospel are listed with no judgement made concerning their precise identity.

Seven Sayings of Jesus on the Cross

As He breathed His last

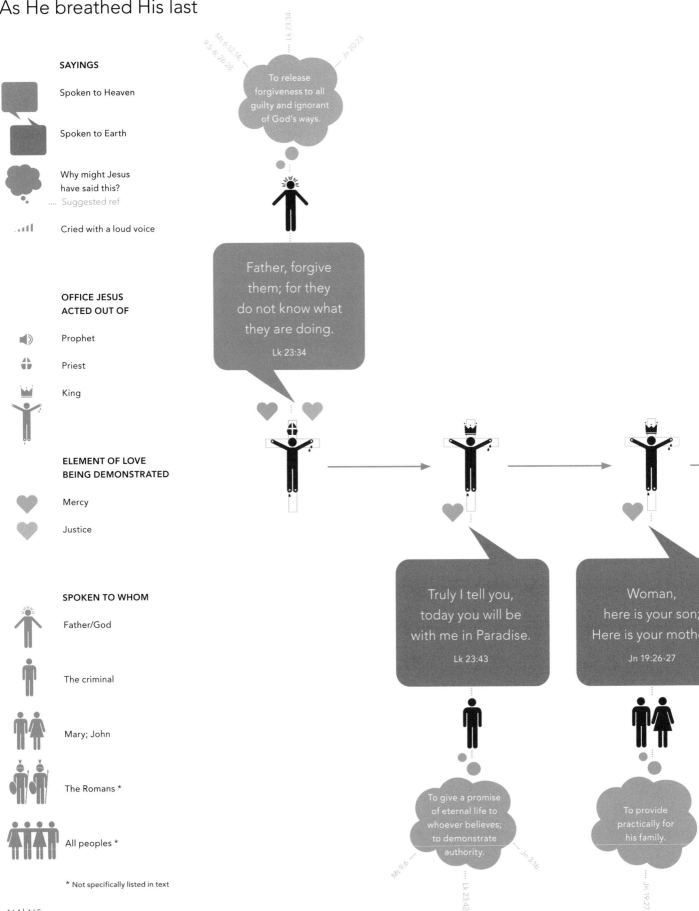

SAYINGS

Spoken to Heaven

Spoken to Earth

Why might Jesus have said this?
.... Suggested ref

..ıtl Cried with a loud voice

OFFICE JESUS ACTED OUT OF

Prophet

Priest

King

ELEMENT OF LOVE BEING DEMONSTRATED

Mercy

Justice

SPOKEN TO WHOM

Father/God

The criminal

Mary; John

The Romans *

All peoples *

* Not specifically listed in text

To release forgiveness to all guilty and ignorant of God's ways.

Father, forgive them; for they do not know what they are doing.
Lk 23:34

Truly I tell you, today you will be with me in Paradise.
Lk 23:43

Woman, here is your son; Here is your mother.
Jn 19:26-27

To give a promise of eternal life to whoever believes; to demonstrate authority.

To provide practically for his family.

see pp88-89, 132-133

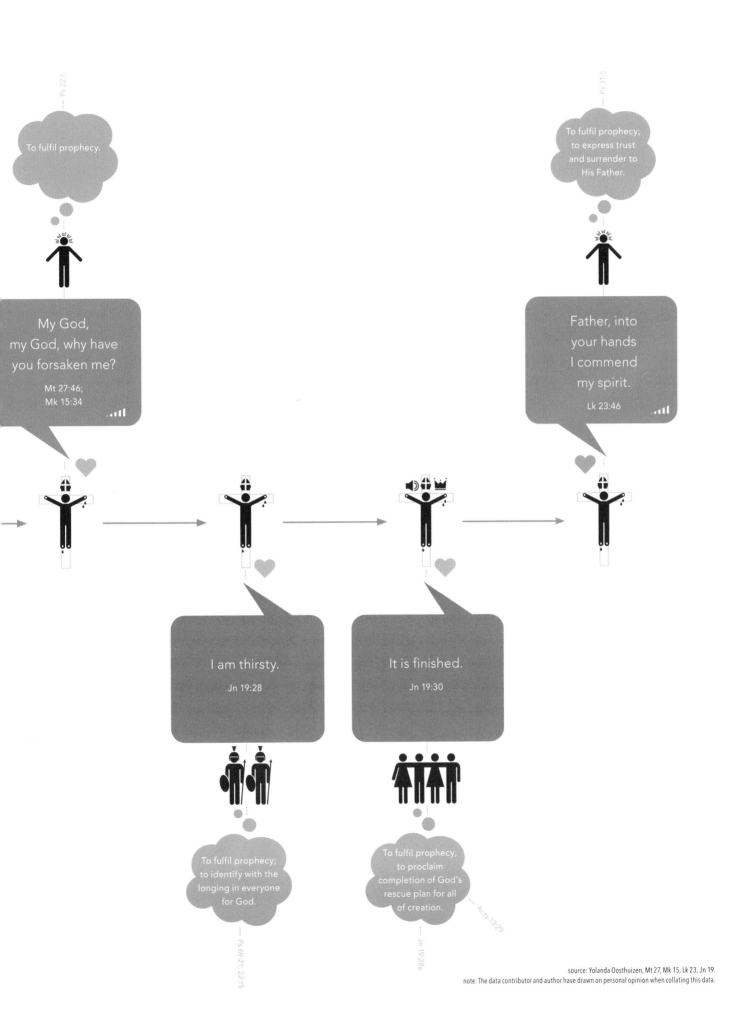

source: Yolanda Oosthuizen, Mt 27, Mk 15, Lk 23, Jn 19.
note: The data contributor and author have drawn on personal opinion when collating this data.

Motifs of the Cross
Problems faced and solutions offered

MOTIFS IN BIBLICAL ORDER

see pp72-73, 200-201

MOTIFS BY THEME

FOR RECONCILIATION 8%

×

Humanity had broken
off their relationship
with God

+

God restored
His relationship
with humanity

FOR FREEDOM 24%

×

Humanity was enslaved
or held for ransom

+

God set humanity free or
paid the ransom demand

FOR VICTORY 12%

×

Enemies were out to
destroy humanity

+

Jesus won a war

FOR MAKING US CLEAN 42%

×

God saw those wrongs like
stains on humanity

+

Jesus' blood removed the
stain on humanity

FOR AMNESTY 14%

×

Humanity's list of offences
was enormous

+

God as judge fully
acquitted humanity

source: Dr Stuart C. Weir. Isa, Zech, Mt, Mk, Lk, Jn, Acts, Rom, 1 & 2 Cor, Gal, Eph, Phil, Col, 1 Pet, 1 Thess, 1 Tim, Titus, Heb, 2 Pet, 1 Jn, Rev.

In Jesus

we gain…

the potential to become like Jesus in character

total acquittal
transformation
truth
victory
wisdom
a destiny
a heavenly Father
a life set apart for Him
a new life
a privileged life
a united community
a well done from Jesus
absolute security in God our Creator
access to God
all His promises fulfilled
all the fullness of God
an inheritance
approval
authenticity
authority
becoming alive to God
becoming established in life
becoming heirs
becoming messengers of reconciliation
being chosen
being cleaned up by Jesus
being established
being His creation
being made fully clean
belonging
blessing
certainty
complete wellbeing
confidence
empowering
encouragement
equality
faith
Father God's pleasure
firm faith
firm foundations for life
forgiveness
freedom
freedom from condemnation
freedom from shame
fullness of life
God as our source of life
God's love
God's power
good reputation
heaven's perspective
healing
grace
His generous provision
His heavenly splendour
His irrevocable commitment
His kindness
His rescue
His strength
His tangible presence
His teaching and advice
His way of living
Holy Spirit
honour
hope
inclusion
innocence
insight
knowing God's will
life
love
loving training for maturity
maturity
morale
our ransom
position of authority and rest
purpose
reconciliation with God
refreshing
restoration
resurrection life
role models
same mind as Jesus
strength
strength through surrender to Him
strong structure for life
support
team

We can participate in everything
Jesus Christ is and has by being in Him
— all because of what
He has done.

TIMES MENTIONED: 1 2 3 4 5 6 8

168 | 169

see pp110-111

source: Yolanda Oosthuizen and Miriam Lowe. Acts, Rom, 1 & 2 Cor, Gal, Eph, Phil, Col, 1 & 2 Thess, 1 & 2 Tim, Philem, 1 Pet, 1 Jn.
note: The contributors have, at times, drawn on personal opinion when collating this data.

Resurrection Appearances
'All mapped out…'

LOCATION

- **A** Tomb, Garden at Golgotha, Jerusalem
- **B** Road to Emmaus; house in a village near Jerusalem
- **C** Jerusalem
- **D** House in Jerusalem
- **E** House in Jerusalem
- **F** Sea of Galilee
- **G** Mountain in Galilee
- **H** Unknown
- **I** Unknown
- **J** Unknown
- **K** Road to Damascus

Damascus

? Location unknown

Sea of Galilee

Mountain in Galilee

Emmaus

Jerusalem

Dead Sea

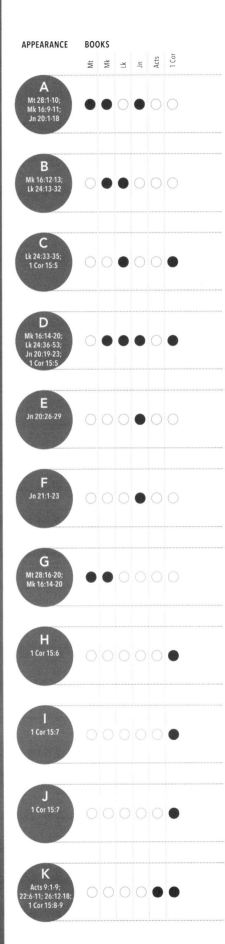

APPEARANCE	BOOKS					
	Mt	Mk	Lk	Jn	Acts	1 Cor
A Mt 28:1-10; Mk 16:9-11; Jn 20:1-18	●	●	○	●	○	○
B Mk 16:12-13; Lk 24:13-32	○	●	●	○	○	○
C Lk 24:33-35; 1 Cor 15:5	○	○	●	○	○	●
D Mk 16:14-20; Lk 24:36-53; Jn 20:19-23; 1 Cor 15:5	○	●	●	●	○	●
E Jn 20:26-29	○	○	○	●	○	○
F Jn 21:1-23	○	○	○	●	○	○
G Mt 28:16-20; Mk 16:14-20	●	●	○	○	○	○
H 1 Cor 15:6	○	○	○	○	○	●
I 1 Cor 15:7	○	○	○	○	○	●
J 1 Cor 15:7	○	○	○	○	○	●
K Acts 9:1-9; 22:6-11; 26:12-18; 1 Cor 15:8-9	○	○	○	○	●	●

source: Professor James Crossley, Mt, Mk, Lk, Jn.
note: The Gospel writers and Paul may not be describing the same resurrection appearances. The classification of appearances according to similarity depends on educated guesswork. Appearances in Mark's Gospel have been taken from the longer ending (Mk 16:9-20).

Resurrection Encounters Keeping it real, from doubt & fear to affirmatio

WHO DID JESUS APPEAR TO?	WAS JESUS' IDENTITY HIDDEN AT FIRST?	WHAT DID THEY FEEL?	WHAT DID THEY DO?
Mary Magdalene and the other Mary	(hidden – crossed out)	Fear, Joy	Worshipped Jesus, physical touch
Two followers, one named Cleopas	(hidden – crossed out)	Sadness, Hearts burning within	Invited Jesus to eat with them
Simon Peter/Cephas	(not hidden)	Amazement	Told 11 disciples
The eleven/twelve disciples and their companions	(not hidden)	Doubt, Terror	None recorded
Disciples, including Thomas	(not hidden)	Doubt	Worshipped Jesus, physical touch
Disciples, including Simon Peter, Thomas, Nathanael, sons of Zebedee, two other disciples, Beloved Disciple	(hidden – crossed out)	Excitement, Confusion, Hurt	Simon Peter gets dressed and swims to Jesus from a boat
The eleven disciples	(not hidden)	Doubt	Worshipped Jesus
500 brothers	(not hidden)	None recorded	None recorded
James	(not hidden)	None recorded	None recorded
All the apostles	(not hidden)	None recorded	None recorded
Saul of Tarsus/Paul	(hidden – crossed out)	Confusion	Falls off horse, goes blind, fasts; requests identity

see p114-115

HOW DID JESUS REPLY?	WHAT DID JESUS DO?	THEIR COMMISSION FROM JESUS	APPEARANCE
Gives reassurance; explains the situation, confirms His & their identity	Breaks off physical touch	Tell 11 disciples of the encounter	**A** Mt 28:1-10; Mk 16:9-11; Jn 20:1-18
Criticises their understanding; interprets Scripture	Walks, eats with them	None recorded	**B** Mk 16:12-13; Lk 24:13-32
None recorded	None recorded	None recorded	**C** Lk 24:33-35; 1 Cor 15:5
Scolds them for their unbelief; gives reassurance	Invites physical touch, eats with them; breathes on them	Tell the good news	**D** Mk 16:14-20; Lk 24:36-53; Jn 20:19-23; 1 Cor 15:5
Gives reassurance	Invites physical touch	Believe in me	**E** Jn 20:26-29
Speaks a miracle, restores Simon Peter	Makes breakfast	Follow me	**F** Jn 21:1-23
None recorded	Taken to heaven	Tell the good news	**G** Mt 28:16-20; Mk 16:14-20
None recorded	None recorded	None recorded	**H** 1 Cor 15:6
None recorded	None recorded	None recorded	**I** 1 Cor 15:7
None recorded	None recorded	None recorded	**J** 1 Cor 15:7
Confirms His identity, instructs	None recorded	Tell the good news to the world	**K** Acts 9:1-9; 22:6-11; 26:12-18; 1 Cor 15:8-9

source: Dr Stuart C. Weir. Mt 28, Mk 16, Lk 24, Jn 20-21, Acts 9; 22; 26, 1 Cor 15
note: Some scholars doubt the veracity of Mark 16:10-20, claiming it was a later addition to the original writing of Mark. As a result, some translations relegate these verses to a footnote.

see pp149-152, 153

Galilee: Economy & Fishing
Followers fishing fish & men

FISHING TECHNIQUES IN THE GOSPELS

1. Angling with rod and line. Mt 17:27
2. The drag net. Mt 13:47-48
3. Casting with nets. Mk 1:16-17

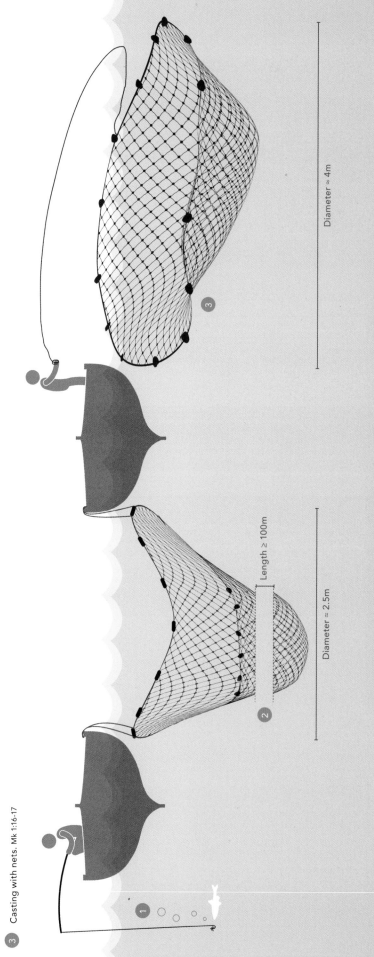

Diameter ≈ 4m

Length ≥ 100m

Diameter ≈ 2.5m

THE GALILEAN FISHING ECONOMY: HIERARCHY AT THE TIME OF JESUS

THE EMPEROR
Augustus/ Tiberius/ Claudius

THE LOCAL RULER
Herod Antipas

CHIEF TAX COLLECTORS
e.g. Zacchaeus

TOLL
COLLECTORS

SHIPPERS &
DISTRIBUTORS

RAW GOODS SUPPLIERS

TAX COLLECTORS   e.g. Levi

PROCESSORS
e.g. Fish salters & sellers

FISHING SYNDICATES
& FAMILIES
e.g. Zebedee

CRAFTSMEN

HIRED
LABOUR

Tribute
money

Money

Money

Licence to collect tolls

Toll payments & import tax

Use of
ports,
roads &
bridges

Fish

Money

Tax

Processed fish & tax

Money

Goods

Money

Licence

Fish

Money

Licence to collect tax

Money

Tax

Fish & tax

Goods &
services

Permission to rule

Licence to collect tax

Licence to fish

Labour

Money

Fish

source: Nick Page, Gospel of Matthew, Gospel of Mark

The Galilean Fishing Economy adapted by Nick from the 'The Galilean Fishing Economy and the Jesus Tradition' by K. C. Hanson. Originally published in *Biblical Theology Bulletin* 27 (1997)

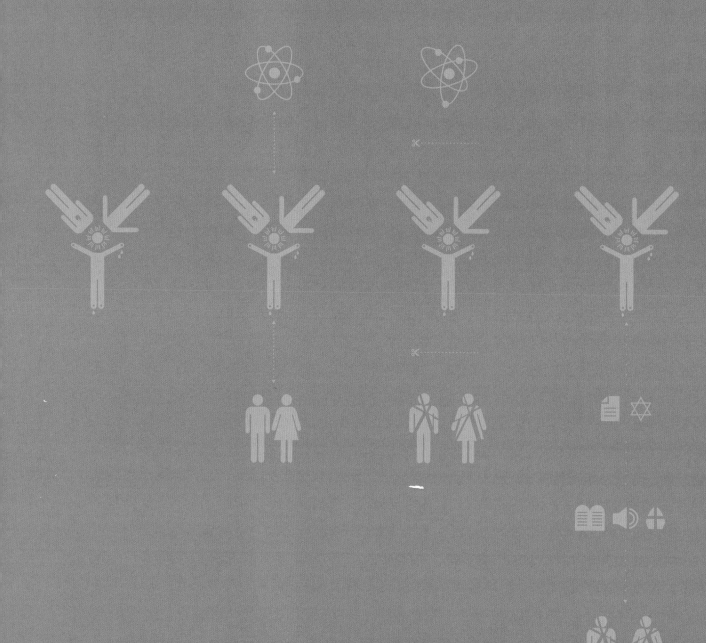

THE OLD TESTAMENT

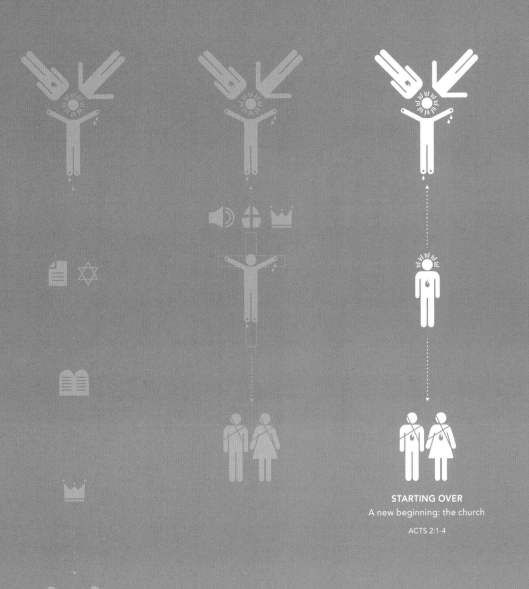

STARTING OVER

A new beginning: the church

ACTS 2:1-4

THE NEW TESTAMENT

Pentecost
The Coming of the Spirit

Then afterwards
I will pour out my spirit
on all flesh; your sons
and your daughters
shall prophesy, your
old men shall dream
dreams, and your
young men shall see
visions. Even on the
male and female
slaves, in those days,
I will pour out
my spirit.

[JOEL 2:28-29]

JOEL

**COMING OF
HOLY SPIRIT PROPHESIED**

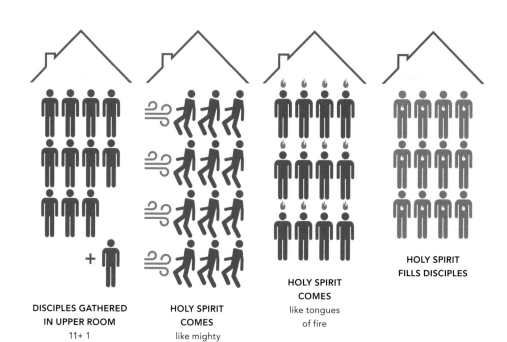

**DISCIPLES GATHERED
IN UPPER ROOM**
11+ 1

**HOLY SPIRIT
COMES**
like mighty
rushing wind

**HOLY SPIRIT
COMES**
like tongues
of fire

**HOLY SPIRIT
FILLS DISCIPLES**

see pp186, 187

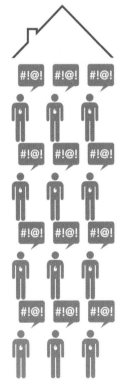

**HOLY SPIRIT
ENABLES THEM
TO SPEAK NEW
LANGUAGES**

**THEY SPILL
OUT OF THE
BUILDING ONTO
THE STREETS**

**THEY TALK
WITH VISITORS**
in 16 different languages

**CROWD ACCUSES
THEM OF
DRUNKENNESS**

JOEL
2:28
-32

**PETER
SPEAKS
BOLDLY**
teaching
them the
prophecy
from Joel

**3000 PEOPLE
BELIEVE IN JESUS**
Baptised and filled

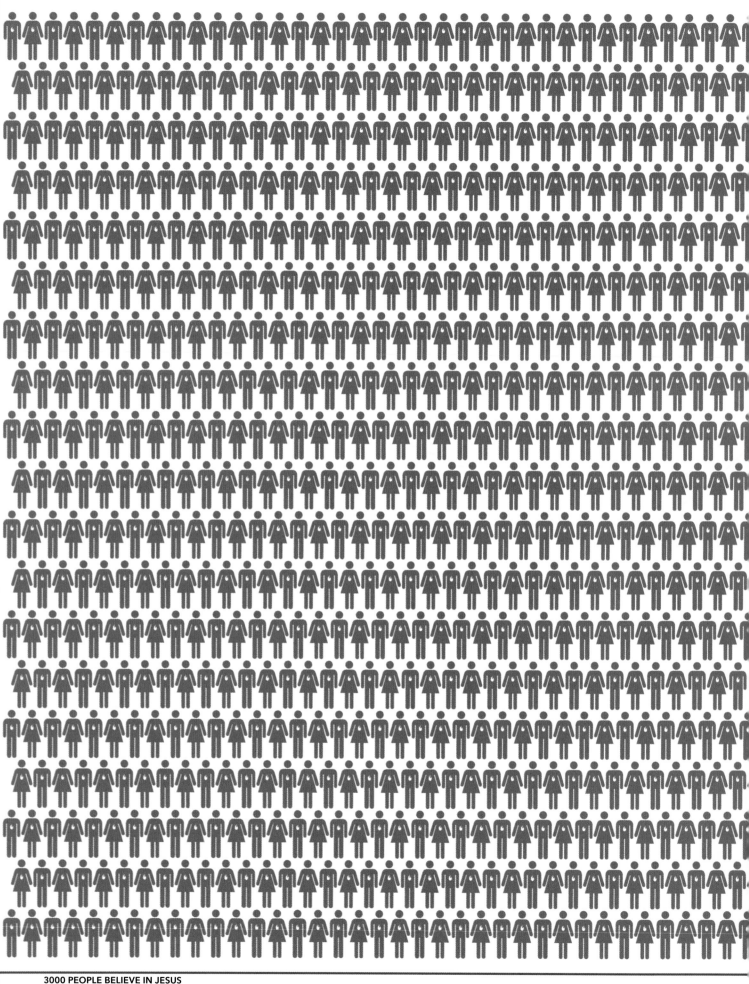

3000 PEOPLE BELIEVE IN JESUS
Baptised and filled

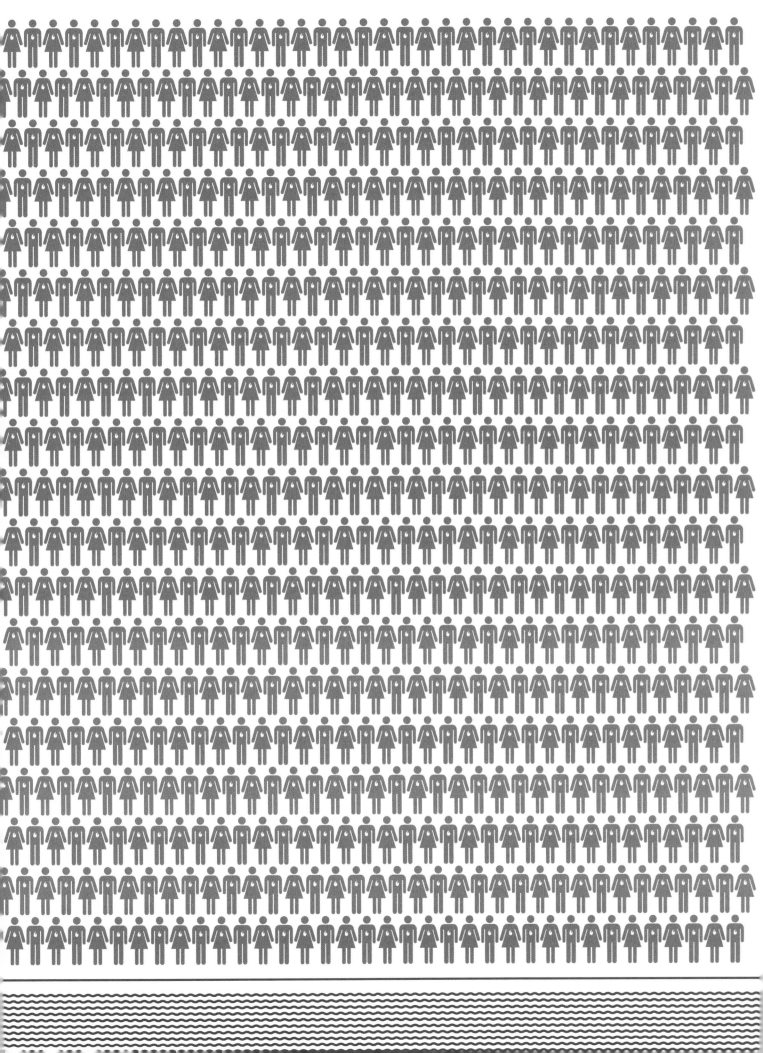

3000 PEOPLE BELIEVE IN JESUS
Baptised and filled

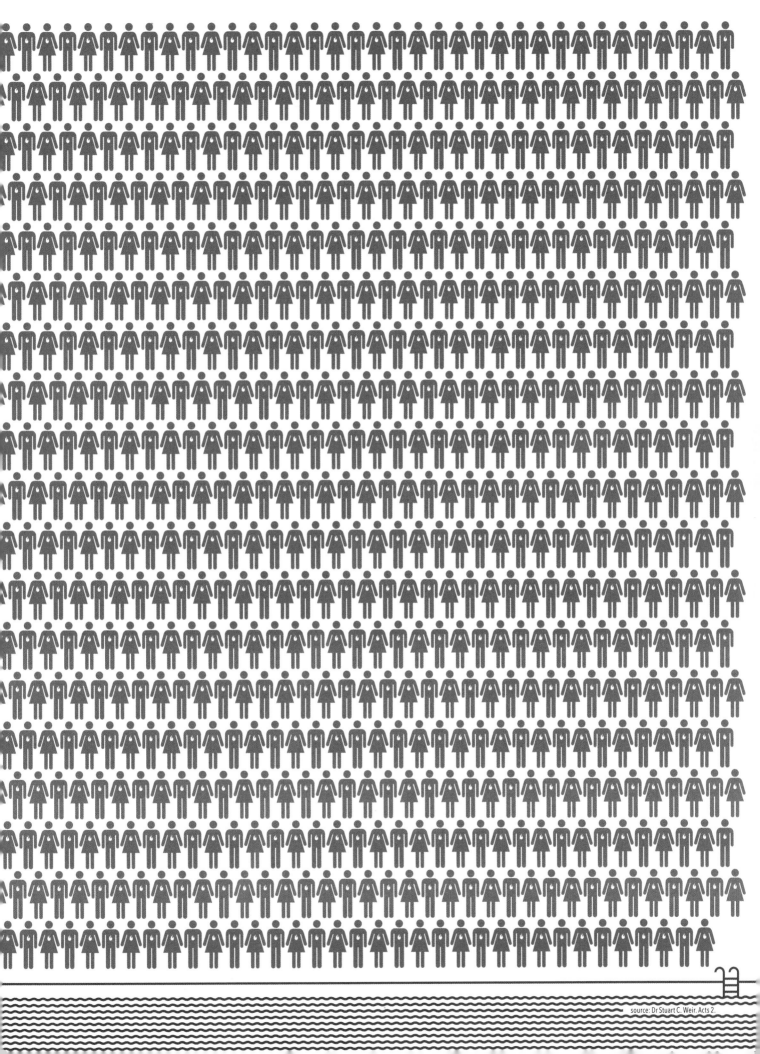

source: Dr Stuart C. Weir. Acts 2.

The Holy Spirit
The source of life... the Helper

He breathed into Adam's nostrils to give him life. Gen 2:7

He is the life force for all living people. Job 33:4

NESHAMA

He hovered over the void and created the world. Gen 1:2

He gave Bezalel and Oholiab, friends of Moses, skills in many crafts for the tabernacle. Ex 31:3

He helped Samson tear a lion apart. Judg 14:6

He is the life force for all living people. Job 33:4

When He leaves a person, they return to being dust. Ps 104:29

RUACH

He promises to be with people for ever. Ez 11:19

He breathed life into an army of skeletons. Ez 37:1-14

He is the source and inspiration of prophecy. Zech 7:12

**HIS IMPACT ON US IN
OLD TESTAMENT TIMES**

 **GIVES
GIFT**

 **PRODUCES
FRUIT**

 NAME OF HOLY SPIRIT USED

HEBREW MEANING:
RUACH; SPIRIT, BLOWING (AS IN WIND OR BREATH), DIVINE POWER INCLUDING LIFE ITSELF
NESHAMA; THE BREATH OF LIFE
GREEK MEANING:
PNEUMA; WIND AND BREATH CHARIS; GRACE

see pp26-27, 132-133, 142

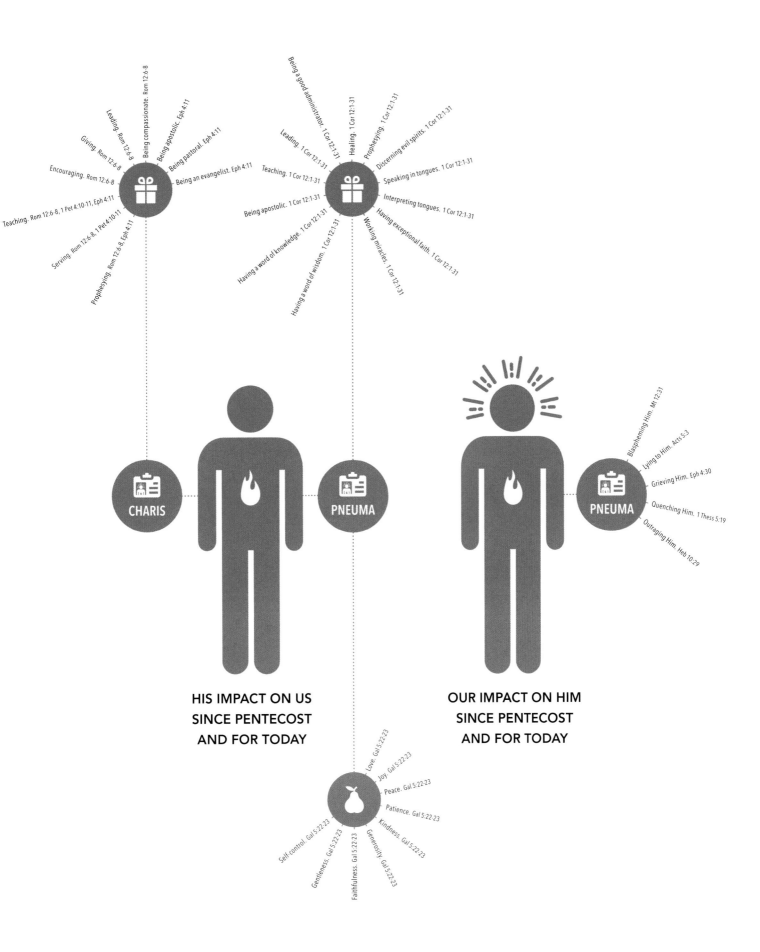

Being compassionate. Rom 12:6-8
Being apostolic. Eph 4:11
Being pastoral. Eph 4:11
Being an evangelist. Eph 4:11
Leading. Rom 12:6-8
Giving. Rom 12:6-8
Encouraging. Rom 12:6-8
Teaching. Rom 12:6-8, 1 Pet 4:10-11, Eph 4:11
Serving. Rom 12:6-8, 1 Pet 4:10-11
Prophesying. Rom 12:6-8, Eph 4:11

Being a good administrator. 1 Cor 12:31
Healing. 1 Cor 12:1-31
Prophesying. 1 Cor 12:1-31
Discerning evil spirits. 1 Cor 12:1-31
Speaking in tongues. 1 Cor 12:1-31
Interpreting tongues. 1 Cor 12:1-31
Having exceptional faith. 1 Cor 12:1-31
Working miracles. 1 Cor 12:1-31
Having a word of wisdom. 1 Cor 12:1-31
Having a word of knowledge. 1 Cor 12:1-31
Being apostolic. 1 Cor 12:1-31
Teaching. 1 Cor 12:1-31
Leading. 1 Cor 12:1-31

CHARIS

PNEUMA

Blaspheming Him. Mt 12:31
Lying to Him. Acts 5:3
Grieving Him. Eph 4:30
Quenching Him. 1 Thess 5:19
Outraging Him. Heb 10:29

PNEUMA

HIS IMPACT ON US
SINCE PENTECOST
AND FOR TODAY

OUR IMPACT ON HIM
SINCE PENTECOST
AND FOR TODAY

Love. Gal 5:22-23
Joy. Gal 5:22-23
Peace. Gal 5:22-23
Patience. Gal 5:22-23
Kindness. Gal 5:22-23
Generosity. Gal 5:22-23
Faithfulness. Gal 5:22-23
Gentleness. Gal 5:22-23
Self-control. Gal 5:22-23

source: Dr Stuart C. Weir. Gen, Ex, Judg, Ps, Job, Ezek, Zech, Mt, Acts, Rom, 1 Cor, Gal, Eph, 1 Thess, Heb, 1 Pet.
note: The data contributor and author have drawn on personal opinions when collating data on the hierarchy and categories of the gifts of the Holy Spirit in the NT.

MISSION AS ORGANISING PRINCIPLE

Mission to the broader society sets the shape and culture of the community.

ORDEAL AND DANGER

Adventuresome community (communitas) is activated in ordeal and challenge.

LIMINALITY & COMMUNITAS

Risk, danger and adventure create a sense of comradeship and belonging in the community.

ACTS 2:42-47

MISSIONAL ECCLESIOLOGY

Our expression of church is shaped by Jesus and His mission.

INCARNATIONAL (DEEPENING)

Jesus, as God, lived amongst us. We, as followers, live embedded in local community.

INCARNATIONAL MISSION

The capacity to contextualise the message and spread it rapidly.

JN 20:21

MISSIONAL (OUTWARD)

Jesus was sent out, so are His followers.

JESUS IS LORD

Centralising Jesus as King over all in His followers' lives.

1 COR 8:6

APEST CULTURE

Ministry and discipleship format which are crucial in releasing and equipping all followers.

EPH 4:1-16

DISCIPLESHIP & DISCIPLE MAKING

Knowing Jesus.
Being His follower.
Becoming like Him.

JN 8:31-32

ORGANIC SYSTEMS

Creating simple, adaptable, reproducible structures that flourish.

ACTS 2:14-42

CHRISTLIKENESS

Becoming like Jesus, in character and ways.

EMBODIMENT

Embodying the message of Jesus every day, everywhere.

MOVEMENT ETHOS

The movement has s structures that a innately reproduci

SPIRITUAL AUTHORITY

Developing followers who have inspirational power and influence.

LEADERSHIP

Arises from living the message and from spiritual authority.

see pp188-189, 192-193

Apostolic Genius
The dynamics of spontaneous expansion and missional movement

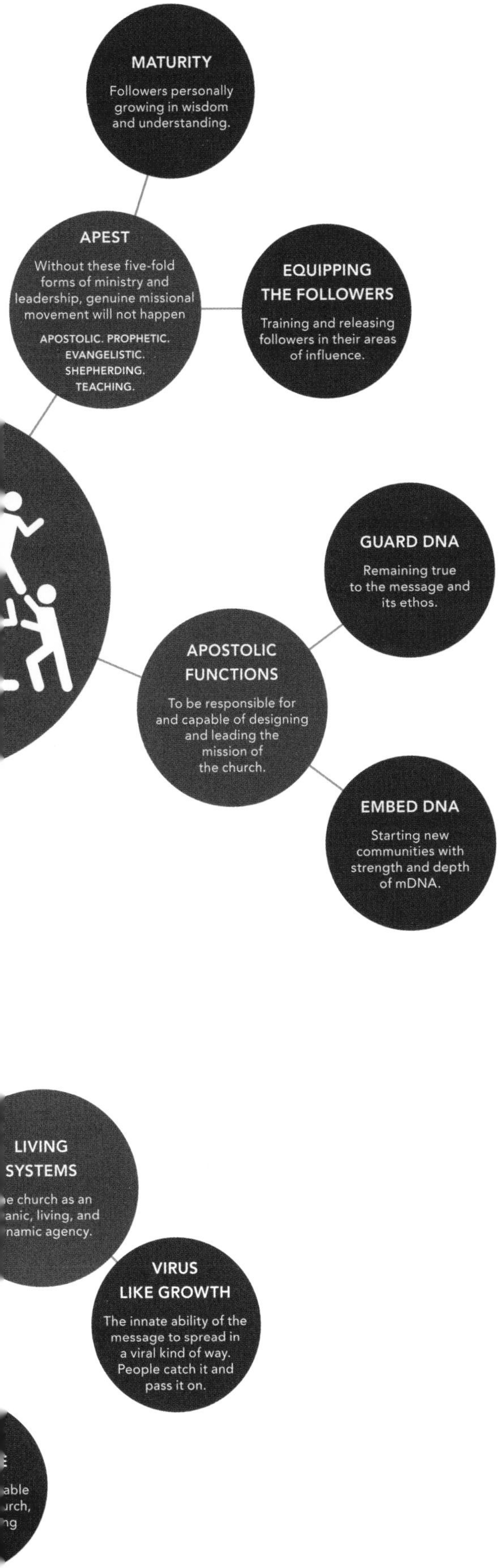

MATURITY
Followers personally growing in wisdom and understanding.

APEST
Without these five-fold forms of ministry and leadership, genuine missional movement will not happen
APOSTOLIC. PROPHETIC. EVANGELISTIC. SHEPHERDING. TEACHING.

EQUIPPING THE FOLLOWERS
Training and releasing followers in their areas of influence.

GUARD DNA
Remaining true to the message and its ethos.

APOSTOLIC FUNCTIONS
To be responsible for and capable of designing and leading the mission of the church.

EMBED DNA
Starting new communities with strength and depth of mDNA.

LIVING SYSTEMS
e church as an anic, living, and namic agency.

VIRUS LIKE GROWTH
The innate ability of the message to spread in a viral kind of way. People catch it and pass it on.

able urch, ng

Apostolic Genius is a way of understanding and adopting the key elements of rapid and exponential growth first shown in the early church and in every other apostolic movement since then.

Expansive movement occurs when the six elements of movement DNA (mDNA as shown in the graphic) come together to activate and then go on to produce the kind of movement that was first shown in the original church.

source: Alan Hirsch. www.alanhirsch.org. 100 www.100movements.com. Jn, Acts, 1 Cor, Eph.
note: This concept of Apostolic Genius and mDNA is the work and creation of Alan Hirsch.

Church Planting
God's (wild!) gardening

MULTIPLICATION

HEARING GOD'S PROPHETIC CALL IN THE WILDERNESS TO REACH HIS PEOPLE

IDENTIFICATION, TRAINING AND COMMISSION OF A LEADER

THE TRAINING OF DISCIPLES WHO DISCIPLE OTHERS

PREACHING THE GOSPEL

SPIRITUAL ATTACK, DELIVERANCE AND RECOVERY PERSONALLY AND CORPORATELY

HEALING THE SICK

EACH ONE PLAYS THEIR PART

FAVOUR OF THE PEOPLE

GATHERING A TEAM

'We can't stop planting'

'Go for I will send you'

'We trust you. God sends you. Go!' (Elders to Timothy)

The church broke new ground reaching new people groups.

Paul called by God to many more people.

Timothy commissioned by elders. *

'Watch me, then go'

Paul coached Timothy.

Paul explained the gospel to Greek leaders.

'Let me explain'

'This is a battle is a spiritual one'

The church are reminded that this battle is not an earthly one but a spiritual one.

Peter and John healed a man in Jesus name.

'In Jesus' name be healed

'I'll go there, you go here', God will bring it together.

Paul explained that church planting is a team effort powered by God

New people joined the believers every day.

The hostile crowd became receptive toward the gospel.

'We're in'

'This is good'

ACTS 22:21
ACTS 10:47
1 TIM 4:14
2 TIM 3:10
ACTS 17:24
EPH 6:12
ACTS 3:1-10
1 COR 3:6
ACTS 2:47

CHURCH PLANTING STEP

'NT call'

NT example

NT SOURCE

* This was done by laying on of hands.

186 | 187

see pp176-181
for 'The Church & the Kingdom' see pp149-152, 176-181

source: Revd Graham Singh. Executive Director of Church Planting Canada and Pastor at St Jax, Montréal. church planting churchplantingcanada.org. Acts, 1 Cor, Eph, 1 Tim, 2 Tim.
note: This sequential cycle diagram, based primarily on a pattern found in the Book of Acts, has been created by the contributor and author for the purposes of this graphic.
Sequential steps that are similar, but not identical, to these have occurred many times throughout church history.

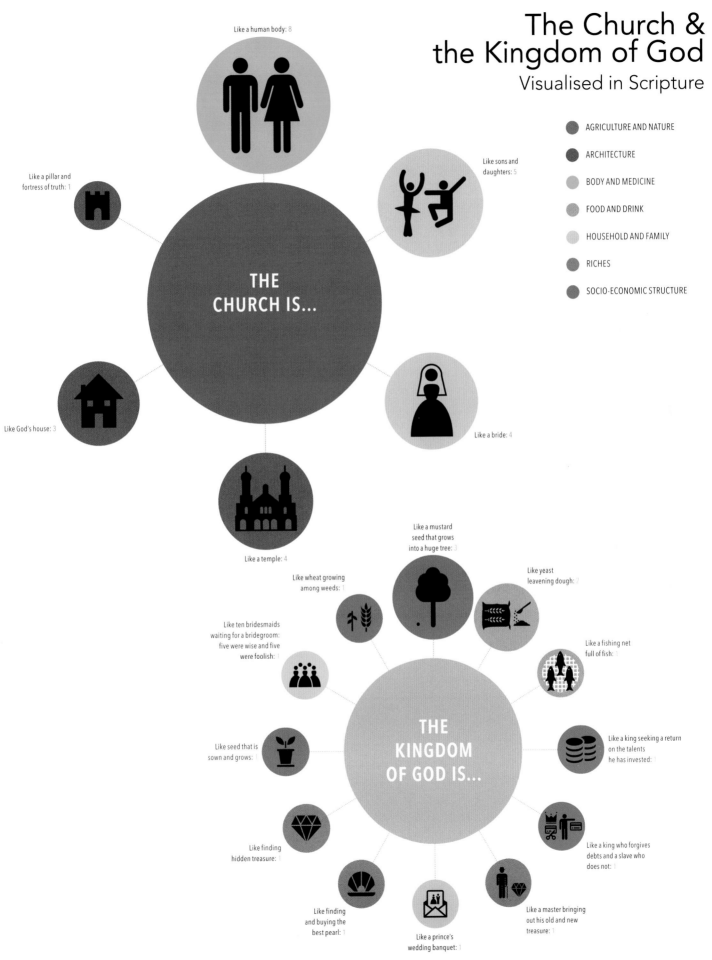

The Church &
the Kingdom of God
Visualised in Scripture

Like a human body: 8

Like sons and daughters: 5

Like a pillar and fortress of truth: 1

THE CHURCH IS...

Like God's house: 3

Like a bride: 4

Like a temple: 4

AGRICULTURE AND NATURE

ARCHITECTURE

BODY AND MEDICINE

FOOD AND DRINK

HOUSEHOLD AND FAMILY

RICHES

SOCIO-ECONOMIC STRUCTURE

Like a mustard seed that grows into a huge tree: 3

Like wheat growing among weeds: 1

Like yeast leavening dough: 2

Like ten bridesmaids waiting for a bridegroom: five were wise and five were foolish: 1

Like a fishing net full of fish: 1

THE KINGDOM OF GOD IS...

Like seed that is sown and grows: 1

Like a king seeking a return on the talents he has invested: 1

Like finding hidden treasure: 1

Like a king who forgives debts and a slave who does not: 1

Like finding and buying the best pearl: 1

Like a master bringing out his old and new treasure: 1

Like a prince's wedding banquet: 1

source: Dr Stuart C. Weir. Mt, Mk, Lk, Rom, 1 Cor, 2 Cor, Gal, Eph, Col, 1 Tim, Heb, 1 Pet, Rev
note: The contributor and author have drawn on their own opinions when categorising the visual language used for the purposes of this graphic.

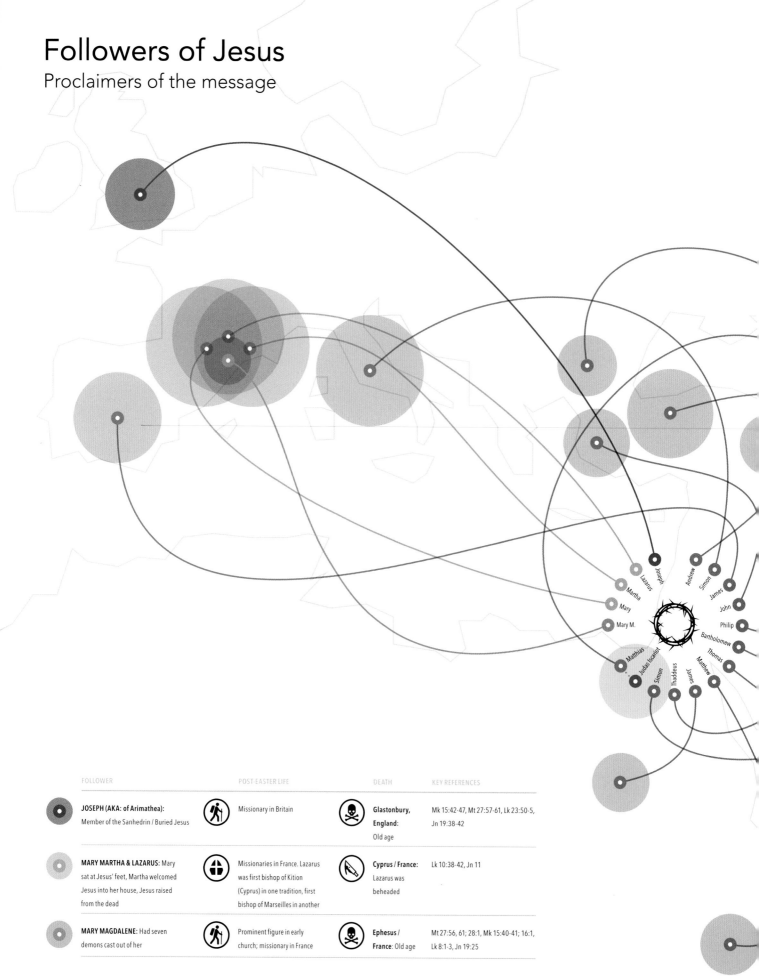

Followers of Jesus
Proclaimers of the message

Joseph
Lazarus
Martha
Mary
Mary M.
Andrew
Simon
James
John
Philip
Bartholomew
Thomas
Matthew
James
Thaddeus
Simon
Judas Iscariot
Matthias

FOLLOWER		POST-EASTER LIFE		DEATH	KEY REFERENCES
	JOSEPH (AKA: of Arimathea): Member of the Sanhedrin / Buried Jesus		Missionary in Britain	**Glastonbury, England:** Old age	Mk 15:42-47, Mt 27:57-61, Lk 23:50-5, Jn 19:38-42
	MARY MARTHA & LAZARUS: Mary sat at Jesus' feet, Martha welcomed Jesus into her house, Jesus raised from the dead		Missionaries in France. Lazarus was first bishop of Kition (Cyprus) in one tradition, first bishop of Marseilles in another	**Cyprus / France:** Lazarus was beheaded	Lk 10:38-42, Jn 11
	MARY MAGDALENE: Had seven demons cast out of her		Prominent figure in early church; missionary in France	**Ephesus / France:** Old age	Mt 27:56, 61; 28:1, Mk 15:40-41; 16:1, Lk 8:1-3, Jn 19:25

see pp176-181, 184-185

Direction of travel	Number of verses referenced			

FOLLOWER	POST-EASTER LIFE	DEATH	KEY REFERENCES
SIMON SON OF JONAH (AKA: Peter / Cephas / 'The rock'): Denied Jesus; declared Jesus as Messiah	Leader in Jerusalem church; first Bishop of Rome	**Rome:** Crucified upside down	Mk 1:16-20, 29-31; 3:13-19, Mt 4:18-20; 8:14-22; 10:1-4, Lk 4:38; 5:1-9; 6:13-16, Jn 1:35-42
ANDREW: Followed John the Baptist	Missionary in Thrace, Achaia, Scythia, Black Sea, Kiev, Novgorod and Byzantium	**Patras:** Crucified upside down on X-shaped cross	Mk 1:16-20, 29-31; 3:13-19, Mt 4:18-20; 10:1-4, Lk 6:13-16, Jn 1:35-42
JAMES (AKA: Son of Zebedee; one of the 'Sons of thunder'): Witnessed Transfiguration	Missionary in Iberia	**Jerusalem:** Killed by sword during Herod Agrippa's church persecution	Mk 1:19-20; 3:13-19, Mt 4:21-22; 10:1-4, Lk 5:10; 6:13-16
JOHN (AKA: Son of Zebedee; one of the 'Sons of thunder'): Witnessed Transfiguration	Moved to Ephesus and Patmos; wrote John's Gospel, Johannine letters and Revelation	**Ephesus:** Old age	Mk 1:19-20; 3:13-19, Mt 4:21-22; 10:1-4, Lk 5:10; 6:13-16
PHILIP: Met Greeks who wanted to see Jesus	Missionary in Greece, Phrygia and Syria	**Hierapolis:** Crucified upside down with hooks	Mk 3:13-19, Mt 10:1-4, Lk 6:13-16, Jn 1:43
BARTHOLOMEW (AKA: Nathanael): Witnessed the Ascension; Nathanael declared Jesus King of Israel	Missionary in India, Ethiopia, Mesopotamia, Parthia, Lycaonia and Armenia	**Albanopolis:** Flayed and crucified upside-down, or beheaded	Mk 3:13-19, Mt 10:1-4, Lk 6:13-16
THOMAS (AKA: Didymus / 'The twin'): Doubted the Resurrection until he saw Jesus	Missionary in India and Parthia	**India:** Speared	Mk 3:13-19, Mt 10:1-4, Lk 6:13-16
MATTHEW (AKA: Levi): Witnessed the Ascension	Missionary to Jews; author of Matthew's Gospel	**Ethiopia or Parthia:** Disputed	Mk 3:13-19, Mt 9:9; 10:1-4, Lk 6:13-16
JAMES (AKA: Son of Alphaeus)	Missionary in Egypt	**Ostrakine:** Crucifixion	Mk 3:13-19, Mt 10:1-4, Lk 6:13-16
THADDEUS (AKA: Judas son of James / Some manuscripts give his first name as Lebbaeus): Had to be distinguished from Judas Iscariot	Missionary in Judea, Samaria, Idumaea, Syria, Libya, Mesopotamia and Armenia	**Beirut:** Old age, beaten with clubs, or crucifixion	Mk 3:13-19, Mt 10:1-4, Lk 6:13-16, Jn 14:22
SIMON (AKA: The Zealot, The Cananaean)	Missionary in Egypt, Persia, Armenia and Syria	**Syria:** Sawn in half	Mk 3:13-19, Mt 10:1-4, Lk 6:13-16
JUDAS ISCARIOT: Betrayed Jesus	Fail. Betrayed Jesus for 30 pieces of silver	**Jerusalem:** Suicide by hanging	Mk 3:13-19, Mt 10:1-4; 27:3-10, Lk 6:13-16, Acts 1:18
MATTHIAS: Replaced Judas	Missionary in Judea and Colchis	**Jerusalem or Colchis:** Beheaded and stoned, or crucified	Acts 1:15-26

source: Professor James Crossley, Gospel of Matthew; Gospel of Mark; Gospel of Luke; Gospel of John; Acts of the Apostles; Christian traditions

note: The identity of some named followers is not clear. The same person may be given different names within the Gospel texts (e.g. Mary Magdalene and Mary of Bethany). Followers detailed here are among the more prominent of those mentioned in the Gospels. Later stories, traditions and legends about their lives after the resurrection of Jesus are numerous and often contradictory. A flavour of only some of these is given here.

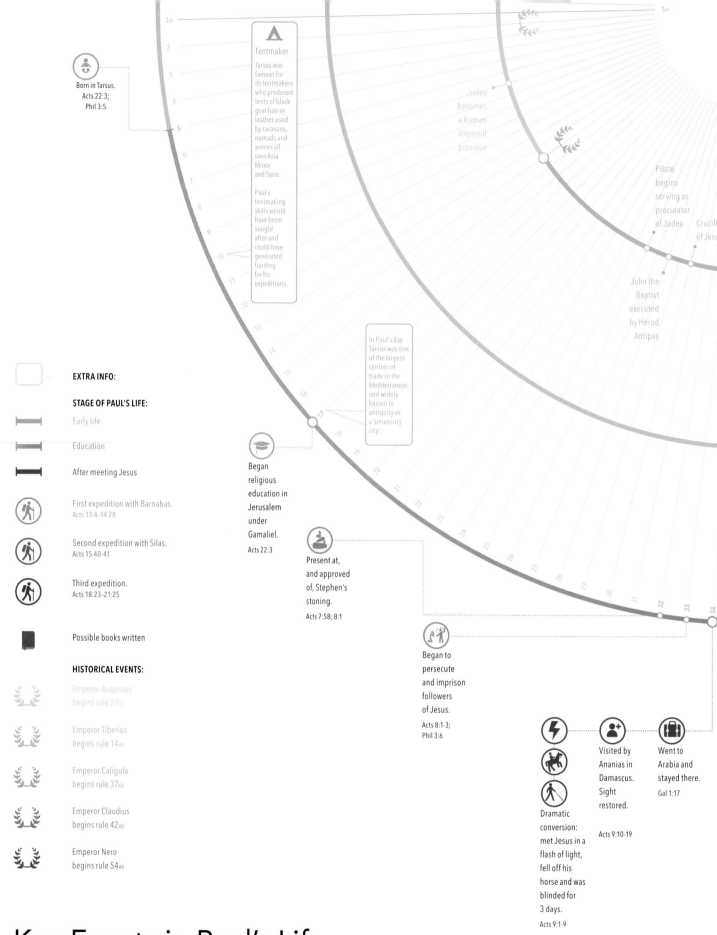

Born in Tarsus.
Acts 22:3; Phil 3:5

Tentmaker
Tarsus was famous for its tentmakers who produced tents of black goat hair or leather used by caravans, nomads and armies all over Asia Minor and Syria.

Paul's tentmaking skills would have been sought after and could have generated funding for his expeditions.

In Paul's day Tarsus was one of the largest centres of trade in the Mediterranean and widely known in antiquity as a 'university city'.

Judea becomes a Roman imperial province

Pilate begins serving as procurator of Judea

Crucifixion of Jesus

John the Baptist executed by Herod Antipas

Began religious education in Jerusalem under Gamaliel.
Acts 22:3

Present at, and approved of, Stephen's stoning.
Acts 7:58; 8:1

Began to persecute and imprison followers of Jesus.
Acts 8:1-3; Phil 3:6

Dramatic conversion: met Jesus in a flash of light, fell off his horse and was blinded for 3 days.
Acts 9:1-9

Visited by Ananias in Damascus. Sight restored.
Acts 9:10-19

Went to Arabia and stayed there.
Gal 1:17

EXTRA INFO:

STAGE OF PAUL'S LIFE:

Early life

Education

After meeting Jesus

First expedition with Barnabas.
Acts 13:4-14:28

Second expedition with Silas.
Acts 15:40-41

Third expedition.
Acts 18:23-21:25

Possible books written

HISTORICAL EVENTS:

Emperor Augustus begins rule 27BC

Emperor Tiberius begins rule 14AD

Emperor Caligula begins rule 37AD

Emperor Claudius begins rule 42AD

Emperor Nero begins rule 54AD

Key Events in Paul's Life
A chosen instrument, counting all a loss, often in chains

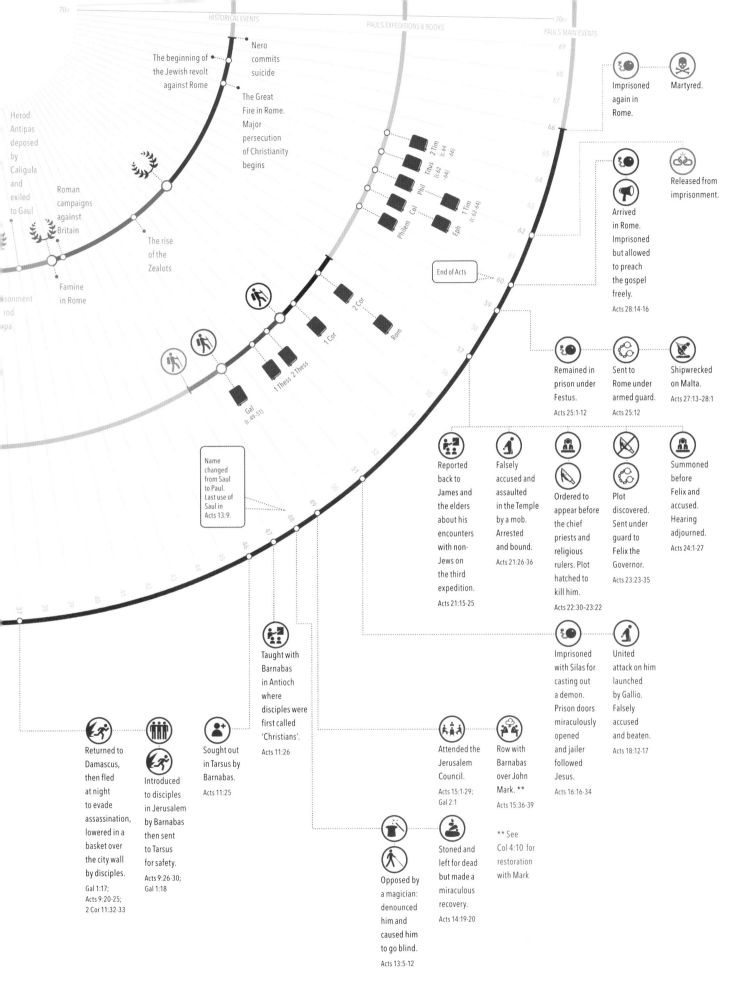

70

69

68

67

66

65

64

63

62

61

60

59

58

57

56

55

54

53

52

51

50

49

48

47

46

45

44

42

41

40

39

38

37

Nero commits suicide

The beginning of the Jewish revolt against Rome

The Great Fire in Rome. Major persecution of Christianity begins

Herod Antipas deposed by Caligula and exiled to Gaul

Roman campaigns against Britain

The rise of the Zealots

Famine in Rome

[...]sonment [...]rod [...]pa

2 Tim (c. 64 -66)

Titus (c. 62 -64)

Phil

Philem Col 1 Tim (c. 62-64)

Eph

2 Cor

1 Cor

Rom

1 Thess 2 Thess

Gal (c. 49-51)

Name changed from Saul to Paul. Last use of Saul in Acts 13:9.

End of Acts

Imprisoned again in Rome.

Martyred.

Released from imprisonment.

Arrived in Rome. Imprisoned but allowed to preach the gospel freely.
Acts 28:14-16

Remained in prison under Festus.
Acts 25:1-12

Sent to Rome under armed guard.
Acts 25:12

Shipwrecked on Malta.
Acts 27:13-28:1

Reported back to James and the elders about his encounters with non-Jews on the third expedition.
Acts 21:15-25

Falsely accused and assaulted in the Temple by a mob. Arrested and bound.
Acts 21:26-36

Ordered to appear before the chief priests and religious rulers. Plot hatched to kill him.
Acts 22:30–23:22

Plot discovered. Sent under guard to Felix the Governor.
Acts 23:23-35

Summoned before Felix and accused. Hearing adjourned.
Acts 24:1-27

Imprisoned with Silas for casting out a demon. Prison doors miraculously opened and jailer followed Jesus.
Acts 16:16-34

United attack on him launched by Gallio. Falsely accused and beaten.
Acts 18:12-17

Returned to Damascus, then fled at night to evade assassination, lowered in a basket over the city wall by disciples.
Gal 1:17;
Acts 9:20-25;
2 Cor 11:32-33

Introduced to disciples in Jerusalem by Barnabas then sent to Tarsus for safety.
Acts 9:26-30;
Gal 1:18

Sought out in Tarsus by Barnabas.
Acts 11:25

Taught with Barnabas in Antioch where disciples were first called 'Christians'.
Acts 11:26

Attended the Jerusalem Council.
Acts 15:1-29;
Gal 2:1

Row with Barnabas over John Mark. ✱✱
Acts 15:36-39

✱✱ See Col 4:10 for restoration with Mark

Opposed by a magician: denounced him and caused him to go blind.
Acts 13:5-12

Stoned and left for dead but made a miraculous recovery.
Acts 14:19-20

source: Dates of Paul's main events, Paul's expeditions and books and historical events derived from: Apostle Paul's Timeline retrieved from https://www.blueletterbible.org/study/paul/timeline.cfm. Stage of Paul's life and extra info David Painting and Karen Sawrey.
note: It is not always possible to be precise with dates for Paul's life; dates are contested. Author has used personal opinion when selecting this data. ✱ Scholars generally agree that Jesus was crucified between AD 30 and AD 36.

Paul's Journeys
And so we came to Rome

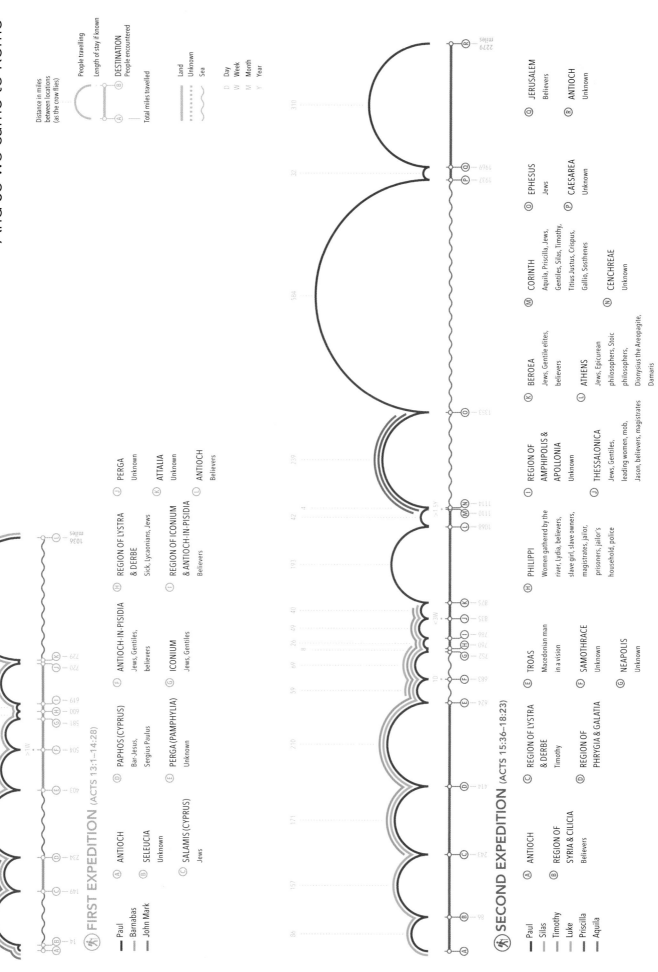

Distance in miles between locations (as the crow flies)

People travelling
Length of stay if known

Ⓐ **DESTINATION**
Ⓑ People encountered

Total miles travelled

Land
Unknown
Sea

D Day
W Week
M Month
Y Year

FIRST EXPEDITION (ACTS 13:1–14:28)

— Paul
— Barnabas
— John Mark

Ⓐ **ANTIOCH**

Ⓑ **SELEUCIA**
Unknown

Ⓒ **SALAMIS (CYPRUS)**
Jews

Ⓓ **PAPHOS (CYPRUS)**
Bar-Jesus,
Sergius Paulus

Ⓔ **PERGA (PAMPHYLIA)**
Unknown

Ⓕ **ANTIOCH-IN-PISIDIA**
Jews, Gentiles,
believers

Ⓖ **ICONIUM**
Jews, Gentiles

Ⓗ **REGION OF LYSTRA & DERBE**
Sick, Lycaonians, Jews

Ⓘ **REGION OF ICONIUM & ANTIOCH-IN-PISIDIA**
Believers

Ⓙ **PERGA**
Unknown

Ⓚ **ATTALIA**
Unknown

Ⓛ **ANTIOCH**
Believers

SECOND EXPEDITION (ACTS 15:36–18:23)

— Paul
— Silas
— Timothy
— Luke
— Priscilla
— Aquila

Ⓐ **ANTIOCH**

Ⓑ **REGION OF SYRIA & CILICIA**
Believers

Ⓒ **REGION OF LYSTRA & DERBE**
Timothy

Ⓓ **REGION OF PHRYGIA & GALATIA**

Ⓔ **TROAS**
Macedonian man
in a vision

Ⓕ **SAMOTHRACE**
Unknown

Ⓖ **NEAPOLIS**
Unknown

Ⓗ **PHILIPPI**
Women gathered by the
river, Lydia, believers,
slave girl, slave owners,
magistrates, jailor's
prisoners, jailor's
household, police

Ⓘ **REGION OF AMPHIPOLIS & APOLLONIA**
Unknown

Ⓙ **THESSALONICA**
Jews, Gentiles,
leading women, mob,
Jason, believers, magistrates

Ⓚ **BEROEA**
Jews, Gentile elites,
believers

Ⓛ **ATHENS**
Jews, Epicurean
philosophers, Stoic
philosophers,
Dionysius the Areopagite,
Damaris

Ⓜ **CORINTH**
Aquila, Priscilla, Jews,
Gentiles, Silas, Timothy,
Titius Justus, Crispus,
Gallio, Sosthenes

Ⓝ **CENCHREAE**
Unknown

Ⓞ **EPHESUS**
Jews

Ⓟ **CAESAREA**
Unknown

Ⓠ **JERUSALEM**
Believers

Ⓡ **ANTIOCH**
Unknown

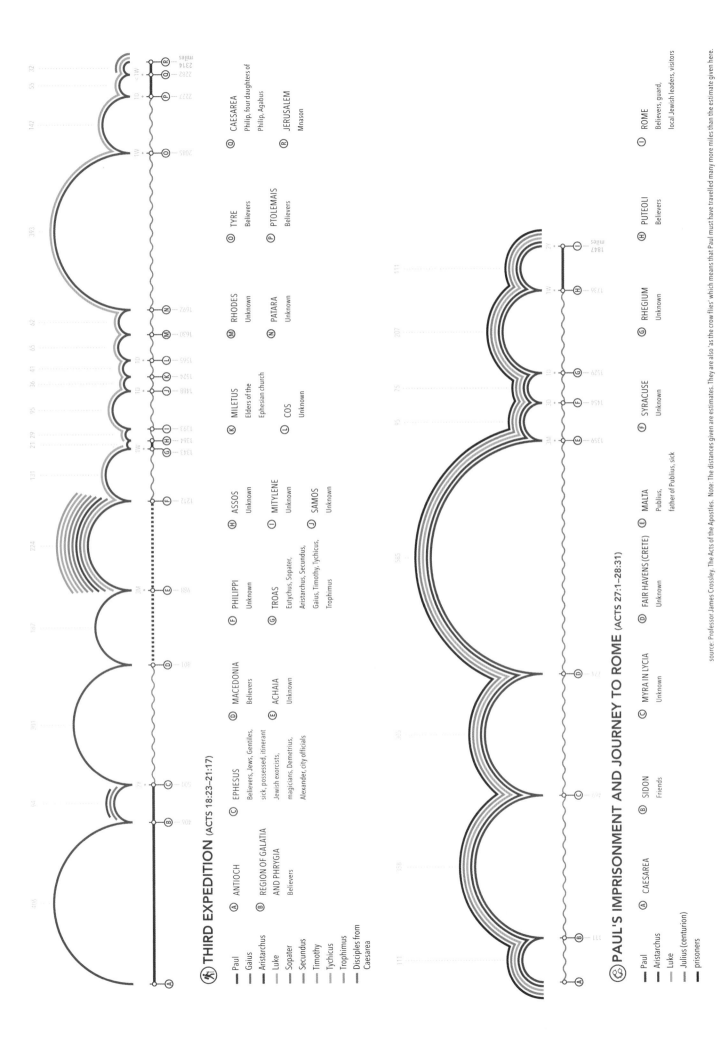

THIRD EXPEDITION (ACTS 18:23–21:17)

Paul
Gaius
Aristarchus
Luke
Sopater
Secundus
Timothy
Tychicus
Trophimus
Disciples from Caesarea

Ⓐ ANTIOCH

Ⓑ REGION OF GALATIA AND PHRYGIA
Believers

Ⓒ EPHESUS
Believers, Jews, Gentiles, sick, possessed, itinerant Jewish exorcists, magicians, Demetrius, Alexander, city officials

Ⓓ MACEDONIA
Believers

Ⓔ ACHAIA
Unknown

Ⓕ PHILIPPI
Unknown

Ⓖ TROAS
Eutychus, Sopater, Aristarchus, Secundus, Gaius, Timothy, Tychicus, Trophimus

Ⓗ ASSOS
Unknown

Ⓘ MITYLENE
Unknown

Ⓙ SAMOS
Unknown

Ⓚ MILETUS
Elders of the Ephesian church

Ⓛ COS
Unknown

Ⓜ RHODES
Unknown

Ⓝ PATARA
Unknown

Ⓞ TYRE
Believers

Ⓟ PTOLEMAIS
Believers

Ⓠ CAESAREA
Philip, four daughters of Philip, Agabus

Ⓡ JERUSALEM
Mnason

PAUL'S IMPRISONMENT AND JOURNEY TO ROME (ACTS 27:1–28:31)

Paul
Aristarchus
Luke
Julius (centurion)
prisoners

Ⓐ CAESAREA

Ⓑ SIDON
Friends

Ⓒ MYRA IN LYCIA
Unknown

Ⓓ FAIR HAVENS (CRETE)
Unknown

Ⓔ MALTA
Publius, father of Publius, sick

Ⓕ SYRACUSE
Unknown

Ⓖ RHEGIUM
Unknown

Ⓗ PUTEOLI
Believers

Ⓘ ROME
Believers, guard, local Jewish leaders, visitors

source: Professor James Crossley, The Acts of the Apostles. Note: The distances given are estimates. They are also 'as the crow flies' which means that Paul must have travelled many more miles than the estimate given here.

New Testament Letters
Signed, sent, received

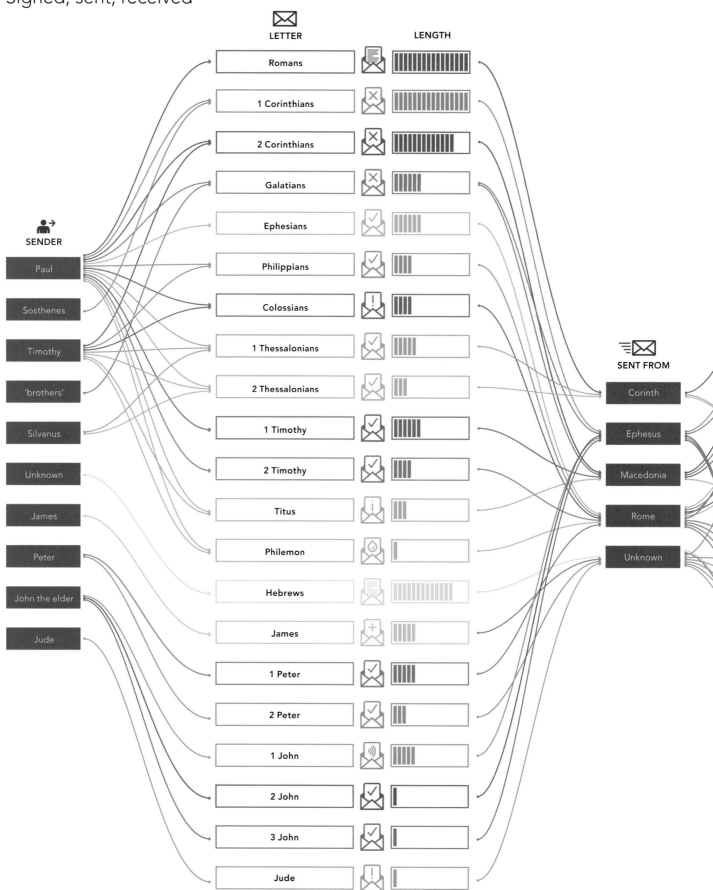

LETTER

LENGTH

SENDER

Paul
Sosthenes
Timothy
'brothers'
Silvanus
Unknown
James
Peter
John the elder
Jude

Romans
1 Corinthians
2 Corinthians
Galatians
Ephesians
Philippians
Colossians
1 Thessalonians
2 Thessalonians
1 Timothy
2 Timothy
Titus
Philemon
Hebrews
James
1 Peter
2 Peter
1 John
2 John
3 John
Jude

SENT FROM

Corinth
Ephesus
Macedonia
Rome
Unknown

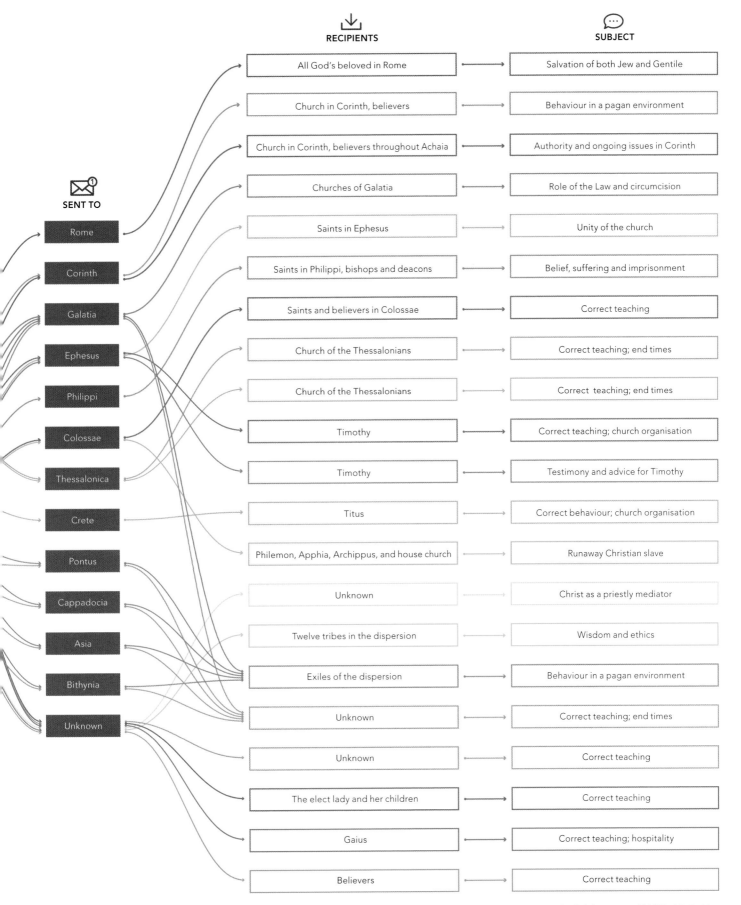

Extended essay   Correction   Encouragement   Warning   Instruction   Teaching   Plea   Manifesto   Number of chapters

RECIPIENTS

SUBJECT

SENT TO

Rome	All God's beloved in Rome	Salvation of both Jew and Gentile
Corinth	Church in Corinth, believers	Behaviour in a pagan environment
Galatia	Church in Corinth, believers throughout Achaia	Authority and ongoing issues in Corinth
Ephesus	Churches of Galatia	Role of the Law and circumcision
Philippi	Saints in Ephesus	Unity of the church
Colossae	Saints in Philippi, bishops and deacons	Belief, suffering and imprisonment
Thessalonica	Saints and believers in Colossae	Correct teaching
Crete	Church of the Thessalonians	Correct teaching; end times
Pontus	Church of the Thessalonians	Correct teaching; end times
Cappadocia	Timothy	Correct teaching; church organisation
Asia	Timothy	Testimony and advice for Timothy
Bithynia	Titus	Correct behaviour; church organisation
Unknown	Philemon, Apphia, Archippus, and house church	Runaway Christian slave

All God's beloved in Rome — Salvation of both Jew and Gentile
Church in Corinth, believers — Behaviour in a pagan environment
Church in Corinth, believers throughout Achaia — Authority and ongoing issues in Corinth
Churches of Galatia — Role of the Law and circumcision
Saints in Ephesus — Unity of the church
Saints in Philippi, bishops and deacons — Belief, suffering and imprisonment
Saints and believers in Colossae — Correct teaching
Church of the Thessalonians — Correct teaching; end times
Church of the Thessalonians — Correct teaching; end times
Timothy — Correct teaching; church organisation
Timothy — Testimony and advice for Timothy
Titus — Correct behaviour; church organisation
Philemon, Apphia, Archippus, and house church — Runaway Christian slave
Unknown — Christ as a priestly mediator
Twelve tribes in the dispersion — Wisdom and ethics
Exiles of the dispersion — Behaviour in a pagan environment
Unknown — Correct teaching; end times
Unknown — Correct teaching
The elect lady and her children — Correct teaching
Gaius — Correct teaching; hospitality
Believers — Correct teaching

source: Professor James Crossley. New Testament and early Christian interpretations; Felix Just, 'New Testament Statistics', http://catholic-resources.org/Bible/NT-Statistics-Greek.htm
note: Authorship of a number of New Testament letters is disputed. We make no judgement on authorship and provide the author implied either by the text and/or in early Christian interpretations.
In the cases of Jude and James, it is not clear which Jude and which James are implied.

FOLLOWERS OF JESUS

Paul

Paul, Silas and Timothy

Paul and Timothy

Peter's church

Paul and Silas
Paul and the Ephesian elders
Paul and Tyre disciples
Peter, John, others
Barnabas, Simeon (Niger), Lucius of Cyrene, Manaen and Saul
Jude
Epaphras
Apostles
Disciples and others
Church in Corinth
Writer Unknown

JESUS

Jesus

12 DISCIPLES

Peter

John

Peter and John

JESUS' FAMILY

Mary, mother of Jesus
Zechariah
James

JESUS' FAMILY
& FOLLOWERS OF JESUS

Peter, John, James, Andrew, Philip, Thomas, Bartholomew, Matthew, James, Simon, Judas son of James, women and Mary, mother of Jesus

NAMED INDIVIDUALS

Simeon
Anna

GENERAL PUBLIC

Worshippers in the Temple
Sailors

ROMAN AUTHORITIES

Cornelius

FOLLOWERS OF JOHN THE BAPTIST

John the Baptist's disciples

SPIRITUAL BEINGS

Angels

Prayers in the New Testament   Who, when, and how?

196 | 197

see pp106-107, 136-137

WHEN: Source scripture > event of prayer >> follow-up event

HOW:

- **Adoration and thanksgiving:** praising God
- **Confession:** asking for forgiveness
- **Corporate prayer:** praying with others
- **Cry from the heart:** a gut-wrenching plea
- **Intercession:** asking God to help others
- **Petition:** asking God for things we need
- **Prayer for healing**
- **Private prayer:** an individual praying alone
- **Spiritual warfare:** asking God to fight against evil
- **Submission:** following God's will
- **Unknown words:** we don't know what was said but we know they were praying
- **Waiting and listening:** hearing from God

WHEN	Adoration & thanksgiving	Confession	Corporate prayer	Cry from the heart	Intercession	Petition	Prayer for healing	Private prayer	Spiritual warfare	Submission	Unknown words	Waiting & listening
Acts 22:17 > Paul tells a crowd about his vision >> Paul is put in the barracks											X	
Acts 26:29 > Paul prays for people in court >> Paul is declared not guilty by Agrippa					X							
Acts 28:8-9 > Paul prays for Publius' father >> Paul cures the rest of the island							X					
Rom 1:10 > Paul prays to see the Romans >> Teaching on Gentiles						X						
Rom 10:1 > Paul prays for Israelites to be saved >> Teaching on Gentiles						X						
Rom 11:33-36 > Paul praises God in prayer	X											
Rom 15:31 > Paul asks the Romans to pray for him					X							
Rom 16:25-27 > Paul ends his letter to the Romans in prayer	X											
2 Cor 13:7-9 > Paul prays for the church in Corinth	X				X	X						
2 Cor 13:13 > Paul prays a blessing for the church in Corinth	X				X							
Eph 1:15-19 > Paul thanks God for the church in Ephesus	X				X							
Eph 3:14-20 > Paul prays for the church in Ephesus					X							
Phil 1:3-6 > Paul thanks God for Philippi	X				X							
Phil 1:9-11 > Paul prays for Philippi					X							
2 Tim 1:3 > Paul thanks God for Timothy	X				X							
Philem 4-6 > Paul thanks God for Philemon	X				X							
1 Thess 1:2-3 > Paul, Silas and Timothy thank God for the Thessalonians	X				X							
1 Thess 3:10-13 > Paul, Silas and Timothy pray for the Thessalonians					X							
2 Thess 1:11-12 > Paul, Silas and Timothy pray for the Thessalonians					X							
Col 1:3-4 > Paul and Timothy thank God for the church in Colossae	X				X							
Col 1:9-14 > Paul and Timothy pray for Colossae					X							
Acts 12:5 > Peter in prison >> Peter released from prison			X									
Acts 12:12 > Peter appears to Rhoda			X									
Acts 16:25 > Paul and Silas in prison >> Earthquake	X		X								X	
Acts 20:36 > Paul says goodbye to the Ephesian elders >> Paul gets on a boat to Tyre			X									
Acts 21:6 > Paul says goodbye to the disciples at Tyre >> Paul gets on a boat to Ptolemais			X									
Acts 4:24-25 > Peter and John released from prison			X								X	
Acts 13:1-3 > Barnabas and Saul commissioned			X							X		
Jude 24-25 > Jude praises God in prayer	X											
Col 4:12 > Paul tells Colossae of Epaphras' prayers					X							
Acts 2:42 > The early church prays together in fellowship			X								X	
Acts 6:4-6 > Choosing seven disciples to be administrators >> Stephen seized			X									X
2 Cor 1:10-11 > Paul gives thanks for prayers of others	X										X	
Heb 13:20-21 > Writer prays for the Hebrew church					X							
Mt 6:9-13 THE LORD'S PRAYER > Jesus gives the Beatitudes sermon	X					X			X	X		
Mt 11:25-30 > Jesus gives the Galilee sermon	X									X		
Mt 14:23 > Jesus goes to a mountain to pray >> Jesus and Peter walk on water								X		X		
Mt 26:36-46 > Jesus and disciples pray in the garden of Gethsemane >> Jesus' arrest								X	X	X		
Mt 27:45-50 > Jesus' crucifixion >> Death, Temple curtain rips, earth shakes, rocks split				X								
Mk 1:35 > Jesus goes to a solitary place to pray in the early morning >> Preaching and driving out demons								X		X		
Mk 6:41 > Jesus blesses the loaves and the fish	X											
Mk 6:46 > Jesus goes to a mountain to pray >> Jesus walks on water								X				
Mk 9:25 > Jesus heals a boy who has an evil spirit							X					
Mk 14:32-42 > Jesus and disciples pray in the garden of Gethsemane >> Jesus' arrest								X		X		
Mk 15:34 > Jesus' crucifixion >> Death, Temple curtain rips, centurion believes				X						X		
Lk 3:21 > Jesus' baptism >> Holy Spirit descends as dove								X		X		
Lk 5:16 > Jesus heals a man with leprosy								X				
Lk 6:12 > Jesus chooses His disciples								X		X		
Lk 9:18 > Peter acknowledges Jesus as Christ								X				
Lk 9:28 > Jesus, Peter, John and James go up a mountain to pray >> The Transfiguration								X		X		
Lk 10:21-22 > Jesus praises God	X											
Lk 11:1 > Jesus prays alone								X		X		
Lk 11:2-4 THE LORD'S PRAYER > Jesus teaches others his prayer	X	X				X			X	X		
Lk 22:40-45 > Jesus and disciples pray in the garden of Gethsemane >> Angel appears, Jesus' arrest					X			X	X	X		
Lk 23:46 > Jesus' crucifixion >> Death				X						X		
Lk 24:30 > Jesus breaks bread	X											
Jn 17 > Jesus prays for himself, his disciples and followers >> Jesus' arrest					X	X		X		X		
Heb 5:7 > Writer describes Jesus' prayers				X						X		
Acts 9:40 > Peter raises Tabitha from the dead							X					
Acts 10:9 > Peter sees a vision												X
3 Jn 2 > John prays for Gaius					X							
Rev 1:5-6 > John's vision	X											
Acts 8:14-17 > Peter and John pray for believers to receive Holy Spirit >> Simon the Sorcerer confronted					X						X	
Lk 1:46-55 MAGNIFICAT > Mary sings praise to God after seeing angel	X											
Lk 1:67-75 > Zechariah sings praise and prophesies after officially naming John	X											
Jas 5:13-16 > Prayers of faith			X				X					
Acts 1:14 > Disciples select a replacement for Judas Iscariot >> Replacement elected			X								X	
Acts 1:24 > Believers elect a leader from the disciples >> Leader elected			X									X
Lk 2:29-32 > Jesus' circumcision	X											
Lk 2:37 > Jesus' circumcision >> Anna prophesies											X	
Lk 1:10 > People pray while the priest enters the Holy Place >> Angel of the Lord appears to Zecharaiah											X	
Acts 27:29 > Sailors on boat with Paul pray about the storm >> Paul feeds the sailors					X							
Acts 10:2-6 > Cornelius sees an angel >> Cornelius summons Peter											X	X
Acts 10:30-32 > Cornelius explains his vision												X
Lk 5:33 > Religious rulers question Jesus about fasting										X	X	
Lk 2:14 > Angels visit shepherds to tell of Jesus' birth	X											

In people's homes
4 prayers: 3%

In the synagogue/Temple
4 prayers: 3%

In gardens
4 prayers: 3%

At the beach/lake
3 prayers: 2%

In Prison
2 prayers: 2%

In the countryside
1 prayer: 1%

On the Cross
8 prayers: 7%

In the cities,
towns & villages
15 prayers: 12%

In the mountains
16 prayers: 13%

WHERE:

Not mentioned
in scripture
67 prayers: 54%

Prayers in the New Testament   Where and what?

see pp106-107, 136-137

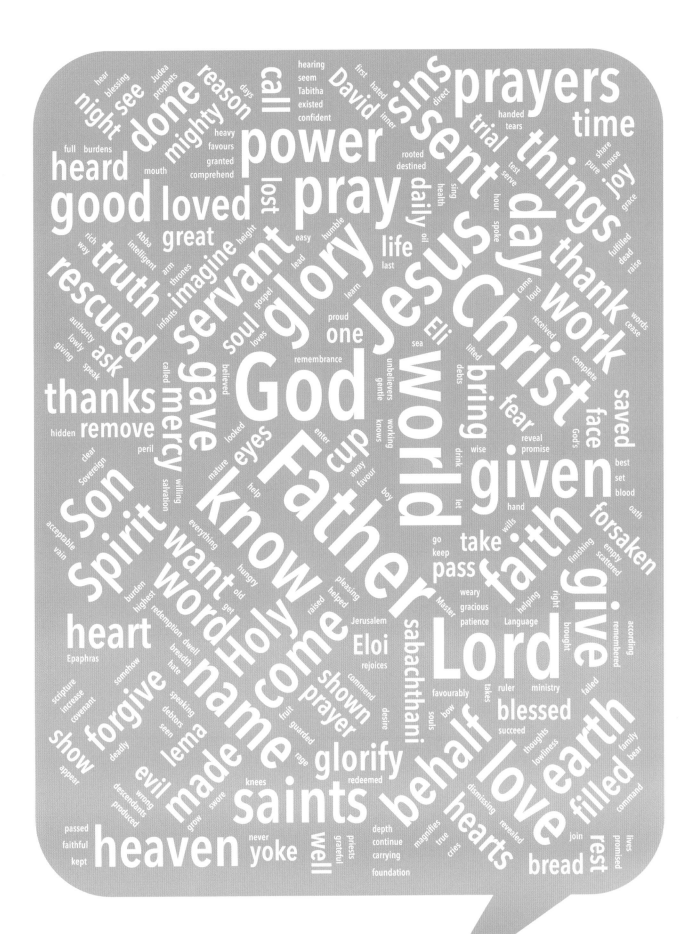

WHAT WAS MOST PRAYED

source: Jess Bailey. 24-7 PRAYER www.24-7prayer.com. Mt, Mk, Lk, Jn, Acts, Rom, 1 Cor, 2 Cor, Gal, Eph, Phil, Col, 1 Thess, 2 Thess, 1 Tim, 2 Tim, Philem, Heb, Jas, 3 Jn, Jude, Rev.
note: The data contributor and author have drawn on personal choices when collating and categorising this data.

Hebrews

Jesus: come not to abolish but to complete

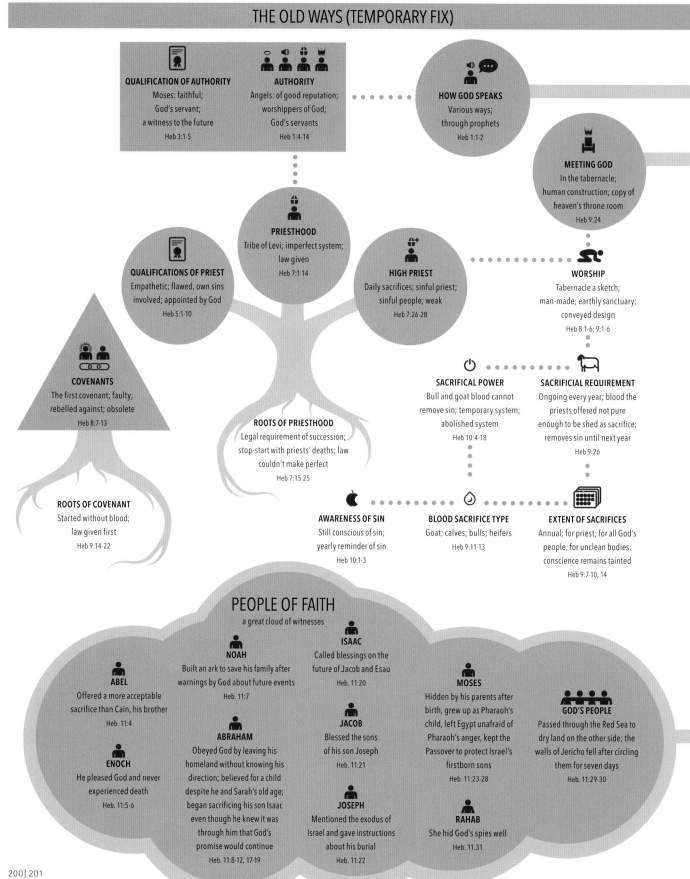

THE OLD WAYS (TEMPORARY FIX)

QUALIFICATION OF AUTHORITY
Moses: faithful;
God's servant;
a witness to the future
Heb 3:1-5

AUTHORITY
Angels: of good reputation;
worshippers of God;
God's servants
Heb 1:4-14

HOW GOD SPEAKS
Various ways;
through prophets
Heb 1:1-2

MEETING GOD
In the tabernacle;
human construction; copy of
heaven's throne room
Heb 9:24

QUALIFICATIONS OF PRIEST
Empathetic; flawed, own sins
involved; appointed by God
Heb 5:1-10

PRIESTHOOD
Tribe of Levi; imperfect system;
law given
Heb 7:1-14

HIGH PRIEST
Daily sacrifices; sinful priest;
sinful people; weak
Heb 7:26-28

WORSHIP
Tabernacle a sketch;
man-made; earthly sanctuary;
conveyed design
Heb 8:1-6; 9:1-6

COVENANTS
The first covenant; faulty;
rebelled against; obsolete
Heb 8:7-13

ROOTS OF PRIESTHOOD
Legal requirement of succession;
stop-start with priests' deaths; law
couldn't make perfect
Heb 7:15-25

SACRIFICAL POWER
Bull and goat blood cannot
remove sin; temporary system;
abolished system
Heb 10:4-18

SACRIFICIAL REQUIREMENT
Ongoing every year; blood the
priests offered not pure
enough to be shed as sacrifice;
removes sin until next year
Heb 9:26

ROOTS OF COVENANT
Started without blood;
law given first
Heb 9:14-22

AWARENESS OF SIN
Still conscious of sin;
yearly reminder of sin
Heb 10:1-3

BLOOD SACRIFICE TYPE
Goat; calves; bulls; heifers
Heb 9:11-13

EXTENT OF SACRIFICES
Annual; for priest; for all God's
people; for unclean bodies;
conscience remains tainted
Heb 9:7-10, 14

PEOPLE OF FAITH
a great cloud of witnesses

NOAH
Built an ark to save his family after
warnings by God about future events
Heb. 11:7

ISAAC
Called blessings on the
future of Jacob and Esau
Heb. 11:20

ABEL
Offered a more acceptable
sacrifice than Cain, his brother
Heb. 11:4

ABRAHAM
Obeyed God by leaving his
homeland without knowing his
direction; believed for a child
despite he and Sarah's old age;
began sacrificing his son Isaac
even though he knew it was
through him that God's
promise would continue
Heb. 11:8-12, 17-19

JACOB
Blessed the sons
of his son Joseph
Heb. 11:21

MOSES
Hidden by his parents after
birth, grew up as Pharaoh's
child, left Egypt unafraid of
Pharaoh's anger, kept the
Passover to protect Israel's
firstborn sons
Heb. 11:23-28

GOD'S PEOPLE
Passed through the Red Sea to
dry land on the other side; the
walls of Jericho fell after circling
them for seven days
Heb. 11:29-30

ENOCH
He pleased God and never
experienced death
Heb. 11:5-6

JOSEPH
Mentioned the exodus of
Israel and gave instructions
about his burial
Heb. 11:22

RAHAB
She hid God's spies well
Heb. 11:31

see pp72-73, 166-167

JESUS (PERMANENT FIX)

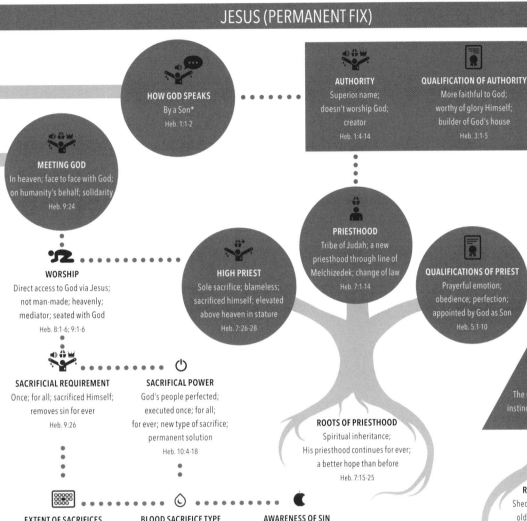

HOW GOD SPEAKS
By a Son*
Heb. 1:1-2

AUTHORITY
Superior name;
doesn't worship God;
creator
Heb. 1:4-14

QUALIFICATION OF AUTHORITY
More faithful to God;
worthy of glory Himself;
builder of God's house
Heb. 3:1-5

MEETING GOD
In heaven; face to face with God;
on humanity's behalf; solidarity
Heb. 9:24

PRIESTHOOD
Tribe of Judah; a new
priesthood through line of
Melchizedek; change of law
Heb. 7:1-14

WORSHIP
Direct access to God via Jesus;
not man-made; heavenly;
mediator; seated with God
Heb. 8:1-6; 9:1-6

HIGH PRIEST
Sole sacrifice; blameless;
sacrificed himself; elevated
above heaven in stature
Heb. 7:26-28

QUALIFICATIONS OF PRIEST
Prayerful emotion;
obedience; perfection;
appointed by God as Son
Heb. 5:1-10

SACRIFICIAL REQUIREMENT
Once; for all; sacrificed Himself;
removes sin for ever
Heb. 9:26

SACRIFICAL POWER
God's people perfected;
executed once; for all;
for ever; new type of sacrifice;
permanent solution
Heb. 10:4-18

COVENANTS
The new covenant; intuitive;
instinctive; God's mercy flowing
Heb. 8:7-13

ROOTS OF PRIESTHOOD
Spiritual inheritance;
His priesthood continues for ever;
a better hope than before
Heb. 7:15-25

ROOTS OF COVENANT
Shed blood begins covenant;
old covenant redeemed by
Jesus' death; blood purifies;
forgiveness
Heb. 9:14-22

EXTENT OF SACRIFICES
Spiritual; sacrificed Himself;
unblemished; cleanses
consciences; purifies;
enables true worship
Heb. 9:7-10, 14

BLOOD SACRIFICE TYPE
His own blood;
uncreated; perfect life
Heb. 9:11-13

AWARENESS OF SIN
Clears conscience;
awareness of past gone
Heb. 10:1-3

PEOPLE OF FAITH
a great cloud of witnesses

GOD'S PEOPLE
Jesus makes their faith perfect
Heb. 11:29-30

MOSES
Jesus makes their faith perfect
Heb. 11:23-28

ISAAC
Jesus makes their faith perfect
Heb. 11:20

JACOB
Jesus makes their faith perfect
Heb. 11:21

NOAH
Jesus makes their faith perfect
Heb. 11:7

ABEL
Jesus makes their faith perfect
Heb. 11:4

RAHAB
Jesus makes their faith perfect
Heb. 11:31

JOSEPH
Jesus makes their faith perfect
Heb. 11:22

ABRAHAM
Jesus makes their faith perfect
Heb. 11:8-12, 17-19

ENOCH
Jesus makes their faith perfect
Heb. 11:5-6

source: Dr Stuart C. Weir. Hebrews 1; 3; 5; 7-10.
note: *Although God speaks through his Son, this does not mean that prophecy has ceased.

THE OLD TESTAMENT

RELATIONSHIP RESTORED
A new heaven and earth
REV 21:1-3

THE NEW TESTAMENT

STAGE 5   STAGE 6   STAGE 7   STAGE 8

Revelation: the Hope of Things to Come
Biblical promises and anticipation fulfilled

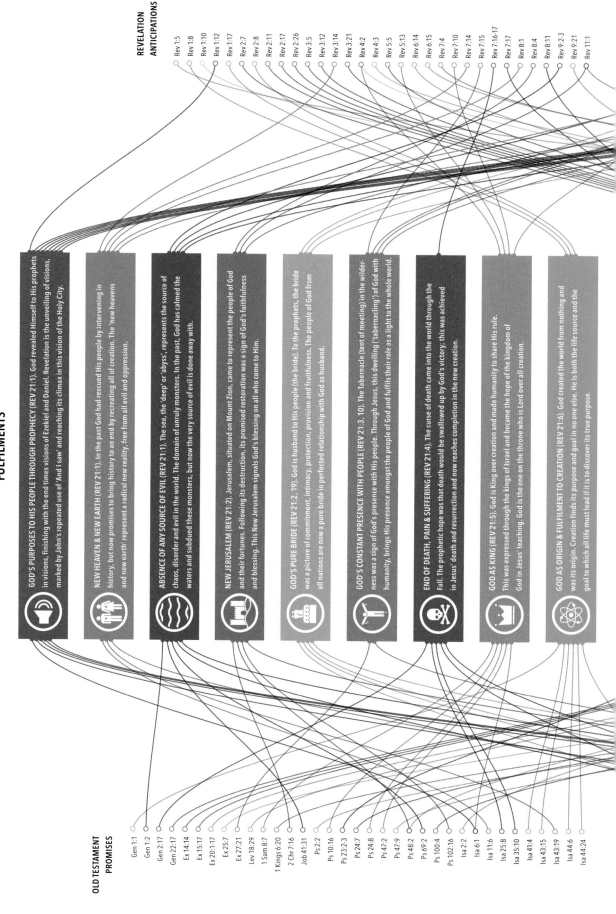

FULFILMENTS

REVELATION ANTICIPATIONS

OLD TESTAMENT PROMISES

see pp32-33, 126-127

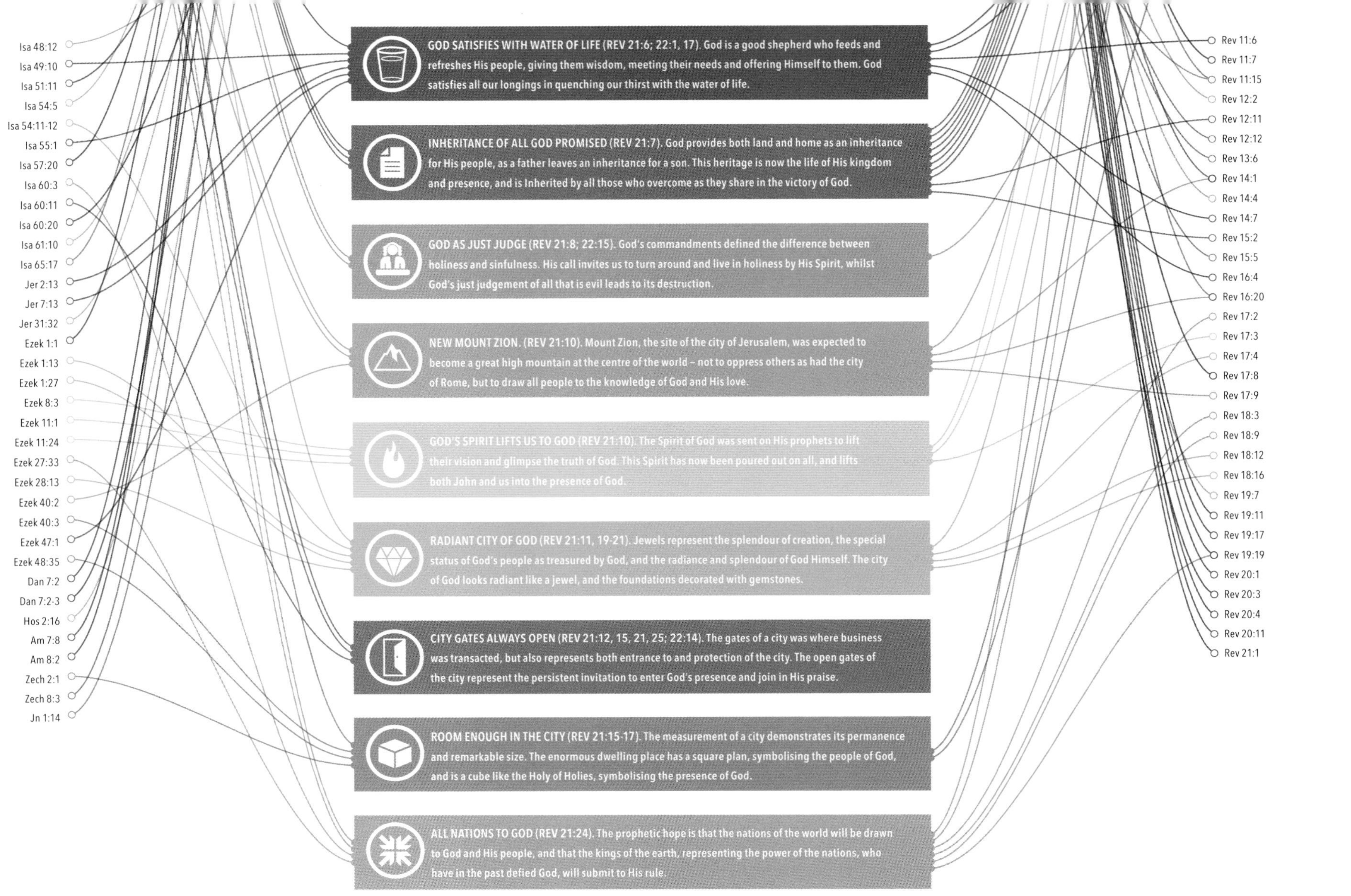

Top reference labels (Revelation verses):
Rev 11:6, Rev 11:7, Rev 11:15, Rev 12:2, Rev 12:11, Rev 12:12, Rev 13:6, Rev 14:1, Rev 14:4, Rev 14:7, Rev 15:2, Rev 15:5, Rev 16:4, Rev 16:20, Rev 17:2, Rev 17:3, Rev 17:4, Rev 17:8, Rev 17:9, Rev 18:3, Rev 18:9, Rev 18:12, Rev 18:16, Rev 19:7, Rev 19:11, Rev 19:17, Rev 19:19, Rev 20:1, Rev 20:3, Rev 20:4, Rev 20:11, Rev 21:1

GOD SATISFIES WITH WATER OF LIFE (REV 21:6; 22:1, 17). God is a good shepherd who feeds and refreshes His people, giving them wisdom, meeting their needs and offering Himself to them. God satisfies all our longings in quenching our thirst with the water of life.

INHERITANCE OF ALL GOD PROMISED (REV 21:7). God provides both land and home as an inheritance for His people, as a father leaves an inheritance for a son. This heritage is now the life of His kingdom and presence, and is inherited by all those who overcome as they share in the victory of God.

GOD AS JUST JUDGE (REV 21:8; 22:15). God's commandments defined the difference between holiness and sinfulness. His call invites us to turn around and live in holiness by His Spirit, whilst God's just judgement of all that is evil leads to its destruction.

NEW MOUNT ZION. (REV 21:10). Mount Zion, the site of the city of Jerusalem, was expected to become a great high mountain at the centre of the world – not to oppress others as had the city of Rome, but to draw all people to the knowledge of God and His love.

GOD'S SPIRIT LIFTS US TO GOD (REV 21:10). The Spirit of God was sent on His prophets to lift their vision and glimpse the truth of God. This Spirit has now been poured out on all, and lifts both John and us into the presence of God.

RADIANT CITY OF GOD (REV 21:11, 19-21). Jewels represent the splendour of creation, the special status of God's people as treasured by God, and the radiance and splendour of God Himself. The city of God looks radiant like a jewel, and the foundations decorated with gemstones.

CITY GATES ALWAYS OPEN (REV 21:12, 15, 21, 25; 22:14). The gates of a city was where business was transacted, but also represents both entrance to and protection of the city. The open gates of the city represent the persistent invitation to enter God's presence and join in His praise.

ROOM ENOUGH IN THE CITY (REV 21:15-17). The measurement of a city demonstrates its permanence and remarkable size. The enormous dwelling place has a square plan, symbolising the people of God, and is a cube like the Holy of Holies, symbolising the presence of God.

ALL NATIONS TO GOD (REV 21:24). The prophetic hope is that the nations of the world will be drawn to God and His people, and that the kings of the earth, representing the power of the nations, who have in the past defied God, will submit to His rule.

Bottom reference labels:
Isa 48:12, Isa 49:10, Isa 51:11, Isa 54:5, Isa 54:11-12, Isa 55:1, Isa 57:20, Isa 60:3, Isa 60:11, Isa 60:20, Isa 61:10, Isa 65:17, Jer 2:13, Jer 7:13, Jer 31:32, Ezek 1:1, Ezek 1:13, Ezek 1:27, Ezek 8:3, Ezek 11:1, Ezek 11:24, Ezek 27:33, Ezek 28:13, Ezek 40:2, Ezek 40:3, Ezek 47:1, Ezek 48:35, Dan 7:2, Dan 7:3, Hos 2:16, Am 7:8, Am 8:2, Zech 2:1, Zech 8:3, Jn 1:14

source: Revd Dr Ian Paul www.psephizo.com. Revelation.

note: The information here comes from Ian Paul's own study and research, but is in line with mainstream scholarly views on Revelation.

The Bible's Big Picture From beginning to end … God is Love

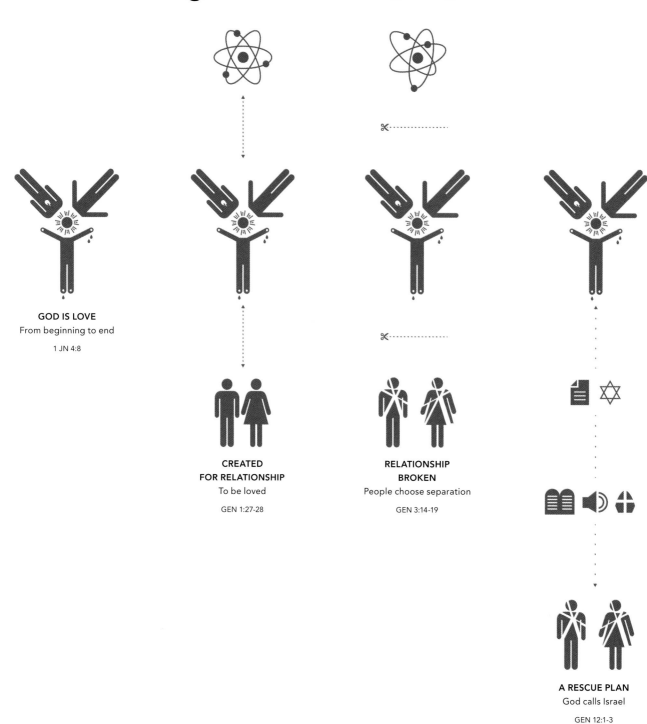

GOD IS LOVE

From beginning to end

1 JN 4:8

**CREATED
FOR RELATIONSHIP**

To be loved

GEN 1:27-28

**RELATIONSHIP
BROKEN**

People choose separation

GEN 3:14-19

A RESCUE PLAN

God calls Israel

GEN 12:1-3

THE OLD TESTAMENT

STAGE 1 ———————————————— STAGE 2 ———————————— STAGE 3 ———————————— STAGE 4 ————

see pP32-33, 166-167, 187

RELATIONSHIP RESTORED

A new heaven and earth

REV 21:1-3

JESUS COMES

God is King

JN 1:10-14

STARTING OVER

A new beginning: the church

ACTS 2:1-4

THE PLAN REJECTED

People choose a king

1 SAM 8:5-7

THE NEW TESTAMENT

STAGE 5   STAGE 6   STAGE 7   STAGE 8

source: David Painting, Alister MacInnes, Karen Sawrey. The Bible.

note: There are many themes that could be used when describing the 'big picture' of the Bible. The author and contributors have chosen to use the theme of God's love and His commitment to relationship.

ABOUT THE BIBLE:
TODAY'S TALLY

Scripture Distribution

Languages with Translations of Scripture

see pp 184-185, 188-189

Scripture Distribution
Spreading the word:
by country, continent and globe

ESTIMATED TOTAL SCRIPTURES DISTRIBUTED ANNUALLY:
Calculated by WCD as total number of Bibles (+/- the Deuterocanon) + distinct
New Testaments + distinct Bible portions (single books of the Bible, usually a Gospel).

Legend:

- 10,000, 001 - 100,000,000+
- 1,000,001 - 10,000, 000
- 100,001 - 1,000,000
- 10,001 -100,080
- 1,001 - 10,000
- 101 - 1,000
- 0 - 100
- No Data

source: Todd M. Johnson and Gina A. Zurlo, eds., World Christian Database (Leiden/Boston: Brill, accessed August 2017).
note: Calculation for scripture distribution (Bibles, New Testaments and Bible portions) by country is based on an annual average 2012-2016 plus a factor in each country for commercial and other distribution.
Where UBS figures are given for a region or group of countries, the distribution has generally been allocated to individual countries according to the number of Christians in each country.

Scripture Distribution

Ranking the liberty index and distributions per capita

GLOBE: ▯ = 266,414,000   👫 = 7,466,964,000   🛉 = 0.03568

ESTIMATED TOTAL SCRIPTURES DISTRIBUTED ANNUALLY:
Calculated by WCD as total number of Bibles (+/- the Deuterocanon) + distinct New Testaments + distinct Bible portions (single books of the Bible, usually a Gospel).

- 10,000,001 - 100,000,000+
- 1,000,001 - 10,000,000
- 100,001 - 1,000,000
- 10,001 - 100,000
- 1,001 - 10,000
- 101 - 1,000
- 0 - 100
- No Data

POPULATION

ESTIMATED TOTAL SCRIPTURES DISTRIBUTED PER CAPITA

* Includes Hong Kong, Macao and Taiwan

RELIGIOUS LIBERTY INDEX:
The freedom to practise one's religion with the full range of religious rights specified in the UN's 1948 Universal Declaration of Human Rights. The index is a scale of 1 to 10 with 10 representing the greatest freedom.

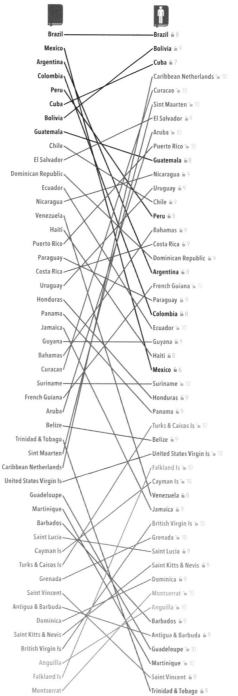

LATIN AMERICA: ▯ = 82,172,000

NORTH AMERICA: ▯ = 59,527,000

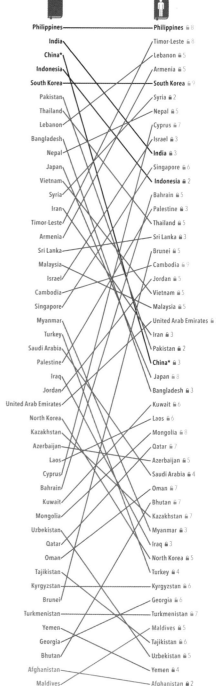

ASIA: ▯ = 81,542,000

see pp 184-185, 188-189

EUROPE: 📖 = 31,201,000

Spain	Spain 📖 7
United Kingdom	United Kingdom 📖 6
Germany	Greece 📖 5
Greece	Isle of Man 📖 10
Russia	Germany 📖 6
France	Channel Is 📖 10
Ukraine	Norway 📖 8
Netherlands	Monaco 📖 9
Italy	France 📖 5
Portugal	Ukraine 📖 7
Romania	Netherlands 📖 8
Sweden	Finland 📖 9
Norway	Gibraltar 📖 10
Austria	Estonia 📖 9
Belgium	Portugal 📖 9
Finland	Faeroe Is 📖 10
Czech Republic	Iceland 📖 8
Poland	Malta 📖 9
Switzerland	Denmark 📖 8
Denmark	Sweden 📖 6
Serbia	Latvia 📖 8
Hungary	Austria 📖 8
Croatia	Croatia 📖 8
Moldova	Serbia 📖 7
Bulgaria	Russia 📖 2
Latvia	Moldova 📖 6
Albania	Czech Republic 📖 8
Estonia	Montenegro 📖 8
Lithuania	Switzerland 📖 8
Belarus	Liechtenstein 📖 8
Slovenia	Belgium 📖 7
Slovakia	Slovenia 📖 9
Ireland	Albania 📖 9
Macedonia	Andorra 📖 9
Bosnia-Herzegovina	Lithuania 📖 8
Malta	Romania 📖 5
Montenegro	Luxembourg 📖 9
Channel Is	Hungary 📖 7
Isle of Man	Bulgaria 📖 6
Iceland	Italy 📖 7
Luxembourg	Macedonia 📖 8
Kosovo	Slovakia 📖 8
Monaco	Ireland 📖 8
Faeroe Is	Poland 📖 8
Gibraltar	Bosnia-Herzegovina 📖 7
Andorra	Belarus 📖 6
Liechtenstein	Kosovo 📖 6
San Marino	San Marino 📖 10
Holy See	Holy See 📖 3

AFRICA: 📖 = 10,901,000

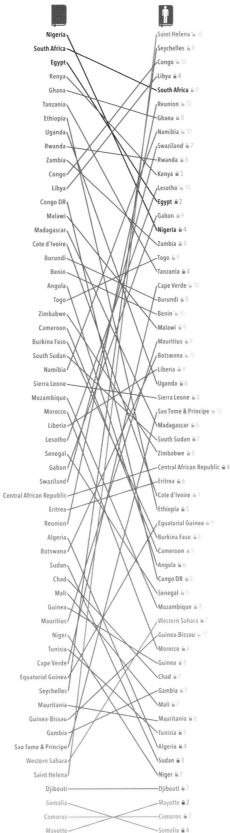

Nigeria	Saint Helena 📖 10
South Africa	Seychelles 📖 9
Egypt	Congo 📖 10
Kenya	Libya 📖 4
Ghana	South Africa 📖 9
Tanzania	Reunion 📖 10
Ethiopia	Ghana 📖 8
Uganda	Namibia 📖 10
Rwanda	Swaziland 📖 7
Zambia	Rwanda 📖 8
Congo	Kenya 📖 5
Libya	Lesotho 📖 10
Congo DR	Egypt 📖 2
Malawi	Gabon 📖 9
Madagascar	Nigeria 📖 4
Cote d'Ivoire	Zambia 📖 8
Burundi	Togo 📖 9
Benin	Tanzania 📖 4
Angola	Cape Verde 📖 10
Togo	Burundi 📖 8
Zimbabwe	Benin 📖 10
Cameroon	Malawi 📖 9
Burkina Faso	Mauritius 📖 9
South Sudan	Botswana 📖 10
Namibia	Liberia 📖 9
Sierra Leone	Uganda 📖 6
Mozambique	Sierra Leone 📖 8
Morocco	Sao Tome & Principe 📖 10
Liberia	Madagascar 📖 8
Lesotho	South Sudan 📖 7
Senegal	Zimbabwe 📖 8
Gabon	Central African Republic 📖 4
Swaziland	Eritrea 📖 6
Central African Republic	Cote d'Ivoire 📖 9
Eritrea	Ethiopia 📖 5
Reunion	Equatorial Guinea 📖 9
Algeria	Burkina Faso 📖 8
Botswana	Cameroon 📖 9
Sudan	Angola 📖 6
Chad	Congo DR 📖 8
Mali	Senegal 📖 9
Guinea	Mozambique 📖 8
Mauritius	Western Sahara 📖 7
Niger	Guinea-Bissau 📖 10
Tunisia	Morocco 📖 6
Cape Verde	Guinea 📖 8
Equatorial Guinea	Chad 📖 7
Seychelles	Gambia 📖 9
Mauritania	Mali 📖 7
Guinea-Bissau	Mauritania 📖 6
Gambia	Tunisia 📖 5
Sao Tome & Principe	Algeria 📖 4
Western Sahara	Sudan 📖 3
Saint Helena	Niger 📖 7
Djibouti	Djibouti 📖 7
Somalia	Mayotte 📖 2
Comoros	Comoros 📖 7
Mayotte	Somalia 📖 4

OCEANIA: 📖 = 1,071,000

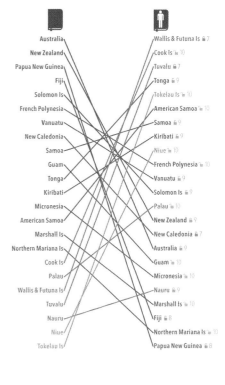

Australia	Wallis & Futuna Is 📖 7
New Zealand	Cook Is 📖 10
Papua New Guinea	Tuvalu 📖 7
Fiji	Tonga 📖 9
Solomon Is	Tokelau Is 📖 10
French Polynesia	American Samoa 📖 10
Vanuatu	Samoa 📖 9
New Caledonia	Kiribati 📖 9
Samoa	Niue 📖 10
Guam	French Polynesia 📖 10
Tonga	Vanuatu 📖 9
Kiribati	Solomon Is 📖 9
Micronesia	Palau 📖 10
American Samoa	New Zealand 📖 9
Marshall Is	New Caledonia 📖 7
Northern Mariana Is	Australia 📖 9
Cook Is	Guam 📖 10
Palau	Micronesia 📖 10
Wallis & Futuna Is	Nauru 📖 9
Tuvalu	Marshall Is 📖 10
Nauru	Fiji 📖 8
Niue	Northern Mariana Is 📖 10
Tokelau Is	Papua New Guinea 📖 8

source: Todd M. Johnson and Gina A. Zurlo, eds.,
World Christian Database (Leiden/Boston: Brill, accessed August 2017)

Population source: United Nations, Department of Economic and Social Affairs,
Population Division (2017). World Population Prospects: The 2017 Revision.

note: Calculation for scripture distribution (Bibles, New Testaments and Bible
portions) by country is based on an annual average 2012-2016 plus a factor in
each country for commercial and other distribution. Where UBS figures are given
for a region or group of countries, the distribution has generally been allocated
to individual countries according to the number of Christians in each country.

Languages with Translations of Scripture

The count by hub continent with current global mother tongue speakers

Continent totals — :Population — :Total scriptures distributed annually — :Religious liberty index — :Hub languages with scripture — :Hub languages without scripture

Current Global mother tongue speakers — Hub language with translations *(language listed only in its main location)*

Africa

:1225081000

:10901000

:6

1915:**164**
1965:**417**
2017:**894**

:1292

Africa

894

16100 ‡Kx'au||'ein. 292000 Aari. 276000 Abé. 87600 Abidji. 44200 Abua. 1997000 Acholi. 38400 Adele. 684000 Adhola. 167000 Adioukrou. 2561000 Afar. 6227000 Afrikaans. 456000 Agatu. 41000 Aghem. 36800 Agwagwune. 187000 Ahanta. 700000 Aja. 9767000 Akan. 82900 Akebu. 148000 Akoose. 99900 Alago. 39900 Alladian. 1820000 Alur. 121000 Ama. 42700 Amba. 27544000 Amharic. 205000 Anuak. 191000 Anufo. 1375000 Anyin. 27765000 Arabic, Algerian Spoken. 2284000 Arabic, Chadian Spoken. 66579000 Arabic, Egyptian Spoken. 22479000 Arabic, Moroccan Spoken. 88400 Arabic, Sudanese Creole. 34458000 Arabic, Sudanese Spoken. 10772000 Arabic, Tunisian Spoken. 1164000 Aringa. 742000 Asu. 88500 Atsam. 661000 Attié. 36400 Avikam. 114000 Avokaya. 11000 Awak. 637000 Awngi. 1141000 Baatonum. 42100 Babanki. 266000 Bacama. 430000 Bade. 98200 Bafia. 105000 Bafut. 1100 Baga Sitemu. 8100 Bainouk-Gunyaamolo. 48000 Baka. 71200 Baka. 109000 Balanta-Ganja. 536000 Balanta-Kentohe. 5277000 Bamanankan. 34700 Bambalang. 538000 Bamun. 37200 Bamunka. 198000 Bana. 205000 Banda, South Central. 329000 Banda-Ndélé. 132000 Bandi. 16900 Bandial. 1251000 Bangala. 176000 Bangi. 10600 Bangwinji. 3038000 Baoulé. 714000 Bari. 285000 Basa. 576000 Basaa. 115000 Basketo. 597000 Bassa. 35500 Batanga. 1855000 Bedawiyet. 140000 Bedjond. 53200 Beembe. 173000 Bekwarra. 81200 Beli. 4817000 Bemba. 587000 Bembe. 1078000 Bena. 169000 Bena. 431000 Bench. 8000 Benga. 354000 Bera. 1134000 Berom. 226000 Bété, Daloa. 226000 Bété, Guiberoua. 126000 Bete-Bendi. 33200 Bhele. 146000 Biali. 37400 Bidyogo. 96000 Bilen. 159000 Bimoba. 243000 Binji. 211000 Birifor, Malba. 166000 Birifor, Southern. 1037000 Bisa. 19800 Bobo Madaré, Southern. 143000 Boghom. 155000 Boko. 52300 Bokobaru. 250000 Bokyi. 143000 Bolia. 7600 Boloki. 671000 Bomu. 79200 Bondei. 10900 Bongili. 309000 Buamu. 83700 Bube. 373000 Budu. 198000 Buli. 7400 Bullom So. 1101000 Bulu. 31700 Bum. 7100 Burak. 444000 Bura-Pabir. 85700 Burji. 54200 Burun. 68200 Burunge. 50700 Busa. 238000 Bushoong. 358000 Bwa. 109000 Bwamu, Láá Láá. 63200 Cen. 123000 Cerma. 143000 Che. 13075000 Chichewa. 569000 Chidigo. 469000 Chiduruma. 2810000 Chiga. 583000 Chopi. 89000 Chumburung. 1765000 Chuwabu. 143000 Cishingini. 155000 C'lela. 2611000 Cokwe. 133000 Comorian, Maore. 363000 Comorian, Ndzwani. 501000 Comorian, Ngazidja 9800 Coptic. 255000 Crioulo, Upper Guinea. 79200 Daasanach. 29500 Daba. 51100 Dadiya. 924000 Dagaare, Southern. 481000 Dagara, Northern. 1044000 Dagbani. 75100 Daju, Dar Daju. 1848000 Dan. 84500 Dangaléat. 1459000 Dangme. 276000 Datooga. 444000 Dawida. 674000 Dawro. 116000 Day. 728000 Dazaga. 35600 Deg. 23500 Delo. 171000 Dendi. 28000 Denya. 73400 Dera. 72000 Dghwede. 57800 Dhimba. 5163000 Dholuo. 176000 Dida, Yocoboué. 70900 Didinga. 118000 Dii. 42600 Dikaka. 951000 Dinka, Northeastern. 761000 Dinka, South Central. 731000 Dinka, Southeastern. 1842000 Dinka, Southwestern. 51700 Diriku. 199000 Ditammari. 70400 Dogon, Donno So. 102000 Dogon, Toro So. 38900 Dogosé. 41200 Doyayo. 219000 Duala. 20200 Dugun. 9300 Duupa. 83700 Duya. 27600 Dzùùngoo. 1941000 Ebira. 161000 Ebrié. 1778000 Edo. 682000 Efik. 234000 Eggon. 187000 Ejagham. 67600 Ekajuk. 2976000 Ekegusii. 97800 Eleme. 15000 Elip. 206000 Emai-Iuleha-Ora. 45000 Engenni. 514000 Esan. 50100 Esimbi. 80000 Eten. 5269000 Éwé. 1553000 Ewondo. 634000 Ezaa 8400 Fa d'Ambu. 50100 Fali, South. 1482000 Fang. 1130000 Farefare. 310000 Fe'fe'. 484000 Fipa. 3600 Firan. 2805000 Fon. 39400 Foodo. 3891000 Fulfulde, Adamawa. 518000 Fulfulde, Borgu. 6209000 Fulfulde, Central-Eastern Niger. 1183000 Fulfulde, Maasina. 6196000 Fulfulde, Nigerian. 1850000 Fulfulde, Western Niger. 464000 Fuliiru. 827000 Ga. 76300 Ga'anda. 65600 Gabri. 1378000 Gamo. 7628000 Ganda. 1131000 Gbagyi. 69900 Gban. 127000 Gbanu. 611000 Gbari. 20400 Gbaya. 599000 Gbaya, Northwest. 245000 Gbaya, Southwest. 236000 Gbaya-Bossangoa. 38800 Gbaya-Mbodomo. 1211000 Gedeo. 1000 Geez. 11000 Geji. 584000 Gen. 649000 Ghomálá'. 162000 Gidar. 7276000 Gikuyu. 13800 Gikyode. 112000 Giziga, South. 52300 Glavda. 45900 Godié. 453000 Goemai. 451000 Gofa. 2371000 Gogo. 154000 Gokana. 297000 Gonja. 119000 Gor. 1388000 Gourmanchéma. 95300 Grebo, Gboloo. 143000 Grebo, Northern. 200000 Gude. 89000 Guduf-Gava. 381000 Gulay. 317000 Gumuz. 1080000 Gun. 111000 Gungu. 578000 Guro. 77200 Gwak. 595000 Gwere. 6800 Gyele. 1541000 Ha. 1552000 Hadiyya. 9000 Hanga. 330000 Hangaza. 52017000 Hausa. 2359000 Haya. 43200 Hdi. 1401000 Hehe. 10600 Heiban. 82000 Herdé. 372000 Herero. 27400 Holoholo. 56700 Holu. 310000 Huba. 578000 Hunde. 610 Hungana. 159000 Hun-Saare. 57100 Hwana. 167000 Hyam. 107000 Ibani. 996000 Idoma. 375000 Ifè. 1422000 Igala. 22107000 Igbo. 404000 Igede. 13300 Igo. 178000 Ijo, Southeast. 36200 Ika. 353000 Ikizu. 49600 Ikoma-Nata-Isenye. 249000 Ikposo. 571000 Ikwere. 279000 Ikwo. 135000 Ila. 749000 Iraqw. 76100 Irigwe. 824000 Isekiri. 669000 Isoko. 2000 Isu. 57100 Ivbie North-Okpela-Arhe. 86000 Izere. 580000 Izii. 2138000 Izon. 5000 Jiba. 52300 Jibu. 8800 Jimi. 286000 Jita. 535000 Jju. 32800 Jola-Felupe. 534000 Jola-Fonyi. 60400 Jola-Kasa. 19100 Jowulu. 43700 Ju|'hoan. 8500 Jukun Takum. 4604000 Jula. 151000 Jur Modo. 14100 Kaansa. 104000 Kaba. 93200 Kaba Démé, Sara. 81600 Kaba Náà, Sara. 1145000 Kabiyè. 954000 Kabuverdianu. 16200 Kabwa. 4132000 Kabyle. 1035000 Kafa. 323000 Kagulu. 171000 Kako. 344000 Kakwa. 486000 Kalabari. 25200 Kalamsé. 464000 Kalanga. 5147000 Kamba. 764000 Kambaata. 36200 Kamo. 541000 Kamwe. 6500000 Kanuri, Central. 1413000 Kanuri, Manga. 415000 Kanyok. 433000 Kaonde. 69500 Karaboro, Eastern. 51400 Karang. 131000 Kare. 360000 Kasem. 154000 Katcha-Kadugli-Miri. 664000 Kela. 57400 Kélé. 462000 Kele. 38700 Keliko. 79100 Kenga. 0 Kenyan Sign Language. 100000 Kenyang. 77,100 Kenzi. 115000 Kera. 220000 Kerewe. 49300 Kgalagadi. 428000 Khana. 14000 Khwe. 916000 Kiembu. 1119000 Kigiryama. 35800 Kim. 6040000 Kimbundu. 2626000 Kimîîru. 26600 Kimré. 204000 Kinga. 112000 Kipfokomo. 2320000 Kipsigis. 402000 Kirike. 307000 Kisi, Southern. 652000 Kissi, Northern. 209000 Kitharaka. 4906000 Kituba. 543000 Kituba. 354000 Klao. 107000 Koalib. 4100 Kolbila. 299000 Kom. 62300 Koma. 18500 Kombe. 620000 Komo. 56700 Komo. 524000 Konabéré. 1500000 Kongo, San Salvador. 761000 Konkomba. 5000 Konni. 329000 Kono. 305000 Konso. 1069000 Konzo. 4964000 Koongo. 45400 Koonzime. 195000 Koorete. 0 Korana. 266000 Koromfé. 69000 Kota. 107000 Koti. 17600 Kouya. 486000 Kpelle, Guinea. 846000 Kpelle, Liberia. 83100 Krahn, Eastern. 102000 Krahn, Western. 851000 Krio. 52200 Krongo. 0 Krumen, Plapo. 53600 Krumen, Tepo. 199000 Kukele. 169000 Kulango, Bondoukou. 42900 Kulung. 243000 Kumam. 238000 Kunama. 269000 Kunda. 7000 Kung-Ekoka. 22800 Kuo. 234000 Kupsapiiny. 513000 Kuranko. 901000 Kuria. 596000 Kusaal. 20100 Kushi. 74000 Kutep. 99000 Kutu. 21700 Kuwaa. 9000 Kuwaataay. 38800 Kwambi. 128000 Kwangali. 39200 Kwanja. 43300 Kwasio. 159000 Kwaya. 269000 Kwere. 104000 Kwese. 150000 Laari. 145000 Laka. 864000 Lala-Bisa. 79200 Lala-Roba. 320000 Lama. 68800 Lamang. 433000 Lamba. 154000 Lambya. 308000 Lamnso'. 539000 Langi. 2489000 Lango. 52200 Laro. 1084000 Lega-Shabunda. 67100 Lele. 72000 Lelemi. 1279000 Lendu. 301000 Lenje. 95200 Lijili. 133000 Lika. 50000 Likuba. 434000 Limba, West-Central. 190000 Limbum. 3684000 Lingala. 119000 Lobala. 889000 Lobi. 495000 Logo. 207000 Lokaa. 206000 Loko. 207000 Lolo. 209000 Loma. 2213000 Lomwe. 1355000 Lomwe, Malawi. 91300 Longuda. 1082000 Lozi. 4724000 Luba-Kasai. 3113000 Luba-Katanga. 1701000 Lubukusu. 690000 Lucazi. 1739000 Lugbara. 1072000 Luguru. 709000 Luidakho-Luisukha-Lutirichi. 93100 Luimbi. 113000 Lukpa. 733000 Lulogooli. 35900 Lumbu. 30900 Lumun. 120000 Luna. 837000 Lunda. 62500 Lusengo. 2862000 Luvale. 188000 Luwo. 460000 Lyélé. 1871000 Maasai. 1285000 Maay. 193000 Mabaan. 593000 Machame. 171000 Mada. 42500 Mada. 437000 Ma'di. 348000 Mafa. 349000 Mahou. 23000 Majang. 180000 Makaa. 4749000 Makhuwa. 2693000 Makhuwa-Meetto. 780000 Makhuwa-Shirima. 2326000 Makonde. 802000 Malagasy, Bara. 739000 Malagasy, Masikoro. 11124000 Malagasy, Plateau. 1805000 Malagasy, Tsimihety. 118000 Male. 94800 Malila. 16200 Mambai. 54700 Mambila, Cameroon. 189000 Mambila, Nigeria. 852000 Mambwe-Lungu. 304000 Mampruli. 124000 Mamvu. 32900 Manda. 2058000 Mandinka. 414000 Mandjak. 1587000 Mangbetu. 153,000 Mango. 3949000 Maninkakan, Eastern. 1316000 Maninkakan, Western. 97000 Mankanya. 417000 Mano. 21300 Mansoanka. 1299000 Manyika. 293000 Marba. 199000 Marghi Central. 208000 Marghi South. 429000 Marka. 215000 Markweeta. 1946000 Masaaba. 512000 Masana. 45100 Matal. 187000 Mayogo. 28300 Mazagway. 737000 Mbala. 543000 Mbandja. 221000 Mbay. 71700 Mbe. 211000 Mbembe, Cross River. 131000 Mbembe, Tigon. 17500 Mbuko. 82300 Mbukushu. 107000 Mbula-Bwazza. 138000 Mbum. 508000 Mbunda. 392000 Medumba. 190000 Me'en. 1928000 Mende. 4900 Ménik. 25000 Merey. 46900 Mesme. 218000 Meta'. 204000 Mgbolizhia. 56600 Migaama. 54900 Miya. 19000 Miyobe. 12500 Mmaala. 389000 Moba. 1134000 Mochi. 67800 Mofu, North. 95800 Mofu-Gudur. 145000 Mokole. 80600 Mokpwe. 15900 Moloko. 176000 Mom Jango. 4976000 Mongo-Nkundu. 10214000 Mòoré. 573000 Morisyen. 76900 Moro. 200000 Moru. 137000 Mpoto. 608000 Mpuono. 29600 Mukulu. 718000 Mumuye. 485000 Mundang. 74600 Mundani. 62800 Mündü. 125000 Mungaka. 159000 Murle. 435000 Musey. 208000 Musgu. 37500 Muyang. 516000 Mwaghavul. 23300 Mwan. 179000 Mwani. 760000 Mwera. 57300 Myene. 175000 Nafaanra. 335000 Nama. 131000 Nambya. 167000 Nancere. 2654000 Nande. 1124000 Nandi. 8500 Narim. 18100 Naro. 95200 Nateni. 172000 Nawdm. 18500 Nawuri. 432000 Ndali. 16000 Ndam. 121000 Ndamba. 2628000 Ndau. 2085000 Ndebele. 780000 Ndebele. 585000 Ndo. 33300 Ndogo. 1288000 Ndonga. 48700 Ndut. 739000 Ng'akarimojong. 121000 Ngam. 1536000 Ngambay. 103000 Ngamo. 459000 Ngando. 103000 Ngangam. 681000 Ngas. 1520000 Ngbaka. 300000 Ngbaka Ma'bo. 392000 Ngbandi, Northern. 242000 Ngbandi, Southern. 220000 Ngiemboon. 484000 Ngindo. 196000 Ngiti. 20400 Ngom. 97900 Ngomba. 569000 Ngombe. 1704000 Ngoni. 76000 Ngoreme. 290000 Ngulu. 971000 Nilamba. 99900 Ninzo. 188000 Njebi. 9600 Njyem. 36100 Nkonya. 119000 Nkoya. 368000 Nkumbi. 147000 Nkutu. 449000 Nobiin. 15000 Nomaande. 44200 Noon. 37000 Noone. 918000 Nsenga. 255000 Ntcham. 289000 Ntomba. 1962000 Nuer. 76800 Nugunu. 263000 Nuni, Southern. 1665000 Nupe-Nupe-Tako. 73900 Nyabwa. 2109000 Nyakyusa-Ngonde. 513000 Nyamwanga. 1940000 Nyamwezi. 3989000 Nyankore. 1024000 Nyaturu. 479000 Nyemba. 1150000 Nyiha, Tanzania. 500000 Nyole. 1069000 Nyoro. 775000 Nyungwe. 52800 Nzakambay. 155000 Nzanyi. 463000 Nzema. 268000 Obolo. 31100 Odual. 293000 Ogbah. 74600 Oku. 2504000 Oluluyia. 409000 Olunyole. 383000 Oluwanga. 117000 Omi. 53100 Oniyan. 118000 Orma. 213000 Oroko. 8519000 Oromo, Borana-Arsi-Guji. 7490000 Oromo, Eastern. 19110000 Oromo, West Central. 1415000 Oshiwambo. 15900 Otoro. 228000 Otuho. 47400 Paasaal. 43900 Pagibete. 123000 Pana. 179000 Papel. 58000 Päri. 54700 Parkwa. 35900 Peere. 45800 Pero. 65100 Pévé. 979000 Phende. 22400 Phuie. 3259000 Pidgin, Cameroon. 1649000 Pidgin, Nigerian. 36500 Pinyin. 8900 Piya-Kwonci. 407000 Pogolo. 175000 Poke. 861000 Pökoot. 40300 Polci. 123000 Psikye. 5081000 Pulaar. 5579000 Pular. 208000 Punu. 2200 Qimant. 64300 Rendille. 85600 Reshe. 241000 Ron. 805,000 Ronga. 10990000 Rundi. 438000 Ruund. 198000 Rwa. 12467000 Rwanda. 813000 Saamia. 286000 Sabaot. 5300 Safaliba. 348000 Safwa. 29400 Sagalla. 249000 Saho. 203000 Sakata. 190000 Salampasu. 199000 Samba Daka. 144000 Samba Leko. 285000 Samburu. 136000 Samo, Southern. 154000 Sandawe. 1004000 Sanga. 510000 Sango. 165000 Sangu. 32800 Sangu. 53500 Sapo. 437000 Sar. 143000 Saya. 3021000 Sebat Bet Gurage. 346000 Sehwi. 30900 Sekpele. 14900 Selee. 1734000 Sena. 496000 Sena, Malawi. 30500 Sengele. 1602000 Sénoufo, Cebaara. 122000 Sénoufo, Djimini. 1135000 Sénoufo, Mamara. 58800 Sénoufo, Sìcìté. 761000 Sénoufo, Supyire. 240000 Sénoufo, Tagwana. 1761000 Serer-Sine. 93500 Seselwa Creole French. 1067000 Shambala. 99200 Shekkacho. 1525000 Shi. 421000 Shilluk. 8953000 Shona. 7400 Shua. 63900 Siamou. 3875000 Sidamo. 1268000 Silt'e. 61900 Sira. 138000 Sisaala, Tumulung. 39700 Sisaala, Western. 25400 Sissala. 35600 Siwu. 22800 So. 3457000 Soga. 45300 Sokoro. 21182000 Somali. 21800 Somrai. 2339000 Songe. 357000 Songhay, Koyra Chiini. 2048000 Songhay, Koyraboro Senni. 192000 Songo. 2788000 Soninke. 4838000 Sotho, Northern. 6624000 Sotho, Southern. 165000 Suba. 131000 Suba-Simbiti. 158000 Suku. 8494000 Sukuma. 35700 Suri. 1748000 Susu. 4219000 Swahili. 1524000 Swahili, Congo. 2606000 Swati. 1176000 Taabwa. 2307000 Tachawit. 5724000 Tachelhit. 250000 Takwane. 264000 Talinga-Bwisi. 132000 Tamahaq, Tahaggart. 1716000 Tamajaq, Tawallammat. 497000 Tamajeq, Tayart. 666000 Tamasheq. 4851000 Tamazight, Central Atlas. 66800 Tampulma. 238000 Tangale. 4438000 Tarifit. 511000 Tarok. 30400 Taveta. 14400 Téén. 310000 Teke, Ibali. 57500 Teke-Eboo. 36300 Teke-Fuumu. 64200 Teke-Kukuya. 19000 Teke-Tyee. 585000 Tem. 12000 Tembo. 269000 Tembo. 44600 Temi. 12500 Tennet. 160000 Tera. 3059000 Teso. 1748000 Tetela. 1805000 Themne. 77800 Tiene. 1245000 Tigré. 7783000 Tigrigna. 49900 Tikar. 33100 Tira. 4660000 Tiv. 56400 Tobanga. 232000 Toma. 461000 Tonga. 485000 Tonga. 2004000 Tonga. 1052000 Tooro. 304000 Toposa. 66400 Toura. 31100 Toussian, Southern. 143000 Tsikimba. 143000 Tsishingini. 51100 Tsogo. 5548000 Tsonga. 143000 Tsuvadi. 1648000 Tswa. 5731000 Tswana. 51100 Tula. 58900 Tumak. 1773000 Tumbuka. 65500 Tunen. 469000 Tupuri. 59300 Turka. 1216000 Turkana. 15200 Tuwuli. 224000 Tyap. 57100 Ubaghara. 63100 Uduk. 7863000 Umbundu. 32400 Umon. 970000 Urhobo. 63800 ut-Ma'in. 17400 Vagla. 178000 Vai. 18800 Vame. 1269000 Venda. 32400 Vengo. 70400 Vidunda. 545000 Vunjo. 35600 Vute. 132000 Vwanji. 104000 Waama. 128000 Waja. 176000 Wali. 93200 Wandala. 5100 Wannu. 171000 Wapan. 271000 Wè Northern. 464000 Wè Southern. 40700 Wè Western. 31200 Winyé. 2123000 Wolaytta. 5854000 Wolof. 236000 Wolof, Gambian. 19000 Wongo. 26300 Wuzlam. 839000 Xaasongaxango. 10655000 Xhosa. 75000 Yace. 21500 Yaka. 62900 Yaka. 1284000 Yaka. 240000 Yala. 154000 Yalunka. 80700 Yamba. 9300 Yambeta. 2750000 Yao. 46600 Yaouré. 44300 Yauma. 444000 Yekhee. 541000 Yemba. 114000 Yemsa. 376000 Yom. 1878000 Yombe. 36702000 Yoruba. 140000 Zanaki. 2578000 Zande. 1008000 Zaramo. 3605000 Zarma. 738000 Zigula. 304000 Zinza. 37900 Zulgo-Gemzek. 12333000 Zulu.

Asia

:4462676000

:81542000

:4

1915:**187**
1965:**338**
2017:**711**

:1645

Asia

711

129000 Abkhaz. 3900 Abun. 4402000 Aceh. 71300 Achang. 7000 Adasen. 157000 Adi. 182000 Adi, Galo. 810 Agta, Casiguran Dumagat. 1000 Agta, Central Cagayan. 2200 Agta, Dupaninan. 0 Agta, Pahanan. 4600 Agta, Umiray Dumaget. 17400 Agutaynen. 3400 Aimol. 170 Ainu. 606000 Akha. 10300 Alangan. 2000 Alta, Southern. 21000 Alune. 74100 Amarasi. 12200 Ambai. 146000 Amis. 24900 Anal. 36300 Anong. 35100 Apatani. 15600 Arabic, Judeo-Tunisian. 34211000 Arabic, North Levantine Spoken. 8001000 Arabic, North Mesopotamian Spoken. 14663000 Arabic, South Levantine Spoken. 430000 Arabic, Standard. 18900 Aralle-Tabulahan. 7982000 Armenian. 14300 Asmat, Central. 2800 Asmat, Yaosakor. 20901000 Assamese. 228000 Assyrian Neo-Aramaic. 86900 Atayal. 1400 Atta, Pamplona. 440 Auye. 26826000 Awadhi. 7700 Awyu, Asue. 9000 Awyu, Central. 6100 Ayta, Abellen. 3000 Ayta, Ambala. 13100 Ayta, Mag-antsi. 7000 Ayta, Mag-Indi. 9376000 Azerbaijani, North. 12400 Bada. 318000 Badaga. 9284000 Bagheli. 191000 Bahnar. 81500 Baikeno. 6000 Bakati'. 29500 Bakati', Rara. 4700 Bakati', Sara. 28500 Balangao. 37000 Balantak. 4199000 Bali. 2328000 Balochi, Eastern. 4782000 Balochi, Southern. 2680000 Balochi, Western. 466000 Balti. 33000 Bambam. 131000 Banggai. 80300 Bantoanon. 125000 Bareli, Rathwi. 3400 Batak. 1125000 Batak Angkola. 1913000 Batak Dairi. 900000 Batak Karo. 1482000 Batak Simalungun. 2802000 Batak Toba. 2100 Bauzi. 11200 Behoa. 228197000 Bengali. 65100 Benyadu'. 0 Berawan, Central. 1600 Berik. 11824000 Bhili. 49137000 Bhojpuri. 37200 Biak. 99000 Bidayuh, Biatah. 25500 Biete. 3560000 Bikol, Central. 315000 Bikol, Rinconada. 175000 Binukid. 51700 Bisaya, Brunei. 21900 Bisaya, Sabah. 140000 Bishnupriya. 172000 Blaan, Koronadal. 122000 Blaan, Sarangani. 1648000 Bodo. 58600 Bolinao. 2300 Bonggi. 619000 Bontok, Central. 7100 Bontok, Eastern. 3914000 Bouyei. 4698000 Brahui. 22957000 Braj Bhasha. 164000 Bru, Eastern. 7061000 Bugis. 12700 Buhid. 43300 Bumthangkha. 16162000 Bundeli. 39200 Bunun. 50100 Buriat, Mongolia. 28779000 Burmese. 47100 Buru. 45700 Caluyanun. 20146000 Cebuano. 852000 Chakma. 166000 Chaldean Neo-Aramaic. 84500 Cham, Eastern. 196000 Chambeali. 13100 Chamling. 13100 Changthang. 471000 Chavacano. 53900 Chepang. 17386000 Chhattisgarhi. 34300 Chin, Asho. 19900 Chin, Bawm. 0 Chin, Bualkhaw. 37300 Chin, Daai. 0 Chin, Eastern Khumi. 186000 Chin, Falam. 605000 Chin, Haka. 79700 Chin, Khumi. 0 Chin, Lautu. 65900 Chin, Mara. 76200 Chin, Matu. 218000 Chin, Mro-Khimi. 38800 Chin, Müün. 21400 Chin, Ngawn. 102000 Chin, Paite. 12300 Chin, Siyin. 476000 Chin, Tedim. 345000 Chin, Thado. 50300 Chin, Zotung. 22500 Chin, Zyphe. 41603000 Chinese, Hakka. 918210000 Chinese, Mandarin. 3225000 Chinese, Min Bei. 9958000 Chinese, Min Dong. 68141000 Chinese, Min Nan. 2974000 Chinese, Pu-Xian. 89971000 Chinese, Wu. 84292000 Chinese, Yue. 345000 Chodri. 27100 Chrau. 20500 Chru. 12400 Citak. 390 Citak, Tamnim. 33500 Cua. 207000 Cuyonon. 17600 Damal. 25800 Dani, Lower Grand Valley. 70000 Dani, Mid Grand Valley. 25800 Dani, Upper Grand Valley. 242000 Dani, Western. 10503000 Dari. 19400 Darlong. 24000 Dengka. 61500 Desiya. 211000 Dhanki. 6500 Dhao. 198000 Dhatki. 22200 Dhimal. 209000 Dhodia. 11179000 Dhundari. 138000 Dimasa. 10300 Dobel. 3953000 Dogri. 1662000 Dong, Southern. 114000 Dungan. 262000 Dungra Bhil. 157000 Duri. 377000 Dusun, Central. 253000 Dzongkha. 1600 Edopi. 4500 Eipomek. 155000 Ekari. 12400 Embaloh. 30900 Evenki. 62900 Fordata. 8100 Ga'dang. 7000 Gahri. 111000 Galela. 511000 Gamit. 25500 Gangte. 160000 Garasia, Adiwasi. 131000 Garasia, Rajput. 3822000 Garhwali. 1299000 Garo. 3096000 Georgian. 30200 Ghale, Southern. 10077000 Gondi, Northern. 118000 Gondi, Southern. 1261000 Gorontalo. 59877000 Gujarati. 232000 Gurung, Eastern. 169000 Gurung, Western. 94600 Hajong. 24700 Halang. 1123000 Halbi. 17500 Hanunoo. 5841000 Haroti. 15778000 Haryanvi. 23000 Hatam. 140000 Hawu. 3327000 Hazaragi. 2094000 Hebrew. 0 Hebrew, Ancient. 9400 Helambu Sherpa. 18100 Helong. 0 Hértevin. 43700 Higaonon. 7730000 Hiligaynon. 156753000 Hindi. 2517000 Hindko, Northern. 103000 Hmar. 2204000 Hmong Daw. 543000 Hmong Njua. 1615000 Ho. 33100 Hrangkhol. 137000 Hre. 5000 Hupla. 1500 Iau. 187000 Ibaloi. 651000 Iban. 815000 Ibanag. 1400 Ibatan. 11400 Ida'an. 55300 Ifugao, Amganad. 75400 Ifugao, Batad. 34400 Ifugao, Mayoyao. 40300 Ifugao, Tuwali. 9836000 Ilocano. 85100 Ilongot. 28700 Inabaknon. 570000 Inakeanon. 42263000 Indonesian. 4700 Indo-Portuguese. 115000 Inonhan. 6000 Irarutu. 15900 Iraya. 245000 Irula. 2300 Isirawa. 45700 Isnag. 225000 Itawit. 10100 Itneg, Binongan. 1633000 Iu Mien. 41800 Ivatan. 5300 Jah Hut. 129401000 Japanese. 406000 Jarai. 131000 Jaunsari. 63166000 Javanese. 29700 Jeh. 1028000 Jingpho. 5600 Jirel. 117000 Kadazan, Coastal. 44400 Kadazan, Labuk-Kinabatangan. 272000 Kadu. 1500 Kagate. 34400 Kagayanen. 61500 Kaili, Da'a. 432000 Kaili, Ledo. 88000 Kalagan. 12300 Kalagan, Kagan. 16900 Kalinga, Butbut. 14500 Kalinga, Limos. 33800 Kalinga, Lubuagan. 2400 Kalinga, Majukayang. 17500 Kalinga, Southern. 20400 Kalinga, Tanudan. 26300 Kallahan, Kayapa. 11200 Kallahan, Keley-i. 261000 Kambera. 12122000 Kanauji. 2282000 Kangri. 239000 Kankanaey. 123000 Kankanay, Northern. 46674000 Kannada. 757000 Karakalpak. 519000 Karbi. 21400 Karen, Bwe. 40400 Karen, Geba. 1260000 Karen, Pwo Eastern. 83100 Karen, Pwo Northern. 247000 Karen, Pwo Western. 2084000 Karen, S'gaw. 6996000 Kashmiri. 87500 Katu, Eastern. 570 Kaure. 107000 Kayah, Western. 142000 Kayan. 9000 Kayan, Baram. 24100 Kayaw. 14585000 Kazakh. 5000 Kelabit. 3700 Kemtuik. 11900 Keningau Murut. 36500 Kenyah, Mainstream. 16300 Ketengban. 0 Khalaj. 10600 Khaling. 61200 Kham, Western Parbate. 315000 Kharia. 1284000 Khasi. 63000 Khengkha. 15632000 Khmer, Central. 1442000 Khmer, Northern. 928000 Khmu. 121000 Khün. 28900 Kimaragang. 13500 Kinabatangan, Upper. 575000 Kinaray-a. 80400 Kinnauri. 26100 Kisar. 176000 Koho. 3700 Koireng. 1360000 Kok Borok. 7800 Kola. 151000 Kolami, Northwestern. 741000 Koli, Kachi. 347000 Koli, Parkari. 19100 Kom. 11300 Konda-Dora. 2990000 Konkani. 4877000 Konkani, Goan. 80536000 Korean. 709000 Korku. 10300 Korupun-Sela. 449000 Koya. 1129000 Kui. 1061000 Kukna. 60500 Kulung. 3261000 Kumaoni. 7100 Kupia. 7194000 Kurdish, Central. 13992000 Kurdish, Northern. 3571000 Kurdish, Southern. 2388000 Kurux. 37000 Kurux, Nepali. 574000 Kuvi. 508000 Kuy. 3600 Kwerba. 4795000 Kyrgyz. 203000 Ladakhi. 293000 Ladino. 602000 Lahu. 207000 Lahu Shi. 14200 Lakkia. 7056000 Lambadi. 13700 Lamkang. 4133000 Lampung Api. 3208000 Lao. 35100 Lashi. 35100 Lave. 63200 Lawa, Western. 68100 Lepcha. 175000 Lhao Vo. 9400 Lhomi. 409000 Limbu. 540000 Lipo. 5600 Lishán Didán. 1099000 Lisu. 24000 Lole. 21400 Loloda. 9900 Lotud. 1276000 Lü. 6900 Lua'. 23800 Luang. 56200 Lun Bawang. 181000 Ma'anyan. 13775000 Madura. 17298000 Magahi. 625000 Magar, Eastern. 1197000 Maguindanaon. 3000 Mah Meri. 30000 Mai Brat. 4200 Mairasi. 45102000 Maithili. 2632000 Makasar. 38300 Mal. 130000 Mal Paharia. 32200 Malaccan Creole Portuguese. 355000 Malay, Ambonese. 119000 Malay, Baba. 2695000 Malay, Central. 262000 Malay, Kupang. 1046000 Malay, Manado. 896000 Malay, North Moluccan. 3433000 Malay, Pattani. 2482000 Malay, Sabah. 0 Malay, Standard. 48629000 Malayalam. 12169000 Malvi. 8600 Mamanwa. 192000 Mamasa. 120000 Manchu. 1171000 Mandeali. 18000 Manikion. 80400 Manobo, Agusan. 35800 Manobo, Ata. 34400 Manobo, Cotabato. 22100 Manobo, Dibabawon. 19600 Manobo, Ilianen. 54400 Manobo, Matigsalug. 68800 Manobo, Obo. 61400 Manobo, Sarangani. 16900 Manobo, Western Bukidnon. 77700 Mansaka. 52200 Mapun. 1271000 Maranao. 88666000 Marathi. 257000 Maria, Dandami. 284000 Marwari. 6333000 Marwari. 936000 Masbatenyo. 123000 Mawchi. 209000 Mehri. 1859000 Meitei. 72900 Mentawai. 6301000 Mewari. 22800 Meyah. 437000 Miao, Eastern Qiandong. 1410000 Miao, Large Flowery. 1686000 Miao, Northern Qiandong. 612000 Miao, Southern Qiandong. 8000 Miji. 4491000 Minangkabau. 681000 Mising. 897000 Mizo. 79200 Mnong, Central. 34600 Mnong, Eastern. 10500 Moken. 14300 Molbog. 8500 Moma. 2500 Momuna. 935000 Mon. 2319000 Mongolian, Halh. 5761000 Mongolian, Peripheral. 284000 Mongondow. 27800 Moni. 19600 Mori Atas. 19600 Mori Bawah. 45700 Moronene. 10300 Moskona. 9400 Mpur. 78400 Mru. 324000 Muna. 1382000 Mundari. 1372000 Muong. 154000 Naga, Angami. 286000 Naga, Ao. 75100 Naga, Chang. 4600 Naga, Chothe. 47000 Naga, Khiamniungan. 31500 Naga, Khoibu. 303000 Naga, Konyak. 0 Naga, Leinong. 50800 Naga, Liangmai. 183000 Naga, Lotha. 110000 Naga, Mao. 46100 Naga, Maram. 21900 Naga, Maring. 4100 Naga, Monsang. 4700 Naga, Moyon. 39300 Naga, Mzieme. 17500 Naga, Northern Rengma. 142000 Naga, Phom. 19600 Naga, Pochuri. 69600 Naga, Poumei. 75700 Naga, Rongmei. 103000 Naga, Sangtam. 28300 Naga, Southern Rengma. 298000 Naga, Sumi. 0 Naga, Tangkhul. 175000 Naga, Tangkhul. 116000 Naga, Tase. 29200 Naga, Thangal. 60600 Naga, Wancho. 124000 Naga, Yimchungru. 89900 Naga, Zeme. 13500 Nalca. 7500 Napu. 1604000 Nasu, Wusa. 291000 Naxi. 15500 Nduga. 17319000 Nepali. 941000 Newar. 1101000 Ngaju. 35300 Ngalum. 5200 Nggem. 970000 Nias. 42800 Nicobarese, Car. 12400 Nicobarese, Central. 1000 Nimboran. 3400 Nipsan. 1115000 Nisu, Eastern. 1900 Nuaulu, South. 1170000 Nung. 2541000 Nuosu. 12700 Nusu. 291000 Nyishi. 150 Obokuitai. 1007000 Okinawan, Central. 40221000 Oriya. 241000 Oriya, Adivasi. 2500 Orya. 90500 Ot Danum. 37200 Pacoh. 148000 Pahari, Kullu. 71000 Pai-

see pp50-51, 176-181

Noun icons

Big shout out to an amazing project

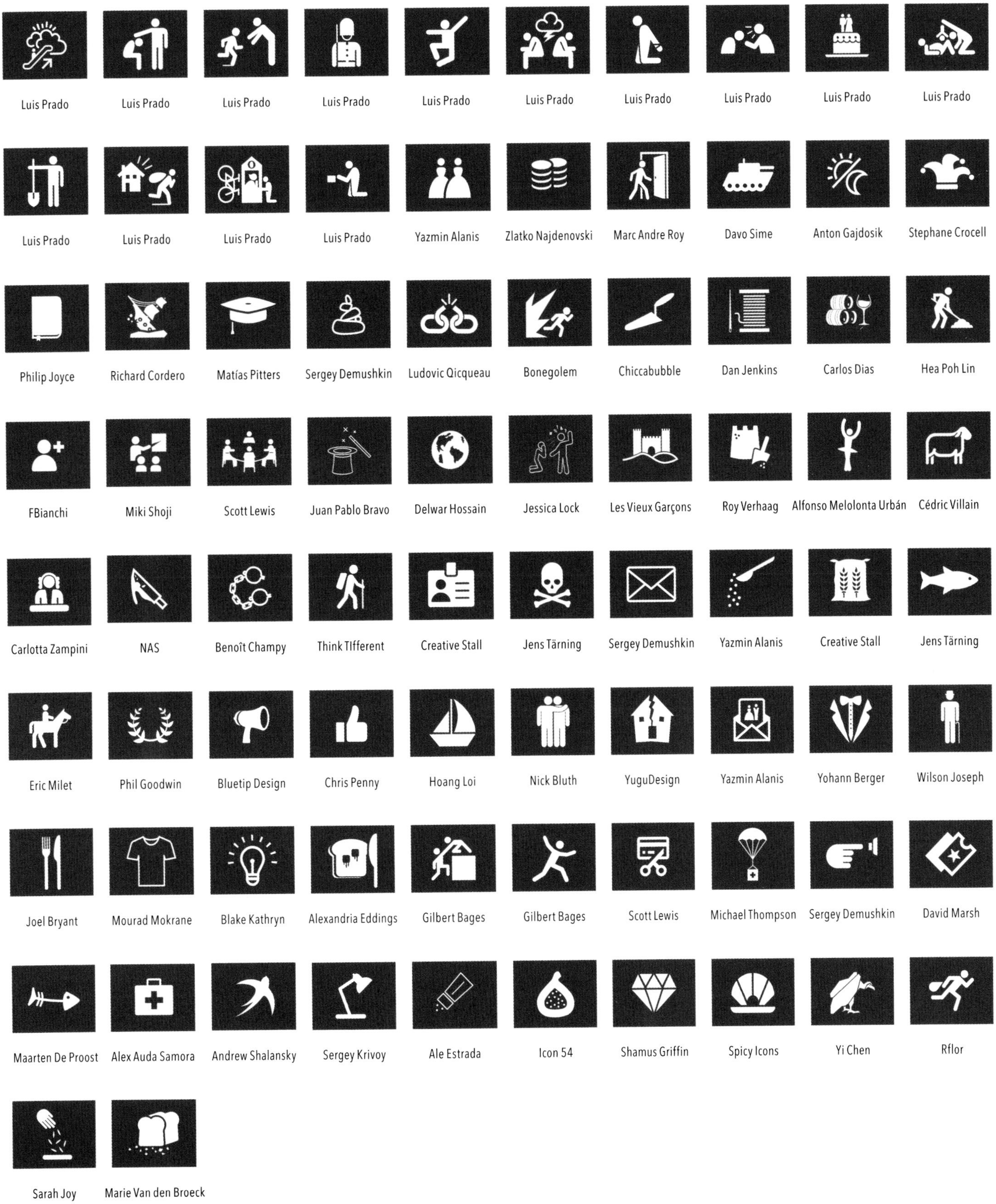
Luis Prado
Luis Prado
Luis Prado
Luis Prado
Luis Prado
Luis Prado
Luis Prado
Luis Prado
Luis Prado
Luis Prado
Luis Prado
Luis Prado
Luis Prado
Luis Prado
Yazmin Alanis
Zlatko Najdenovski
Marc Andre Roy
Davo Sime
Anton Gajdosik
Stephane Crocell
Philip Joyce
Richard Cordero
Matías Pitters
Sergey Demushkin
Ludovic Qicqueau
Bonegolem
Chiccabubble
Dan Jenkins
Carlos Dias
Hea Poh Lin
FBianchi
Miki Shoji
Scott Lewis
Juan Pablo Bravo
Delwar Hossain
Jessica Lock
Les Vieux Garçons
Roy Verhaag
Alfonso Melolonta Urbán
Cédric Villain
Carlotta Zampini
NAS
Benoît Champy
Think TIfferent
Creative Stall
Jens Tärning
Sergey Demushkin
Yazmin Alanis
Creative Stall
Jens Tärning
Eric Milet
Phil Goodwin
Bluetip Design
Chris Penny
Hoang Loi
Nick Bluth
YuguDesign
Yazmin Alanis
Yohann Berger
Wilson Joseph
Joel Bryant
Mourad Mokrane
Blake Kathryn
Alexandria Eddings
Gilbert Bages
Gilbert Bages
Scott Lewis
Michael Thompson
Sergey Demushkin
David Marsh
Maarten De Proost
Alex Auda Samora
Andrew Shalansky
Sergey Krivoy
Ale Estrada
Icon 54
Shamus Griffin
Spicy Icons
Yi Chen
Rflor
Sarah Joy
Marie Van den Broeck

source: www.thenounproject.com

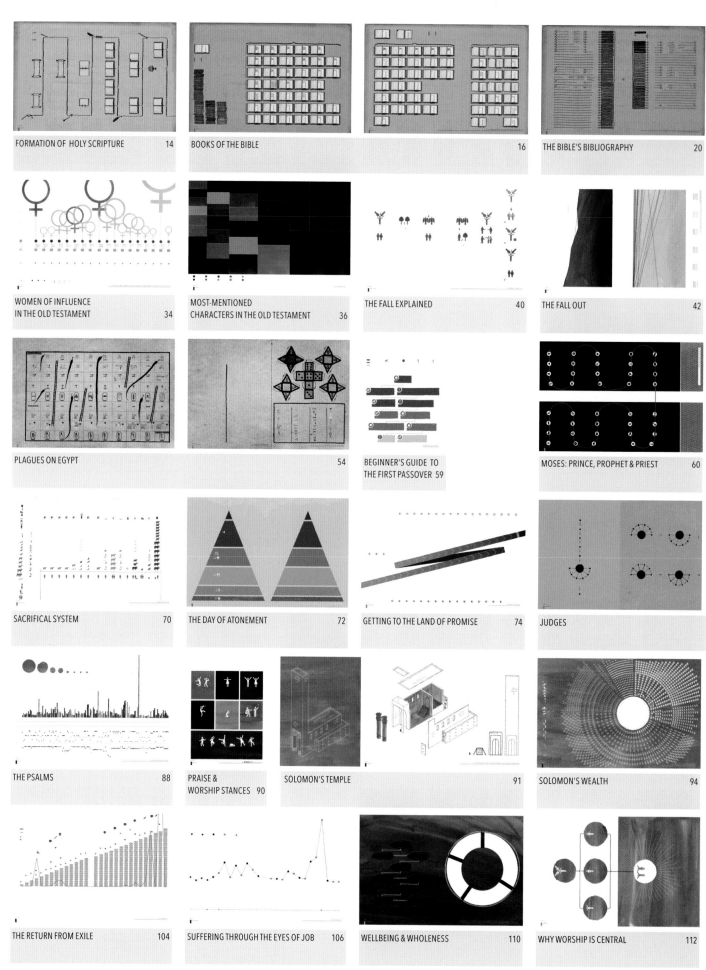

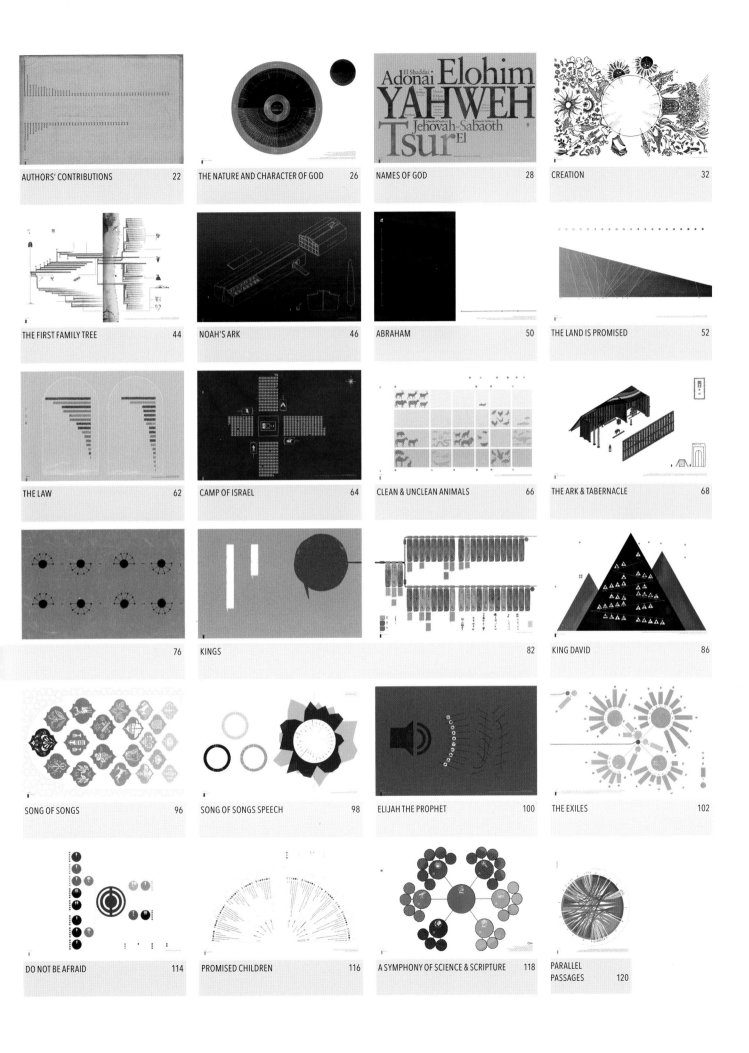

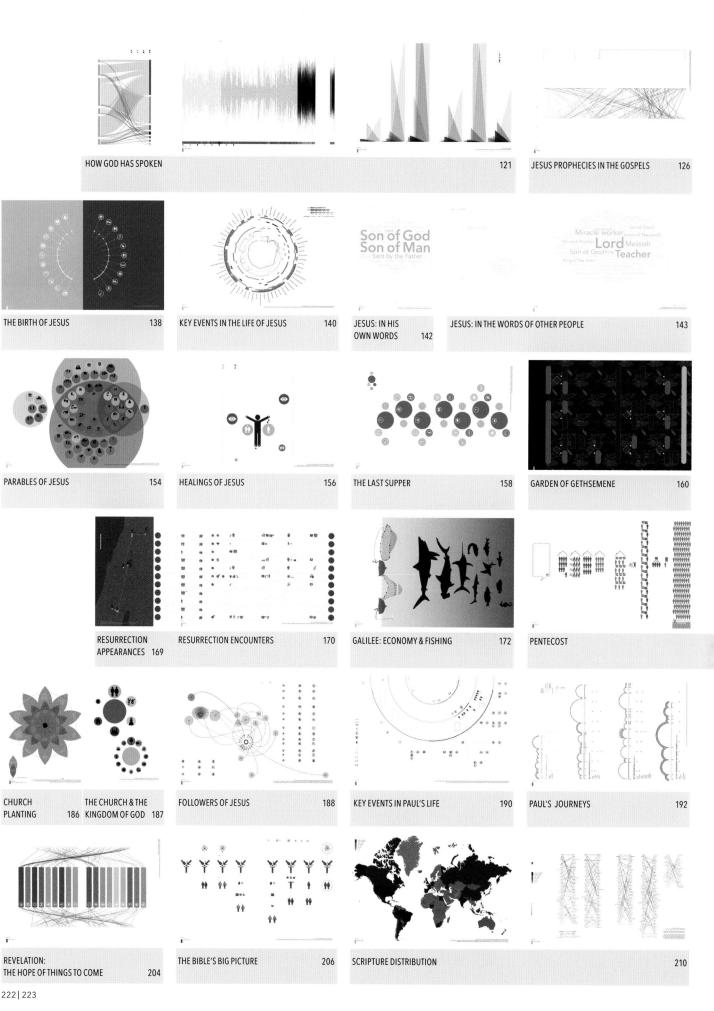

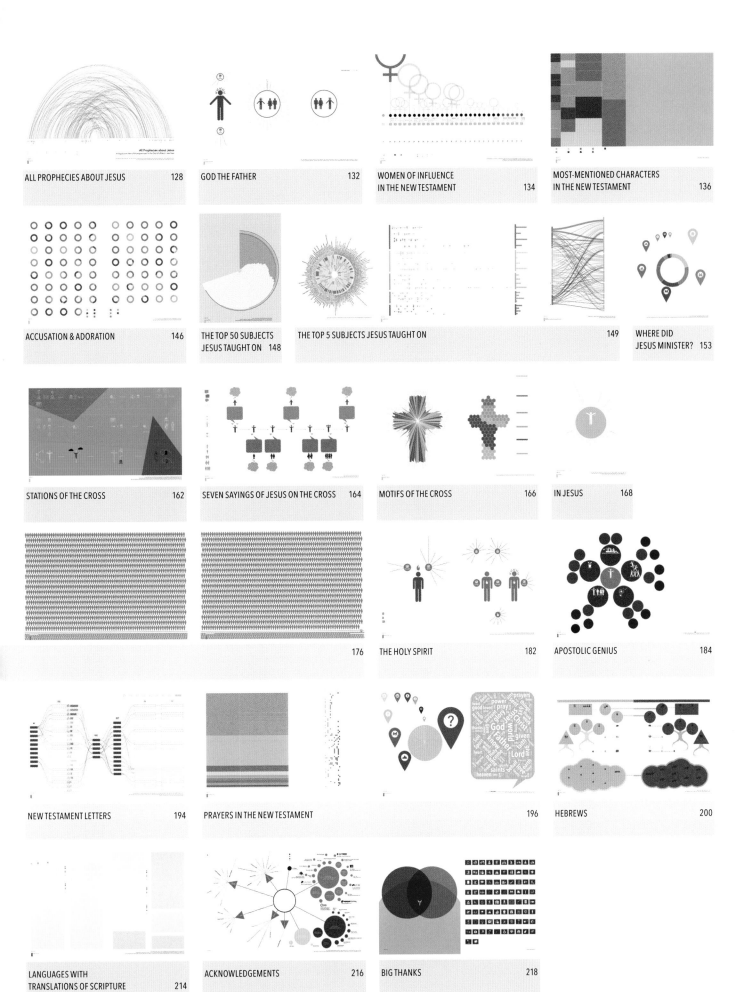

in the words of my beloved John Mcleod
Soli Deo gloria